Hungry for Touch

A Journey from Fear to Desire

Laureen Peltier

This book contains descriptions of molestation that may be triggering for those with a history of PTSD.

Published by Inhoe Press, October 2015

ISBN 978–0–9968228–0–0 (Inhoe Press trade paperback)

ISBN 978–0–9968228–1–7 (Inhoe Press e-book)

Book design by Book Cover Cafe
Edited by Carol A Frisbie

All healing is essentially a release from fear. To undertake this you cannot be fearful yourself. You do not understand healing because of your own fear.

A Course in Miracles

Foreword

I f you have picked up this book, you are looking for something. It might be entertainment. This memoir is engrossing, but it's not a light read, nor is it "fun." *Hungry for Touch: A Journey from Fear to Desire*, describes some very personal and difficult experiences of transformation.

If you are a therapist or helper, you might be looking for information. Ms. Peltier conveys honestly and candidly what she experienced in intensive therapy.

If you are a survivor, you might be looking for hope. The author offers her story of transformation as an example of what might be possible.

Personally, I found this book engaging, compelling, informative and enlightening. Ms. Peltier seeks to share with you her experience of a transformative time in intensive outpatient therapy. In doing so, she hopes to open your eyes to what is possible when it comes to healing psychological trauma. It's not meant to be a how-to book, nor does it prescribe a path or plan of action. It does take the reader along a difficult but rewarding journey. It's not an easy book, but it's an honest one. Some of the material is difficult, but it is treated in a matter-of-fact, non-sensational style. Please note: it may be triggering for some readers.

If you are still with me, I hope I have piqued your interest. Reading this story was an odd experience for me: you see, I am "Dr. Erickson." The work that we did was informed by EMDR (eye movement desensitization and reprocessing), ego-state therapy, schema therapy, inner-child work, object relations, and visualization and guided imagery. Some somatic techniques were also used when the information seem to be trapped in body memories. Some therapist readers might recognize techniques that are reminiscent of NLP (neuro-linguistic programming).

We also made use of the metaphors that the author presented in therapy. They came from dreams, drawings, and even the jewelry she chose to wear. The examples of therapy that are depicted come from her perspective as a client and not myself as a medical professional; thus the book does not convey enough information for the reader to fully understand what I was doing. It was enlightening for me to see our sessions from her personal perspective.

Ms. Peltier is an intelligent, ambitious, creative, and goal-oriented individual whose approach to therapy was informed by years of successful corporate experience. She was not looking to waste time or resources. Her needs fit with my ambition: I was looking to devise a method that would promote the kind of transformation I had experienced in my own psychoanalysis, but with more regularity and greater frequency than a handful of sessions out of hundreds.

Spirituality also informed my work as a therapist. Raised as a Christian, I understood the healing power of that metaphorical system. The archetypal energies do not seem to care about one's state of faith or doubt. To the emotional part of our brain, metaphor is reality. The symbol is the thing. The map is the territory. Changing the map is changing the territory. Explorations in shamanism provided me with a rich metaphorical system and ways of accessing healing that are very practical.

When I was fourteen years old, I decided I would be a therapist when I grew up. I wanted to be a psychiatrist because I was good at math and sciences, and I understood that psychiatry was the best-paid type of therapy, with the most options.

By the time I completed my training fifteen years later, the field of psychiatry had changed. It was becoming more and more preoccupied with biology, and the art of mind therapy was becoming a sideline, almost a joke—certainly not anything I would want to spend my life doing. I took extra training in psychoanalysis. As part of the training I went through personal analysis. In three years of twice- to three-times-a-week therapy, I had a few breakthrough sessions that were wonderfully healing, powerful, transformative and moving.

While this experience was extremely valuable, I came to understand that it was not economically viable. Out of some three hundred and fifty sessions, I experienced only a handful of memorable transformative sessions, and even those sessions were frustrating. We stuck rigidly to a 45-minute hour, even when I had been crying for thirty-five minutes of that time. Afterwards, I went to the lobby and cried for another thirty minutes.

It seemed clear that the pattern of healing did not conform to the convenience of hourly scheduling, which was an arbitrary artifact of Dr. Freud's schedule. My psychoanalytic instructors could not tell me why the session needed to be one hour or less. From my experience of hypnosis, I knew that we go through rhythms of alertness that last ninety minutes or more. And I know from EMDR and hypnotic work that this might be a better allotment of time to accommodate this kind of healing work.

I knew that the sort of transformative work I wanted to do needed to be respectful of the natural rhythms of the psyche. We worked when we started and we worked until we were through. The arbitrary 45-minute hour was like having heart surgery in 45-minute weekly increments: your chest is laid open, then time's up and you're told to return in a week. Sorry, don't have time to close you up this week.

Standard therapy actually trains someone with a trauma history not to talk about it; because it's upsetting and time is so limited, a person learns not to venture there. The intensity and amount of processing that it takes to transform trauma into wisdom doesn't fit itself into the 45-minute hour. Models exist that advocate 90-minute and two-hour sessions.

EMDR, created by Francine Shapiro, is an accelerated information-processing technique. EMDR practitioners need to gain additional training and expertise in somatic techniques and ego-state therapy to treat complex trauma or dissociation safely. DNMS (developmental needs meeting strategy), a therapy developed by Shirley Jean Schmidt, is excellently organized and taught, and incorporates hypnosis, EMDR, CBT (cognitive behavioral therapy), ego-state therapy and some modified bodywork into an integrated and learnable process.

Ericksonian hypnosis (Milton Erickson) is taught through the American Society of Clinical Hypnosis; it supports longer sessions and has some excellent practitioners. NLP also draws heavily on the work of Erickson. Shamanic counseling by Michael Harner's group, Holotropic Breathwork from Stanislav Graf, and sensorimotor psychotherapy from Pat Ogden all have ways of approaching trauma and its healing that incorporate spirituality, bodywork, or both.

Looking for practitioners with training in these methods will provide useful therapy that can hasten effectiveness. These methods are catalytic, meaning they can be intense and will move things along, and might be something you could pursue after you have mastered self-care skills and safety habits through DBT (dialectical behavioral therapy).

Ultimately, healing is the goal of psychotherapy. And healing can be defined as the process of transforming trauma into wisdom.

I should state here that "Erickson" is not my real name. For ethical concerns and for practical reasons, I believe it necessary to be an anonymous presence in this narrative. My practice does not currently include the methodologies that are described in *Hungry for Touch*. The book is my client's work; it is her memoir from her perspective, and her experience of our work together in the journey toward healing. It was not written to provide instruction on how to work this way.

Ms. Peltier has explained how personal and unique the experience of her therapy was for her, and I did not have input into the writing, editing, or production of her book. I also believe that, as a psychiatrist, it is necessary for me to avoid dual relationships with my clients.

I hope you find Ms. Peltier's journey engaging and enlightening, as I have. And, whether you are a therapist, in the helping professions, or someone seeking healing, I hope her personal account adds depth and richness to your journey.

Dr. Erickson
Psychiatrist

Introduction

My intention in writing this book is to share my recovery from post-traumatic stress disorder (PTSD) and educate people as to the complexities of trauma recovery. In doing so, I hope to change the way mental health is perceived and how medical professionals practice healing. Healing does not need to take time, but it does require commitment (both from the therapist and from the client).

It took me thirty years to decide to heal. In that time I was not physically intimate. I refused physical exams, and the mere experience of casual touch caused me great anxiety. This is how I lived my life—unconscious of my behaviors and convinced my life was by choice. I didn't realize there was something lacking until I found myself in the county psychiatric ward.

This was the turning point in my life, a moment when, after thirty years of hiding, I had broken. It was my bleakest and my greatest moment. It was the moment when everything lined up perfectly for me; I had the perfect psychiatrist, who practiced and understood holistic psychiatry, and time off work to heal.

Of course, I could have stayed where I was at, taken the antipsychotic the psychiatrist had prescribed, and gone back to my life. But suddenly it felt empty and meaningless. I was given this incredible opportunity to choose, and I chose to heal without really understanding what was wrong or what healing would look like. In my typical fashion, I jumped in with both feet.

I completed this book a few months after therapy. Using copies of my medical records and my personal journal, I have told as accurate a story as I am able.

You will find in reading this book that there are moments when I dissociated during therapy, or mixed up my memories. This is the normal process of trauma recovery. This book is unique in that I bring you into my therapy sessions and allow you to feel the process of recovery. To that end, some readers may find that the content triggers their own PTSD. I understand triggers to be signals to us to explore deeper, but this can be done safely and effectively with the help of a trained professional.

My experience will not be yours. We are all unique. I understand there are countless ways to heal and this is but one. My purpose here is to inform. When I entered therapy I didn't know what to expect and I hope this book will inform and enlighten, whether you are on your journey to healing, interested in the effect of trauma on the human psyche, or a medical professional intrigued as to how the client processes therapy. At the very least, this book is about overcoming life's events, taking responsibility for our lives and letting go.

Dr. Erickson, the psychiatrist in this book, is very real, but I have changed his name at his request. Also, my therapy sessions were two to three hours in length, and I have condensed them to make the book manageable. Even our phone sessions were over an hour.

Longer sessions were part of the reason I was able to heal successfully in one year. It seems impossible (and cruel) to me to expect people to do trauma-recovery work in forty-five minutes. This is what I hope to change. No other section of medicine has time limits, and mental health should not be an exception. If people want to live more peaceful lives, with healthy relationships, then psychiatry and mental health need to change. I hope my success story offers a model for better therapy.

The main core of this book is my therapy sessions, but I have alternated these chapters with short sections that paint a picture of what was happening in my life outside of therapy, and provide some background. I did not limit myself to Dr. Erickson in my healing, but searched other modalities to help me along the way. Some I found effective, some not. My strong need to succeed and heal guided me to try everything, from aromatherapy to acupuncture to meditation.

While Dr. Erickson assured me that I did seven years of work in one year, I found the process slow and frustrating. Without medication to numb me, I was highly motivated to find my peace and get the change I wanted in life. That discomfort pushed me forward to do the work I needed to do to heal.

Dr. Erickson once told me that most people quit therapy when it gets too difficult. In my experience, people quit because they become confused and overwhelmed. I hope this book will "un-confuse" people and offer hope. My story is not unusual; millions of people share my experience of being molested. What makes my circumstances unique are both the healing journey I undertook and the peace I found at the end of that journey.

Be well and be safe.

July 17

I'm not hearing voices; at least not at the moment. It's small comfort as I sit on a hard chair in the corridor of the psychiatric unit waiting to see the psychiatrist on duty. I've come in voluntarily, I keep repeating to myself, as the unit settles in for the night. All the medication had been dispensed and still it's not quiet. Saturday night in the county hospital psychiatric unit ...

I don't belong here.

I'm a successful financial manager for a prominent, nationwide company. I'm intelligent, capable and articulate, hardly the type to end up in a psych ward, but I haven't stopped crying the entire day. My complete outer shell, the impenetrable veneer that's gotten me through life, has shattered and crumbled. My sister watched as I broke down in a pool of flailing flesh and tears. *Me.*

Stress, my family surmised. But it doesn't feel like stress. I didn't rise to an upper-management position by not being able to handle stress.

I'm suing my company for sexual harassment and I've just finished a two-day deposition that went into all the details of my childhood molestation, most of which, I would learn later, I have buried and hidden from myself.

I don't let situations control my life, and I don't let events define me. The fact that I'm thirty-seven years old and have never experienced sexual intimacy is easier for me to explain as a life choice than an after-effect of sexual abuse.

I have a good life. I have a great career, a beautiful house, excellent health (current situation notwithstanding), and am actively creative in the arts. What can possibly be wrong with my life?

It's a question I can't erase from my mind.

What am I doing wrong?

The opposing attorneys that my company has hired in defense have done a great job of pointing out everything my life lacks: sexual relationships, medical examinations, and my inability to tolerate the touch of others. In two short days they have defined me as someone to be pitied, a victim who was unable to say no to her father's abuse and who is incapable now of preventing her boss from feeling her up.

Two days of intensive questioning, no eating and no sleeping ... and I finally broke. I'd never broken before and didn't recognize that it was happening. I have no experience of what a breakdown feels like. Even sitting here now, waiting for the doctor, I don't understand what's wrong, what's happening to me. It's that confusion and fear that has prompted me to sign myself in. I need to know why.

"Laureen?" The voice is low, soft and gentle.

I look up to see a man standing a good distance from me. I've never met a psychiatrist. The nurses told me how lucky I was to be seeing this particular doctor, that he was the best they'd ever worked with, one who took a lot of time with his patients.

I had come with a mental picture of someone clean cut and well attired, a kind of cross between an intellectual genius and Gandhi. The man who's staring at me now looks more like a throwback to the sixties. His dress is casual; Saturday-night fare, not the shirt and tie the emergency-room doctor had worn. This man's long blond hair is pulled back into a ponytail, and his mustache and goatee are neatly trimmed. He seems a little too far out of the box for my taste.

I realize I'm staring at him and reluctantly I uncurl from the chair. They took my clothes when I was admitted, and I feel inadequate and vulnerable in the oversized gown the nurses fished out of a closet for me. Slowly, and with great hesitancy, I follow him to the end of the hall, where he stops and sorts through the enormous ring of keys attached to his belt.

All the doors in the unit are locked, except the patient rooms. Those doors are left conspicuously open for the rounds the nurses conduct every fifteen minutes. There isn't any pretense of privacy. I suddenly have a wild vision of a scene from *One Flew Over the Cuckoo's Nest.*

You're not actually going to go into a locked room with this man, are you? It's the first sane thought I've had all day.

He's busy unlocking the door, but I know he's watching me and sensing my hesitation. I've waited hours to speak to him in the hope of understanding what's happening to me, and to get something to help me sleep. I'm the type of person who needs information. If I can understand it, I can deal with it. And, quite frankly, he could be Dr. Zhivago as long as he has his prescription pad.

"Do you want someone to go with you?" a nurse asks me, seeing my apprehension.

I immediately think: Do I need someone with me?

I calm my thoughts. The door's open, and the doctor is waiting. What will he think if I say yes? That I'm so shattered and crippled that I can't manage a brief meeting with a psychiatrist? I don't want to have to stay here for the night under evaluation, tagged as a high risk.

I shake my head at the nurse, even though I'm not at all certain of what I'm about to do.

The doctor lets me enter first. The room is small and filled with exercise equipment. It looks like a catchall room, with a small table and chairs; it's not exactly therapeutic.

I curl into one of the chairs, tucking my bare feet under the hem of my gown. I feel unreasonably small.

He sits down. He watches me and I watch him, wondering when he'll speak. He has all the advantages: keys to the doors, shoes on his feet. I don't know what to say or how to start. Shouldn't he offer me comfort?

"You had a court proceeding recently," he says finally.

I nod.

"That was difficult."

I like the sound of his voice; it's almost enough to soothe my uncertainty about his appearance. He just doesn't look like a doctor.

"They asked me lots of questions about being molested as a child." I had stopped crying only an hour ago. My eyes are sore and red, my voice thin and frail. "They wanted to know everything that happened to me and my sisters, and why I never said no to my father. I don't know why they wanted to know all those things."

"Couldn't your attorney have objected?"

"He did, but it didn't stop the deposition. I had to answer the questions."

He sits utterly still, his papers forgotten on the table in front of him. "Feels kind of like a rape, doesn't it?"

I say nothing. My body is drained and empty.

"Karma," he says, nodding in a knowing way.

I wonder how many times the doctor has seen women like me, broken into disparate pieces that no longer connect. How many legal proceedings have delivered their victims to him? There is a worn look to him, a quiet and unassuming look that says he sees something only too familiar in me.

"I don't understand why I reacted this way today," I tell him. "I'm not the kind of person that cries easily. I'm not the kind to crumble."

"The human mind isn't made to withstand that kind of attack. Everybody has things they put away, tuck into storage chests in their minds and bury. Occasionally, items will surface and we're forced to deal with them. But these attorneys went rummaging around in your chests and stirred everything up, things you had put neatly away. That's an assault."

I turn this over in my mind. I do have my childhood abuse buried deep, so deep that it's hardly a part of me anymore. It's a footnote in my life. Or so I think.

"They wanted to know why I'd never had sex, or a gynecological exam. They made it seem like there was something wrong with me for not having sex and not wanting to have a relationship. I don't think there's anything wrong with my life. I don't think I have to have sex."

"Not if it's not a goal of yours." He pauses, studying me. "As you heal the wounds inside of you, you can have a more whole life—if that's what you want."

What I want is to feel better. I want to feel like I felt before the last two days. I want everything back in the locked chest at the bottom of my mind. I want my life back—neat, orderly, and controlled. But as much as I want that, I know I cannot have it, not anymore. I've crossed over into unknown territory and there's no going back.

He asks me if I've been to a therapist before and I tell him I'm seeing one at Five County Mental Health.

His expression brightens into surprise and pleasure. "I'm the psychiatrist there," he says.

Two months earlier, when I was arguing with my company, I took a month's leave of absence to get some help because I hadn't been sleeping. I asked my insurance company to recommend a female therapist who specialized in sexual assault. She was easy to talk to, but it didn't really help. I felt as if I were talking to a girlfriend, not a therapist. I left those sessions feeling vindicated.

This man was different. He seemed deeper, more intense.

"There are only a few things I remember about being molested," I say. "It's always been something in the far past for me. I don't think it's affected my life. Those lawyers just made me feel … less of a person, and then today I couldn't stop crying."

He's silent for a long time as he watches me. "When you think about that, where do you feel it inside?"

It's a strange question. I don't like to feel my body. I hardly ever get sick and so have little cause to take inventory of aches and pains.

When I do get sick, I discipline myself to ignore the discomfort. What he's asking me is the equivalent of asking a blind person to describe color, and yet I find myself looking inside to answer his question.

"My stomach."

"If you were to look inside your stomach, what does it look like? Is there something in there that's making you sick?"

"Metal shavings." They line the inside of my stomach like one of those magnetic toys where you move the wand and collect the shavings into shapes.

"You can open an imaginary hole in your middle and let them flow out," he says. "There's a healing white light that comes from high above. This can only comfort you; it can't hurt you. Let the metal shavings flow into the healing white light."

The metal shavings lining my stomach flow out of me and into a stream of white light.

"Is there anything else in your stomach?" he asks.

Beneath the metal is a yellow liquid. "Yellow liquid, sour liquid," I tell him. It's easy to see when I turn my eyes inward.

"Bitterness," he says. "Do you want to keep that?"

"No."

"Let that flow into the light. When it's all gone, seal up the opening in your middle so that nothing comes back inside. We can send away from you all those things the light took from you. How do you feel now?"

"My chest is tight, like something's squeezing my heart."

"Can you see what it is?"

Thick bands are wrapped around my heart, bands that have been there for years. "Something wrapped around my heart."

"Do you want to let that go, or do you need it for something?"

The thought of unwrapping my heart makes me fearful. I feel instinctively that it wouldn't be a good idea. "I need it."

"It's protecting you," he says with a nod. "Check the rest of your body and see if there's something else you need to attend to."

There isn't. I feel empty, but not undone. Somehow the veneer of myself is still in place, and I feel calm and reassured. I've gotten back something of what I've lost and my thoughts suddenly turn to the question that I've been asking myself all day. "Why do I feel this way?"

"You're having flashbacks," he says simply. "With post-traumatic stress they can be pretty powerful."

"I haven't slept in two days."

He nods. "There's something called Seroquel. It's an anti-psychotic."

Psychotic. I'd been reality tested when I was admitted. I'm fairly certain I answered that I wasn't hearing voices. I take a moment to validate my conviction. No, I haven't heard any voices. My mind spins. I'm trying to figure out how I went from PTSD to psychotic when I realize he's finished speaking.

"I don't like taking drugs," I say.

I don't like the idea of going on antidepressants and anti-anxiety medicine, pharmaceuticals that dull the sensations enough to let people move like shadows through life. But at the moment I'm not opposed to a small dose of Valium.

"Seroquel is the best medication for flashbacks. It should help you get some sleep."

Which would be kind of like Valium, I reason. I am, after all, in the hospital. I checked in to get help. It's been months since I slept through the night. The thought of a drug-induced sleep is intoxicating, but I can't get past the psychotic part.

"What will it do?"

"It calms the emotions, helps to dull the emotional impact of the images." He waits. "Does that sound like something you'd like to try?"

I need sleep. I need to be able to think, neither of which I've been able to do in days. "Okay."

"You can follow up with me at the clinic next week and we'll see how things are."

I look around the room. Things can only improve, can't they?

CHAPTER 1

You may be wondering how a successful woman who managed dozens of people and millions of dollars ended up in the psych ward because a man put his hand under her shirt. I certainly wondered that as I was released from the hospital at midnight. My younger brother picked me up, looking at me as if I might break into a thousand pieces at any moment. And maybe I would have, except the Seroquel had taken effect and I just wanted to sleep.

The next day was my birthday, and that night my sister, with whom I shared my home, threw a party for me. It was too late to cancel, and the house filled with my friends as I rode the numbing effects of the Seroquel, plastered a smile on my face and tried to put the previous night's events in the hospital behind me. If I looked a little too serene and anesthetized, my friends didn't mention it.

I was good at putting things away. In fact, I'd made a career of putting on a stoic mask and playing whatever role suited me at the time: competent manager, unbreakable woman, independent provider. I prided myself on my independence and inability to get hurt. Even as a child I was strangely stoic, impervious to the taunts of other children and never allowing a tear to be shed. I could no longer say those things about myself. I'd been in a lock-down psychiatric unit, stripped, searched and medicated, hardly the experience of a strong woman.

Other women faced much worse and managed to keep themselves out of the hospital. The thing of it was, I'd faced adversity my entire life. Why did I break now? I'd spent a year building a two-story home on ten acres of land. My sister was physically disabled and I supported us, which was a strange reversal of roles considering I was the youngest of five girls and, up until a few years before, she had been the one taking care of me.

My sister had been a surgical scrub tech before an accident on the job disabled her. She had worked hospital trauma centers and loved the fast-paced thrill of emergency surgery. While she was saving lives, I was counting numbers and learning about the financial world. Because she made more money than me, she paid for our vacations and always picked up the tab when we ate out. I deferred to her with ease and without prejudice.

We had been in a good rhythm, sharing the rent and living comfortably in our assigned roles. Then she got an infection from a total knee replacement that almost killed her. She spent months in a hospital bed, and more months restricted to a chair in the living room, her leg bound by an external fixator. She was in and out of the hospital over the years with numerous surgeries.

One day the hospital fired her because she had been on disability too long. Policy, they said. Nothing personal.

Everything changed after that. Slowly our roles shifted.

She couldn't drive and relied on me for transportation. Her wages were cut and I paid more and more of the expenses. I wanted to own a home, and so we talked about building a house together. One thing led to another and the next thing I knew we were drawing up plans and buying land.

We built a house together over the course of a year and made plans like a married couple. She was the one who took care of the house and made the meals while I made the hour-long commute to work each day. I called her Pleasing Sister.

Our dad had also molested Pleasing Sister, long before I was born. She had gone through the physical pain of reconstructive knee surgery, therapy, and loss of her independence and her career, and she'd never faltered. One man put his hand up my shirt and I broke like day-old meringue.

Was I broken now? Would I be able to return to my job with my high salary? Could I continue to support the two of us? Would I be able to put this behind me as I had done with all the other things in my life that had upset me? Could I just carry on, take my Seroquel, and have a happy life?

Maybe.

But I didn't want that, either.

August 3

"I have an image in my mind I can't seem to get rid of," I tell Dr. Erickson. "A snapshot of a memory that's always there, and I can't stop looking at it."

His office is dimly lit. On the wall facing me are two pictures of shamans, medicine men who heal spiritually. I had thought a psychiatrist might decorate with pictures from the masters, Van Gogh, Monet, maybe a classical artist like Michelangelo. Below the shamans, on an end table, is a Kokopelli statue set in a dish of smooth stones. Next to that are two huge bookcases filled with copies of publications from the American Psychiatric Association. At least he seems well read.

"Are you sure it's a memory?" He sits near the opposite wall, filing my evaluation form into a folder. Today he's wearing a shirt and tie. If it weren't for his long hair and ponytail he would seem every bit a doctor.

"Yes. It's something the attorneys brought up during the deposition. Something I haven't thought about in a long time."

He stares at me and says nothing. I realize he isn't going to prod. It seems a strange way to communicate, not asking questions.

"When I was nine I told kids at school that I'd seen my father's penis," I tell him, "that I'd touched it. Only I didn't know to call it that.

They stared at me in shock. That's when I realized there was something wrong with what I was doing. You only know what you're told when you're a child. I didn't know that other kids weren't touching their fathers that way." I pause. "They stopped playing with me after that."

He's quiet for a moment. "That's the image in your mind?"

"Yes, swinging on the playground, laughing. I remember the looks on their faces when I admitted what I was doing. It was all so … innocent."

"How does that make you feel?"

How does it make me feel? The memory is so old, almost thirty years have gone by, but it still seems like yesterday. It's the kind of memory I store in one of those chests at the bottom of my mind, but now I can't seem to put it back.

"Ashamed, sad, like I've done something wrong."

"Do you feel that in your body?"

Another strange question. The memory is in my head. My emotions are in my head, glued to that image of swinging happily, chattering with my friends and having no idea of the impact of my words. My emotions are not imprinted in my body. But I think about the question anyway because I have so much anxiety these days, a tightness in my stomach that feels like a descending roller coaster. Even my nightly dose of Seroquel isn't alleviating it.

"In my stomach," I say.

"Images come forward in your mind to help you get what you want. Your subconscious wants to heal. This is its way of communicating that to you."

"There's something for me to learn from this memory?"

He nods. "There's something called EMDR—eye movement desensitization reprocessing. It's a therapy-like hypnosis that can help speed the processing of memories. It's very effective for PTSD. Once you process the memory, the picture goes away, along with the emotions associated with it."

I'd like to get rid of the snapshot memory, and the sadness and shame it brings with it. It was different before; it was a private memory I could easily tuck away. I could convince myself it was a single incident barely worth my energy to consider. But I had admitted it during the deposition;

I had exposed my shame to a team of attorneys who simply stared at me, stoic and apathetic. I had mirrored their apathy, determined not to allow them to see my pain. I can still see their unimpressed expressions.

"How do I do that," I ask Dr. Erickson.

"I move my hand in front of you and you follow it with your eyes as you think about the memory. Emotions will come to the surface. As you process the emotions, they will be released. The memory will lose its emotional charge."

"Will the image go away then?"

"It should."

Is that what the memory wants—to be felt? Have I tucked away so much of my life that it stubbornly refuses to be hidden any longer? Or is this just a byproduct of the deposition, the aftermath of stress?

What I know is that the memory bothers me. I don't like looking at those faces of my schoolmates staring in shock, and me realizing I did something wrong. I don't like being made to feel bad when the onus should be on someone else. Maybe that's been the problem; the guilt belongs to someone else and not me.

"Okay," I say.

"Okay what?"

"Okay, I want to try that. I want the image to go away."

He moves our chairs closer together, so his left arm will be next to my left arm. We're sitting side by side, but facing in opposite directions. He lets me sit close to the door so I don't feel boxed in. "An escape route," he says. Then he stands back from the chairs like an artist appreciating his work.

I know his deliberate manner is meant to make me feel more comfortable, but his ceremonial style has the opposite effect. I hesitate and glance at the door. Am I going to need an escape route? Do his patients routinely flee the room and he's learned to anticipate it? Or is this merely a psychological strategy?

Nothing will happen with me standing in place, and if it's all been set up by design then I'm failing and the image will remain.

Unwilling to leave and uncertain of how to move forward, I take my seat, knowing that I feel part of the scene rather than an observer.

He gives me a moment before taking the seat next to mine. We're too close for my comfort. I have pretty strict boundaries; I've never been able to allow people to get very close to me physically. It always feels like they're suffocating me with their proximity, as if they've wrapped their arms around me in a crushing embrace.

I can see the ring he wears and the tiny hairs on his arms, and it makes my body tense. He's sitting only a few inches from me; I can feel his gaze studying me, and I become self-conscious and begin to fidget in the chair.

"Think about the image," he instructs. "Think about being on the playground with your friends. Hear their laughter. Think about how you feel as you talk to them. You feel ashamed, sad."

I hate this already. What kind of therapy begins like this?

He moves his left hand horizontally in front of me. I follow it with my eyes, but I don't see his hand.

The playground is noisy. I'm swinging with my friends. It's a Catholic school, and we're all in uniforms: replicas of one another.

"I've never seen a boy's wiener before," Kathy says. Her voice is filled with laughter.

"I've seen my father's. It looks like a bratwurst."

"You have not!"

"Yes. I touched it."

"That's right," Dr. Erickson says in a soothing voice. He's reading the emotions that play across my face. "Stay with it. Let the emotions build and then let them go."

I don't know how to let go. I don't know what I'm supposed to learn from this. It's all old news, pain long past. It doesn't belong with me. I'm an adult now, a grown woman who's made her own way in the world and crafted her own successes. I'm a million years from that little girl on the playground, but the pain is so fresh.

The transformation is rapid. The expressions on the girls' faces morph from playful amusement to confusion, settling on prudence. They're judging me. They know something I don't know. For the first time in my memory, I feel like an outsider, a pariah. Dr. Erickson stops EMDR. I can feel his eyes on me, but I don't look at him. I stare, without seeing, at the carpet.

"I have a question," he says gently. "Whose shame is it?" He moves his hand in front of me, and the image switches.

I'm touching one of my sisters, kissing her on the neck. On Wednesday nights we played a game my father made up, where we had to select small pieces of paper from a hat. On each piece of paper was written something we were supposed to do: kiss a butt, lick a breast, touch a crotch. Each of us would then choose one of our siblings and go into a room with them.

"Where are you?" Dr. Erickson asks. He's stopped his hand movement and is studying me.

"With one of my sisters."

"On the playground?"

"No." Pause. "Every Wednesday my mother would go away and my father would have us sit in a circle, naked. He made up this game." When I finished explaining the bizarre game, I said, "I'm with one of my sisters in a room … kissing her."

"Go with that," he instructs, and begins EMDR again.

It's all giggles and little-girl fun. It doesn't feel sexual, just playful. We're both naked because that's the way our father wanted it.

I don't like touch. It's a mantra I say to myself and it has defined my life. I don't have relationships and I don't let people near. But some part of my brain is wondering why I'm not afraid with my sister, why I don't feel apprehension. I say as much to Dr. Erickson.

"You're judging her as an adult with rights and wrongs. She's feeling the comfort of her sister."

"I liked when we were touching." It's the only time I can recall liking touch, when caressing was comforting and nurturing.

What happened to that feeling? Darkness falls on me as tears well in my eyes. An enormous sadness overwhelms me.

"I like touching my sister, but I don't like touching other people. Men. What kind of a person does that make me?"

"Human."

What I hear is "different."

I like the softness of my sister's skin and the sense of freedom, and I like the closeness as if nothing were going to separate us. Sitting in a psychiatrist's office, trying to come to terms with my life, liking to touch my sister seems wrong.

I've never had a sexual relationship with anyone, male or female. I stopped dating a decade ago; I long since gave up trying to let someone get close. And yet there I was at the tender age of nine, exploring my sister's body. Was that what was wrong with me?

"I want you to think about the healing white light," Dr. Erickson says softly. "It's coming from high above and surrounding you. A brilliant white light taking away all the pain."

The light bathes me with a warm glow. It calms my breathing, eases my tension and, like a drug, dulls the pain the memory created.

"Let those images go. You don't need them anymore."

The memories fade, but they don't disappear. I like the light surrounding me. It takes me far away from my feelings of guilt and shame.

CHAPTER 2

I wasn't working, and the unfamiliar free time was causing me a great deal of anxiety. Without ten-hour workdays, and staff and customers to distract me, I found myself focusing on the therapy session: what I said and didn't say, why I said this or that and what it meant. My body was restless with all the thoughts.

I wanted to walk the country roads, but the isolated environment made me fearful. I wondered what would happen if a man were to force me into his car. Who would rescue me?

I ended up sequestered in my room, listening to Pleasing Sister go through her daily routine of house chores. The screen door banged open loudly each time she took the dogs out. I could hear her ongoing conversation with them, and I realized I felt like an intruder in our home.

Pleasing Sister was giving me room to be myself. We seemed to be out of synch for the first time in our lives. She was lending support by way of omission—asking me little and moving constantly throughout the day. Maybe she hoped I would stop therapy and everything would go back to the way it was before I decided something was wrong.

My friends from work called to check up on me and see how the lawsuit was going. They were still working for the company I'd just left, and they seemed angrier than I was about the company's position in dealing with me. I let their outrage wash over me and said little.

Other than Pleasing Sister and my younger brother, I didn't tell my family about the hospital or therapy. They knew only that I was off work while I pursued my lawsuit. Even in this I'd become passive, letting my attorney take the lead while I examined my life, trying to map where I've been and where I was going.

August 7

I don't like to be touched."

Dr. Erickson stares up at me, pausing from making notes in my file. "Not any kind of touch?"

"Yes. I don't let people touch me."

"Why is that?"

"I don't like it."

I don't feel safe when I'm being touched. Just a few months ago my boss put his hand under my shirt. He was just rubbing my back at first, and I sat still and paralyzed, my thoughts spinning and twisting to find a reason for him doing that, the analytical part of my brain taking over. My silence sent the wrong message. As he got bolder with his touches, I began to disappear, retreating into a gray haze of numbness.

I don't recall how his hands felt, but I know how dangerous I've become to myself. In a way, I've always known. It's because of my inability to defend myself, to get myself free of unwanted touch, that I've designed my life around not touching, keeping an invisible barrier between myself and others. I've decided it will be easier to keep the hands away by not allowing them to get close than to try and outmaneuver them.

It's all about safety. I've gotten good at keeping people away. Men have long since stopped asking me out. My do-not-trespass signs are an extension of myself, as is my inability to allow a man to hold me. What I'm beginning to realize is that no matter how carefully I build those barriers, someone can always cross them. That leaves me with one question: How do I stay safe?

"What about when you were with your sisters?" Dr. Erickson asks. "You said you didn't mind that touch."

"No," I say faintly, "I didn't mind that."

My sisters and I were little girls, and the touching was playful and undemanding; the gentle hugs and easy way we had of wrapping our arms around one another. I can see it in my head so clearly. There were no boundaries; there was no need for them.

"People define absolute statements that identify themselves," Dr. Erickson says. "'I don't like touch,' 'I'm not smart enough,' 'I'm a bad person.' These become reality for them and control their behavior. You say you don't like touch, but there was a time in your life when you did like touch. Was there any other time in your life when you were touched and it felt good?"

I'm eighteen years old and sitting on the couch with a blind date my older sister fixed up for me. She's in the navy and so is the young man next to me, but he seems more worldly than her. His arm is around my side, his thumb caressing the swell of my breast.

"How did that feel?" Dr. Erickson asks.

"Nice." The memory is warm and pleasant. "He wasn't pushy or demanding. His hand just stayed there. It felt good."

He smiles. "Okay, now we've found two times in your life when touch felt good."

"But that was a long time ago."

"The exception isn't the rule. Do your friends touch you?"

"No."

I choose my friends carefully. They both respect and accept my boundaries. I move away when they're too close, or gently pull my arm free from their friendly grasp. It's not a reflection on them; it's simply the way I am. They accept this about me without imposing a change, but now I'm not certain if I can accept myself.

His arms circle me with no effort and I feel his strong hands press against my back, drawing me near. Pressing and taking; trapped and suffocated.

I don't like the feel of his hands on me.

Do I want this life I've constructed? Do I want a life without physical contact, without emotional openness, without intimacy? Does safety have to mean isolation?

"Do you hug your sisters?" Erickson asks.

"Sometimes."

"But you hate it."

"No, I don't hate it."

"But you hate touch," he presses. "You must hate it when they hug you."

"I don't like hands on me," I say crossly. He's deliberately being obtuse and it annoys me. "People can't just take what they want."

"So touching you is taking from you?"

There's a small dish of stones on the end table next to me. I have been wanting to touch them, but now I want to throw them at him. I look down at the armrest, trying to be less annoyed. His words are playing in my head, stirring up thoughts.

Touch is taking. I try to imagine hands on me, what they feel like, what they do. They're reaching from one spot to the next, always moving and searching. I can see it clearly and I know a certain fact from the information I perceive: men only touch when they want something.

"What?" Erickson asks, prompting me.

I try to control my features. I don't like when people can read me, and this man already knows too much about me, but I realize I've been discovered.

"I have a thought, but it's negative," I say shyly.

"Go for it."

Dr. Erickson is unabashed in everything he does, sitting back comfortably as if he's enjoying an evening with friends, unassuming in his posture and unapologetic about his candid manner. We're taught not to stare in society; not only has he made a living doing just that, but he's turned it into an art.

"I think when men touch they have an agenda." I can't look at him when I say this. It sounds immature and sexist, a typical wounded woman's reply.

"And that agenda would be sex?"

I hadn't thought that exactly, but … "Yes."

He's half-smiling as he stands up to get some paper. I can see his mind sharpen and focus. "What about when a doctor takes your pulse? Does he want to have sex with you?"

"No."

"What about the guy who hands you your change at the store?"

That dish of stones is looking real good to me. I wonder how many of his patients have thrown something at him and how good his reflexes have gotten at ducking.

"You're deliberately making this complicated."

"I'm just trying to follow what you're saying. You said when men touch someone they have an agenda, that they want to have sex with that person. I'm just trying to get clarification."

"There are different kinds of touch," I explain. "There are social touches like handshakes and giving change—they're perfunctory. And then there are other touches."

"Like what?"

I exhale sharply. I desperately want out of this conversation. "I'm trying to tell you that I don't like touch."

"Our bodies are wired for touch."

"I want to be safe." *And keeping hands away keeps me safe.*

"You're a decent-sized woman," he says easily. "You could do some damage if you wanted. You need to be able to back up your 'no.' You can take a self-defense class and be more confident about keeping yourself safe."

My head hurts and I'm so tired.

To me, hands seem to take. I try to imagine a gentle touch, a considerate touch, a kind touch, but I only see how calculating and manipulative touch can be. It can be a way of getting close and getting control, like the way my father used control in touching me. Like the way my boss touched me.

"Hands are calculating." My voice sounds distant. Despite his argument, I know what I know. "Hands have agendas. Hands go where hands go."

CHAPTER 3

I love Pleasing Sister. We have lived together for twenty years; neither of us is married and both wanted to get out of the small town in Wisconsin where we were reared. She was twenty-nine and I nineteen when we left home for Phoenix.

I saw our hometown as a means of slow death by boredom; she saw it as a trap. Being the eldest single sibling, she lived at home with Mom and Dad, and supplemented their income. She knew, as I did, that if we didn't get out we'd both be trapped in our roles, and doomed to be responsible for Mom and Dad.

Phoenix was an adventure, but we didn't want to stay. Gang violence and oppressive heat quickly tainted our view and we looked to move again within five years. At that time, I missed the seasons changing and wanted to be closer to our parents, so we focused on Minnesota as our new home.

Only three hours away from Mom and Dad and our two other sisters who also lived there, we made many weekend visits. I liked those short visits to see Mom, but could barely tolerate my dad, whose narcissistic behavior always grated on my nerves. There was never enough of anything for him—not enough love, not enough money, not enough attention. He was like a black hole, a bottomless pit of need that could never be satisfied.

A few years before, when Pleasing Sister and I had built our house together in Minnesota, Dad had helped. During that year he gave us everything we needed, driving early in the morning and staying for days to help plumb or wire the house. I convinced myself he had changed, that everything that had happened in the past was a mistake, a single event that had somehow gotten out of control, that I had … overreacted.

Helping us with the house, he was like a little boy with a new toy, and I relied on him heavily for his expertise and guidance, things any daughter looked to receive from her dad. That year, it was easy for me to put away my disjointed memories and pretend we were a happy family.

Like everything imaginary, it didn't last.

August 14

I want something," I say to Dr. Erickson. I can't look at him. I don't even know the color of his eyes.

"Okay."

For weeks now I've been waiting for life to resume the familiar and comfortable pattern I have established, a pattern painstakingly—albeit misguidedly—designed for my safety. While sorting the information of the past weeks, and reviewing the chain of events that led to residency in the psychiatric unit, I've suddenly realized that I don't want this life anymore.

It came to me with such clarity, a breakthrough moment of dawning recognition when my life made frightening sense. I was sitting in the grass, absorbing the sun and smelling the fresh sent of summer around me. I looked at my beautiful house in the middle of ten acres of woods. I thought of my sister inside the house, knowing she would do anything for me. I watched the chickens busily hunting for bugs and paying no attention to anything else.

A thought came to me: *I am not living; I am hiding.*

How did I get this life when I wanted something else?

"It's strange when you have everything in your life laid out on a table before you," I tell Dr. Erickson. "All the inadequacies and emptiness.

You don't see those things when you're living them, only later when they're pointed out to you, and sometimes not even then."

I didn't *see* during the deposition, when the attorneys were going to great lengths to expose my failings. I didn't *hear* during the years when my friends were telling me that I was cheating myself of a fuller life. I had assumed a role and done what so many women before me had done: I had settled for what I had.

This isn't the life I want, I realize. It's just the life I have.

Now I can remember all the times I've physically pushed men away. All the times I desired an intimate relationship but couldn't let men get close. I go to work and I come home. I plan my vacations and I have my hobbies. And I have to ask myself: is this all there is for me?

"I was thinking about being safe," I say. "We talked about self-defense, but I realized something this week. Being safe isn't keeping the hands away— it's knowing the hands can come close. I can't keep people from touching me. I might be in an accident some day and doctors will have to touch me.

"Despite how careful I've been all these years, someone still touched me. I think about how I reacted to my boss touching me and I don't want that any more. I don't want to have nightmares every time a man touches me. I don't want to shatter because I talked about my abuse."

I don't ever want to repeat the last thirty days.

"I want to be able to have a relationship with a man," I say. I want a whole life, like other people.

"What do you mean by a relationship?"

"A sexual relationship."

"I can help you with that." He studies me. "But it means getting out of your comfort zone. You've been very careful all your life not to let people get close to you. You've done a good job of protecting yourself, but it's come at a terrible price—being alone."

It doesn't sound like me he's talking about. I'm one of eight children and can't remember a time when I've been alone. There isn't room for loneliness in a house filled with noisy children.

I'm still not alone. I'm thirty-eight years old, I live with a sister and I vacation with my family. There are holidays and get-togethers and daily phone calls and opinions and assigned duties. My family is so enmeshed in my life that I can't be alone even when I crave it.

And yet I'm alone in the truest sense of the word. I have isolated not only my body, but my emotions as well.

"We're wired for touch," he says. "Our bodies crave it. It's part of being human. It keeps us healthy."

"I want a different life. I don't want to live like this anymore." Afraid and isolated. "I won't live like this."

He watches me and I wonder if he's trying to figure out how determined I am. Do I want change badly enough to work at it, or am I just seeking a feel-good solution? How many patients does he see that expect him to make them feel better? I'm not willing to turn that kind of control over to anyone, especially a doctor.

"You said images come into our minds to help us get what we want." He nods.

"How do I know what I'm supposed to learn from them?"

The images came to me one morning with such clarity and intensity that it remains impossible to erase them from my mind. That seems so strange to me, because they're familiar images that have long since lost their emotional impact.

"I have two pictures in my mind. They're old images. I've seen them for many years. They're my mental references to being molested. You know, the image that comes to me when I say to myself, *I was molested as a child.*"

He sits quiet and still, waiting.

"When I was nine, we lived in a farmhouse. I told you about the games on Wednesday nights. Sometimes when we played those games, my father would take one of us with him into a room. In this memory, I'm in a room with him. I remember being naked and kneeling on the floor. I have a strong sense of waiting for something, as if he'd promised me a surprise or a present. I remember looking around the room, wondering what the surprise was, what was going to happen.

Suddenly he was kneeling in front of me. I don't remember my father taking off his clothes, but I can feel that he's naked."

I kneel in front of him, seeing his naked chest and nothing more.

"He takes my hands in his. I'm still looking around the room, thinking I'm going to get a present or something, when I look down. My father is naked and aroused. I pull my hands back in shock."

I look at Dr. Erickson. "It was so … confusing. I wondered where that image came from. It seemed to just appear, so large and threatening. He takes my hands and puts them back on him. Then … nothing. I don't remember anything more."

He studies me so carefully. The silence in the room expands and I rush to fill it, thinking about the things he's taught me these past weeks, about recognizing my emotions and finding the information in the images I see.

"I'm not afraid the way I feel with the other images. I'm not ashamed. I'm not being hurt. I know I'm supposed to feel upset, but I don't feel anything. But I realized something. This is the picture that comes up when I push men away. This is what I see in my mind."

He's quiet for a moment. "What's the other picture?"

I hesitate. "Sometimes my father would take us on trips with him."

My father makes me take a shower. I come back to bed and move to the edge of the mattress, far away from him, and pretend to sleep. He reaches for me, his hand catching my middle, and pulls me near. I roll onto my back and float to the ceiling.

Dr. Erickson doesn't bat an eye. It's impossible to interpret his thoughts. "Do you look down from the ceiling?"

"No."

I don't want to look down. I don't want to know what's happening. It has nothing to do with me.

"Which image came first?" he asks.

"Our farmhouse, in the room where I touch my father. I think that was the first time. It has a feel of me not knowing what was happening."

"We can do EMDR," he says, referring to eye movement desensitization and reprocessing.

My stomach tightens and I feel a coil wind inside of me, stretching up my spine, twisting my insides. I hate EMDR. It's like stepping onto a moving train; you simply hang on and hope for the best. Only it's not a train, it's my memories. I'm helpless to stop the images from unfolding once I begin the process. I risk feeling more than I want to feel and knowing more than I want to know.

I like control, and EMDR leaves me none.

"Is there another way of making the image go away?" I ask.

"We can change the picture to something less emotional, something you can live with."

When I was in therapy a few years ago, the counselor used EMDR. I changed the scene in my memory to one where I walk out of the room after telling my father no. I changed the scene so the children at school laughed instead of mocked. It offered relief from the pain of the memory, but it was surface work only; transparent images hiding an ugly truth.

That time, I worked with a counselor. Maybe a psychiatrist did it differently.

"Will that be permanent?"

"No. It lasts for a while, but it's not permanent. You have to process the image, and release the emotions that are attached to it for it to be permanent. Once you release the emotional charge—the energy surrounding the image—the image loses its power and just becomes something that happened in your life."

That's what I thought it was already. "I just want to learn to like touch. Why do I need to feel the image?"

"Because the images are standing in your way of reaching your goal. They're preventing you from having relationships. A man pulls you near and you push away. It's an automatic response to the trauma."

I stand before my date, a nice young man who towers over me. His smile is charming, his demeanor polite. He pulls me into a good-evening embrace. I immediately push away, suddenly filled with an unexplained fear.

"Look at these memories as sources for the changes you want to make. What you need to heal is all right inside of you."

"I want to go forward."

"You can't go forward until you go back."

That doesn't seem fair, having to live it again after having lived it once. I glance at Dr. Erickson. He seems so certain that this is the right path to heal.

"I want to make the image go away permanently. I don't want it surfacing in my life anymore."

"Sounds like you're ready to work the image." He pauses. "But you should be prepared to find out what happens next," he says gently.

What happens next? His words are like a cold blast of air on my face. "What do you mean, what happens next? Nothing happens next." That image is my whole story: beginning, middle and end.

"Do you leave the room?"

I stare at him. Do I leave the room? I try to make that work in my mind, try to get that little girl to get up and walk away, but my mind stubbornly holds the image as it is. "I don't remember."

Is there something more my mind has kept hidden from me? My father was aroused and we were naked …

"Don't worry about that now," Dr. Erickson says quietly. "We don't have time for EMDR today. I want to give you enough time, if that's what you want to do."

I want a normal life. I want to feel the way other people feel. I want to be free. "I never thought about anything more happening," I say softly, my mind drifting. I never even asked the question. "Maybe nothing did."

We both know it's a lie. Suddenly that simple picture I've carried in my mind for thirty years seems larger than life, an all-encompassing event. It has a feel of being more, like I'm only seeing a small corner of the room.

"I don't want you to think too hard about this," he says cautiously.

But I am thinking about it. I'm thinking about how I hate to be touched and how I push men away and how afraid I am of sex. For the first time in my life I wonder why. What happened in that room that stopped me from having intimate relationships?

What did I do?

CHAPTER 4

I haven't said much about my mom and the role she had in all this. Did she know Dad was molesting us? Why didn't she ever question his need to be alone with his daughters? Did she know what was happening, and if so why didn't she do anything to help us?

Those are questions I've asked myself over the past thirty years, but I try not to think too hard on this. I don't fool myself into thinking she didn't know. A mother knows. But I can't blame her for surviving. It's what we all did in our own way. I was molested in the early seventies, a time when child molestation was kept secret. My sisters, who were all older than me, were molested in the early sixties.

Five girls, all molested and each of us with our own label: the angry one, the one who wants to please, the analytical one who has catalogued it all like a scientist, the one who is ashamed, and then there's me, the pretender.

Analytical Sister shared with me that she told her best friend what Dad did. Her friend told her to stop lying. A nun at school told Pleasing Sister the same thing when she confessed. Angry Sister, only two years older than me, thinks that if Mom finds out what Dad did it will kill her. I don't know about Shameful Sister. She's very skilled at being a chameleon. She's kept the secret, but has worn the guilt and sought sympathy from the world.

Me? I pretended nothing had happened.

I realize I haven't painted a flattering picture of my mom. Angry Sister hates her. But Angry Sister hates most everything. Her anger bleeds out into other areas of her life, and she shows no tolerance of others. Her temper is sparked when someone cuts her off in traffic, she becomes red-faced with rage when the bank makes an error, or she bullies others under the guise of being a "strong and powerful" woman who "won't take being treated like that by anybody."

When we were little, Angry Sister would hurt us little kids, twist the skin on our arms, slap and bite us. She loved to sit on us and wouldn't let us up until she was ready.

When I was ten, she sat on me. I put my hands up in defense, and as her weight came on me I heard a snap. My wrist had broken. I started to cry and she immediately got off me. It was one of those moments in childhood that seem disastrous and irreparable. All we could think of was how mad Mom and Dad would be and how much trouble we'd be in.

That's how it was with my sisters and brother; no matter how much hurt there was we would rally around each other when it counted. We knew how to take care of each other.

So we lied to Mom and Dad and said that I was doing handstands when I hurt myself. I went to the emergency room and had it x-rayed. I was stoic, as usual, not wanting anyone to know I was in pain. I remember the technician saying, "It can't hurt that much if you're not complaining." At the hospital they were surprised to find that my wrist was broken.

My mom is passive and kind, and maybe that's part of what Angry Sister hates. I have never felt angry toward Mom. She was always there to make sure we had a meal to eat and clothes to wear. She was the one helping us with our homework and tucking us in at night. I only knew unconditional love from her.

August 21

The picture pushes at me. It is all right there and it takes everything I have to keep it from consuming me. What happens after my hands return to my father's penis? How do I get out of the bedroom in the farmhouse?

Those questions circulate in my brain all week and, suddenly, the image that held no emotion for me is full of fear and uncertainty. I struggle between wanting to know what happens next and wondering why I haven't asked the questions before.

Have I gotten that good at avoiding my life?

"Are we doing EMDR today?" Dr. Erickson asks.

I nod. I sit stiffly in the chair with my legs tightly crossed. I'm always nervous in his office, as though at any moment he's going to discover how truly ill I am and start filling out the commitment papers.

"Are both of those images still in your mind?"

"Yes."

Side by side, like wallpaper: the erect penis rising from between his legs, the white ceiling.

Restlessness settles in and I don't know what to do with my hands. My fingers twist together nervously until I notice and make a conscious effort to still them.

"We can combine them, do both at the same time." He gives me a look that's a cross between anticipation and encouragement. "Two for the price of one?"

I frown and shake my head. "I can't be in two places at the same time."

He smiles. "You can in your mind. Your mind is as large or as small as you make it. It can be as small as this room, or as infinite as space. Time and space don't exist in our minds."

I'm a linear thinker. Things have to be in order. There's a sequence to everything in life, a cause and effect. The thought of being in the hotel room *and* the farmhouse is too complex for me.

"I'm only doing one picture."

He goes to the dry-eraser board. "What do you feel when you think about the bedroom with your father?"

I want to say I don't feel anything, but I know instinctively that he'll reject that idea. I don't like to think too hard about that image. I don't like to be that little girl. But Dr. Erickson has asked me a question and he's waiting, and my mind is already sorting the information.

"Anticipation."

He writes this down on the board and turns, waiting.

"Fear." I know it's there, even if I can't feel it.

"Where do you feel that in your body?"

I stare at him, unable to answer.

"In your chest, your stomach?"

I turn my thoughts inward. "Lower."

"Pelvis?"

"Yes."

"And what does that make you feel?"

Invasion. The word echoes in my mind and I immediately reject it. "Trapped."

"What do you want to feel when you see this picture?"

"I want the fear gone."

"What do you want to feel instead of trapped? What's the opposite of trapped?"

My mind stumbles on this word *trapped*. I stare at it on the board, trying to conjure an answer.

"Safety?" he suggests. "Freedom?"

"Not safety," I whisper. Hands will hurt and catch and take. I can't be held and be safe. Safety is just an illusion. "Freedom."

He writes all these words on the board.

> Anticipation
> Fear
> Invasion
> Trapped
> Freedom

It's my roadmap of what I want out of the EMDR: to eliminate the trapped, helpless feeling the memory gives me; the strong sensations that have bled into other areas of my life, my relationships, jobs. For as long as I can remember, I've wanted to be free. Love has become a suffocating, clinging thing I can't tolerate. Even love from my siblings is too much, a cloying tie that binds and restrains.

"This is about choice," he reminds me. "You have an automatic response: a man pulls you close and you push away. I want you to have a choice: either to allow men to embrace you or not. You don't have a choice now. This image of your father makes you push men away."

"It's just something I do," I explain. "I don't want to. I don't even know I'm doing it."

"I know. You learned an important lesson in that room and you've been applying that lesson to your life ever since. If you can take the lessons you need to learn out of this image, you can be at choice."

He says it as if it were an unquestionable fact, as if everybody has these choices. I haven't thought about choosing, only about getting away.

The idea that I can be held, can melt into a pair of strong arms and relax seems like a fairytale. He's painting a beautiful picture and I want it.

He moves the chairs into the center of the room. "Think about the picture. Think about what the room looks like, how it smells, how it feels."

I kneel on the hardwood floor that's been painted gray. The bedroom is sparsely decorated and seems to have expanded from where we sit. We seem small in comparison to the beds and walls, as if the room has opened up, ready to swallow us.

Dr. Erickson begins. I follow the smooth pattern of his hand with my eyes. It's a strange thing that happens during EMDR, when images are moving in your mind. I'm determined that nothing else happened in my picture. I want to be right about that … but I'm not.

I pull my hands back as I see my father's aroused penis. He captures my hands again and returns them. I don't feel him, but I sense him. It's like an electric current running through the palms of my hands.

Darkness.

My hands are resting on my naked thighs. My father is still kneeling in front of me. He reaches out and opens my legs. I nervously tuck my hands between my thighs to cover my genitals, protecting myself.

I look away from Dr. Erickson's moving hand. I don't want to see any more.

He's persistent, wiggling his fingers to draw my attention back to him. The moment my eyes lock onto his hand, he moves it again, back and forth, back and forth.

I can feel my legs being spread. I'm still on my knees, naked. My hands are pressed close to my genitals. An overwhelming sense of dread wells up, threatening to drown me. I'm breathing heavily, trying to get oxygen into my lungs. My heart is pounding, the blood rushing in my ears.

"I don't …" This isn't me. My father doesn't touch me. This isn't me. "I …" A buzzing fills my ears.

Erickson stops EMDR. "You don't have to tell me the details, but it will help me to help you if I know what's happening, if you're looping the same images or going someplace else." He's watching me, studying me, and he's so close.

"I'm stuck. The picture's not moving." The fingers of my left hand are wrapped tightly around my right wrist, anchoring me.

"You're still sitting with your hand on your father's penis?"

My stomach tightens at the sound of that word: *penis*. It doesn't seem like a word that should be said aloud. I take a deep breath and realize there's sweat running down my back. I don't like talking to Dr. Erickson about this. I would rather he see my pictures and understand for himself.

"No. After my father puts my hands back on him everything goes black. Then I'm sitting with my hands on my thighs … and my father opens my legs … I put my hands between my legs. Then everything stops."

Dr. Erickson is sitting so close to me I can smell the subtle scent of his soap. I'm inches from him, and that's too close. His hand is resting on the arm of the chair, still as a photograph, and yet I sense that it will reach out and grab me. There's something threatening about that still hand, threatening and familiar. I want so badly to move away, to breathe. His presence is sucking all the oxygen from the room, crushing me.

"Stay with that," he says as he recommences EMDR.

My father's hand is between my legs and the image is frozen, but I still feel the fear and dread. That large hand on the inside of my thigh, inches away from my genitals. Invasion!

Suddenly, another girl appears. She's standing in the room, but off to the side, a quiet observer. She looks nothing like me. She has long, straight black hair. Her skin is pale and her face expressionless. Without permission, she steps in front of me, like an opaque image in a science fiction film, and takes my place.

Instantly, the fear and humiliation, the frustration and anger disappear. My muscles relax as I release a breath and study the scene with fascination.

His hand stops.

"She's not supposed to be there," I whisper softly to myself. I know this girl. She's in the hotel room. I call her Feels Nothing because when she steps into my place she feels nothing of what's happening. She's an imaginary playmate that exists only in my memories; I created her long after the event in the farmhouse. Feels Nothing doesn't exist in this time, and she doesn't belong here now. She has entered this picture to give me some relief, but I want resolution. I don't understand why my memories are becoming mixed up.

"I want to do this again," I tell Dr. Erickson. I follow the motions of his hand ...

The hand is on the inside of my thigh and I can sense a strong need from somewhere; an urge and desire building. Feels Nothing steps in to take my place and the fear and shame bleed from me.

I watch the scene unfold without emotion.

"Are you still in the room with your father?" Erickson asks as he stops EMDR again.

I nod.

"You can feel what's happening?"

I shake my head.

"No, you don't want to feel," he says with humor.

"Someone else is here."

"In the room with you?"

"Yes, another little girl, but ... she isn't a part of the memory. I was alone in that room."

"Who is this little girl?"

I shake my head. "She's taking my place."

"Can you ask her to leave?"

I stand next to her in the room. She and my father are on the floor, but she remains unaffected by his invasion.

"I'm supposed to be here, not you," I tell her. She's like a doll, living and breathing, but a shell without insides. "I want you to leave. I want to finish the picture."

She's protecting me. I can feel that about her, and she's stubborn and unbending in her task. The image in my mind does not move and neither does the little girl with the long hair who has taken my place.

"She won't listen," I tell Dr. Erickson.

"Where did this little girl come from?" he asks.

"I don't know. She just stepped into the picture."

"Do you know why she's there?"

I nod, and then frown. "Why do you think she's being hurt?"

"Where did that come from?" he asks, instantly alert.

"You wanted to know why she was there."

"And in answering that question you decided she was hurt?"

Somebody said she was hurt. I can *feel* those words and I know they're true.

"She doesn't feel like other people," I tell him. "She doesn't feel anything at all." So it's all right if she steps into my place. I'm not being cruel in letting her do so. After all, she's not real.

"Your consciousness is being very gentle with you," he says.

My insides feel tight and nervous. Nausea rises and I feel the start of a headache. "Gentle?"

"Some people get information in a flood of images and sensations. That makes it more difficult for them to process the emotions. You're getting information very slowly."

"Is it supposed to be fast?"

"EMDR is very fast, that's one of its benefits. But I'm cool with you going slow."

"Why won't it move?"

"You're blocking." He indicates my hands, which are crossed in front of my body, locked in self-defense.

I release my grip.

"Are you still taking Seroquel?"

"Yes." The medication helps me sleep and quiets the chaos the PTSD has created.

"You might want to think about not taking it a few days before our next session. It might be creating a mental block."

No Seroquel means no sleep. Now I have these new images ... how is all of this work going to bring me to choice?

CHAPTER 5

I was born in the summer of 1966 during a time when society was in upheaval and the family structure was changing with the dawn of the New Age hippie revolution. I was a mere infant when young people were challenging the establishment, and rebelling against the strictures of tradition in the name of personal freedom of choice.

I'm one of eight children, number six in line, with two brothers younger than me. Shortly before I was born, my parents bought a piece of property on Squash Lake in Wisconsin and built a small cabin. It was intended to be temporary housing while Dad designed and built the real house a short fifty feet away. I don't remember the two-story home anymore, but I remember everything about that small cabin.

I shared a room with all my siblings. There were seven of us then: the two eldest girls had their own beds along one wall, and the five of us slept in the two double bunk beds on the opposite wall. The two boys were in the bed below and all three of us younger girls were in the bed above, packed in like a litter of puppies.

There was no running water or electricity. We bathed in the lake during the summer and in an old washtub in the winter. I remember waking my sisters, the ones closest in age to me, to go to the outhouse late at night.

I was no more than three years old and was always afraid of falling in. My sisters would hang onto my hand as I sat on the cold toilet seat that was carefully propped over a hole cut into a piece of plywood.

We were unleashed and unsupervised in those early years, running barefoot and wild in the woods with no one around: the nearest neighbor was over a mile away. My siblings were my best friends and only playmates. I was fearless then, catching rabbits and birds with my bare hands, and climbing trees to explore nests and get a better view of the small patch of world around me.

What, I wondered during the week following my EMDR session, had happened to that little girl?

August 31

*L*et *go*. It's a strange thing, to hear distinct words in my mind and not be afraid. The words are driving and persistent. I think of it as a nagging thought, like when I remember that I've forgotten something but don't know what. I don't know exactly what "let go" means, but I know it has to do with the farmhouse bedroom I was in with my father, because the room is what I see.

Part of me doesn't want to know what happens next in the picture, and part of me does, so letting go seems like a leap of faith. Let go of the fear ... and trust.

I can't remember the last time I let go.

"I have to let go," I tell Dr. Erickson the moment I sit down. "I remembered something. As a little girl I loved to climb trees and jump off. I was always jumping off of something—rooftops, bridges, trees, cliffs—and I always landed safely. I liked jumping. It was okay to jump as long as I had a place to land."

He looks at me with that amused-anticipation expression, as if he's excited by my words. "You're going to let go?"

I nod. I'm determined to move something in the picture. It's taken me the better part of a week to extract the intrusive little girl with the long black hair from my place in the room. I'm ready to resume the memory and my place in it.

It's difficult to put the images away and function during the day. They're like a movie that's always playing, distracting me. Only this movie comes with flashbacks—sudden, unexplainable bouts of fear that punch a hole in my stomach. I don't like the feeling of being on guard, of waiting for the knife to drop.

Dr. Erickson sets up for EMDR, moving the chairs to the center of the room in the same configuration as before, with his left arm alongside my left arm. I want to ask him why we need to be so close, but when I think the question in my head, it sounds paranoid. A powerful sense of his hand reaching out to grab me assaults me again. What is it with his hand that makes me feel so afraid? Thoughts move randomly and are disconnected: he's not in control of his hands, they will hurt me even though he doesn't mean to; his hands want something from me.

I argue with these thoughts. I don't like that they've planted seeds of doubt that spawn distrust. I instinctively know that Dr. Erickson is not going to hurt me and would never cross my boundaries. I sense that he will not touch me. He's always careful about giving me room to enter the office, to find my seat.

I push the voices aside and discipline myself to focus on the task at hand.

"Think about being in the room." His voice is smooth and soft and it instantly relaxes me. "You're kneeling with your father …"

My hands are resting on my naked thighs. My father is kneeling in front of me. He reaches out and opens my legs. I nervously tuck my hands between my thighs to cover my genitals, protecting myself. He takes my right hand and moves it until my palm is pressed to the floor—gentle, always gentle. He keeps his hand on mine, pinning it to the hard floor while his other hand caresses my inner thigh. I can't pull my hand away. His strong fingers keep it pressed firmly to the floor.

I look away to stop EMDR. My fingers are wrapped around my right wrist, bruising my bones.

"Still stuck?" Dr. Erickson asks quietly. He's not more than a foot from me and I have nowhere to hide.

"Yes, my father takes my hand away and holds it to the floor."

"This is after you cover yourself?"

"Yes."

"The other little girl isn't in the image any longer?"

"No, she's standing in the room, watching."

"Stay with this," he says and begins the steady motion of his hand.

I can't pull my hand away from its spot on the floor. Strong fingers keep it pressed firmly in place. My father's hand on my inner thigh moves—

Darkness.

A little girl is on her back. My father pushes his fingers into her. She is crying.

I turn the images over in my mind like a child examining a new toy. "It's strange that she's crying."

"Why is that strange?"

"Because I don't know why she would be crying."

"Are those tears of pain or frustration, humiliation?"

"I don't know," I say quietly, concentrating on the image. "She's just crying."

"You're not associating with this at all," he says, with a tone of concern.

"I told you what the pictures look like." And then I wonder aloud, "Why are there still blank spots?"

"Your subconscious is protecting you. It might be something you don't need to know, or information you're not ready to process. Your subconscious will only give you information you can handle."

Meaning I won't be back in the psych ward, or, at the very least, what I learn won't kill me. I will survive.

"It's good that there are blank spots," Dr. Erickson says. "You're not trying to invent a story to fill in the emptiness."

You read about it all the time, false memory. I only know what's in my mind and what I feel: *that* is my reality.

My fingers encircle my right wrist. "I can feel his fingers on me, holding my hand down on the floor."

He nods. "That's a powerful connection. If I were to hold your wrist, you'd be connected to the memory instantly. You'd be right there."

I frown. I don't want to be *right there*, trapped in the room and powerless to defend myself. It's difficult enough to look at the images unfolding before me and to acknowledge that they're a part of my life, but to *be* that image?

"Does your father say anything to you?"

"He says something," I say easily.

"What is it?"

"I don't know." My thoughts drift. I can hear the murmur of my father's voice, soft and seductive. "Something stupid."

"Why is it stupid?"

"It just would be stupid." Lies and silly words with soft laughter that only confuse me. How do I feel this without betraying myself, and the life I know as my own? "It seems like my goal is a long way away."

"I think for you it's going to take some time."

His words crush me. I don't want it to take a long time. I just want to learn to like touch so I can have a relationship and live a normal life.

"Who's that little girl on the floor?" he asks.

She's lying on her back with my father's hand between her legs, crying. Nobody can hear her. Nobody is coming to help.

"I don't know." What I do know is that little girl is not me.

CHAPTER 6

This most recent image had upset me and I'd begun to think that maybe I'd made it all up. Certainly I couldn't have forgotten that. It didn't mesh with my idea of who I thought I was, of my childhood playing with my siblings and exploring the woods. And I didn't want it to be me. I didn't want to be that person who was molested. It was a story I wasn't willing to write.

I didn't want to talk to Pleasing Sister. Everything was always all right with her. Because she was Dad's favorite, and because she always liked to keep the peace, I thought that having this discussion with her wouldn't be such a great idea. Plus, being in the medical field meant she wasn't keen on psychotherapy. Her physician had recommended it when she became disabled, and that didn't go down too well. She didn't understand how talking about her disability would help anything.

I kept my therapy to myself, and somehow Pleasing Sister and I lived together in stilted peace.

So I called Angry Sister. Dad had molested us individually, in locked rooms and on business trips. Although my sisters and I had never spoken of it with each other, we knew that we shared that experience.

Angry Sister doesn't understand why I'm in therapy. Those had been the first words out of her mouth when I had asked for help.

My answer was simple: "I want what you have, to have a husband and children if I want."

That had shut her up quickly. I asked what Dad did to her, but she wouldn't answer. I tried another approach and shared my memory, and told her I wondered if it was real.

"Yes," she said. "If Dad followed a pattern then what he did to you is real."

That was the end of the conversation.

September 7

I've been thinking this didn't happen to me," I say to Dr. Erickson. It's not what I wanted to talk about, but it's what comes out of my mouth the moment I sit down. "I don't see how I could've forgotten something like this."

He stares at me with an indecipherable expression. Is he angry? Disappointed? He's always relaxed and comfortable in his chair on the opposite side of the room. He folds into it like a cat in a favorite spot. As usual, I rush to fill the void.

"I was thinking this wasn't real and I wanted to know, so I told my sisters what I remembered and asked them if it seemed real. And they said yes, that if Dad had followed a pattern, I was remembering it correctly. The same thing happened to them. You remember I told you about the Wednesday nights? When my father would have us sit around naked and play games?"

He nods. His expression is still guarded.

"I thought there were a lot of Wednesday nights—four or six of them, at least—but they say no, only one night. It was a long night, they said. I was only nine and it was a school night. It went late into the night and we all got tired. Only one night, but I thought it was lots of them.

Now everything's all jumbled and confused. I never thought my father touched me. I only remember touching him. I've always only remembered that one thing. Now I have these other memories and I don't know what to do with them."

"Everything is all jumbled up and you don't know what's real."

"Yes. I don't know where I fit into all of this. I remember going to a hotel once, but my sisters say I went more often than that. And there were times when my father kept me home from school. My sisters say that when he kept them home he would molest them. I don't remember those things."

And yet I know they're true. My sisters wouldn't lie to me. It's my life that's been a lie; a nice lie I've sold myself.

"The human mind is complex," Dr. Erickson explains gently. Something has shifted in his expression, as if he's resolved something of his own. "What you remember of that Wednesday night, stretching it out into lots of nights, is called a screen memory." He stretches out his hands to mime an invisible screen. "It's a shield protecting you from other memories. As long as it was in place you didn't have to think about anything else."

And now that I see it for what it is? Now what?

"All of these images are coming forward for you to heal, so you can be a whole and complete person."

When he says "whole and complete person," it makes me think about being an incomplete person, and that seems like a strange concept to me. I'm very successful at my profession. I manage my finances well. I pay my taxes and obey the laws. I think I have a good life, or is that just something I've been telling myself? Money and a career, a beautiful house and a safe existence … isn't that a good life? And does a good life mean happiness?

"Will I have to remember everything to heal?"

"No. You only need to remember what's important for your healing. There are lessons in those memories you need to learn to have the things you want. You remember your goal?"

I have a picture in my mind of who I want to be: laughing, easy, outreaching, and unafraid. Even as I call up the image in my mind, she seems familiar, like that little girl running around barefoot and jumping out of trees. The girl I was before my father molested me.

"What do you need to do to attain your goal?" he asks.

I know the pictures have to go away. They're distracting and fearful for me. If there's a lesson in these images, I don't know what it can be.

"What is it that you want?" he asks intensely.

"To be free."

"How can you be free?"

"By letting go of the past."

But I don't know how to let go. I only know how to hold on: hold onto the pain, hold onto the fear, hold onto the lies. This is the cage I've built for myself. It's a safe and secure cage. I know every corner of it, and I know I can't be harmed in it because I won't let anyone inside with me.

But that's not the picture of who I want to be. That is the old me.

"You've gotten good at keeping yourself safe," he reminds me. He speaks as if he can see the pictures in my head. "But that safety has come with a very high price—loneliness. If you're free, your life won't be as comfortable. Relationships are complicated. They aren't always pleasant. Have you thought that a relationship might not always be pleasant and happy?"

"Yes, I know. I'm okay that it might not always be happy, but at least it's living. I can take those chances. I want to change things in my life."

"Okay," he says with a small smile. "Are you ready to let go of the past?"

"Yes."

"Let's take a short break."

"I want to talk to you about something." Dr. Erickson says when we resume. He has set aside my chart to give me his full attention. "When you go away in the pictures in your memory, that's called dissociation. When stressful things happen, the mind breaks off. Have I shown you mind maps?"

I shake my head. I don't like where he's going.

He steps to the dry-eraser board and begins drawing. He makes a circle. "This is your mind. To be a good victim you can't be angry, so you stay over here in this section being hurt." He draws a little stick figure in the circle. "Another part of you is over here, a happy little girl who hasn't been hurt. These are all separate places. Children are great at separating things, especially traumas. They survive because in their minds these things haven't happened to them."

I know he's trying to make a point, but for the life of me I don't know what it is. I study the map he's drawn, wondering what people do with all that space in their minds. My own mind seems crowded, a maze of walls, and at the center, a dark hole.

"Is everybody's mind like that?"

"People are different, but this is a general diagram of someone who's been abused."

I don't like things separated the way he's shown it in his drawing. I think everything should be together, simple and uncomplicated. The mind map shows a compartmentalized diagram like a tiny house with rooms. Is that where memories go? And why was I so compelled to change it?

"How do you get things together so they aren't separated?"

"You heal." He says it with such certainty that I almost believe him. "The mind wants to heal. It wants to be whole and complete. When you're ready to heal, like you are now, it begins to show you what you need to do."

"How do you get into those places that are separated off?"

"Those are walls. In our minds, we store all sorts of information. Everything we learn and experience is remembered, even if we 'forget' it. Trauma is stored in walls in our minds. When something happens to trigger those memories, the walls crumble. They are ready to be worked."

I think about my breakdown, of everything falling around me. Now I see I have lots of walls in my mind, placed like in an elaborate maze.

"You can find this wall in your mind." His voice is soft and hypnotic.

A great stone wall stands before me. It has a tiny hole at the bottom, a way to escape through to the other side.

"There might be feelings in this wall, or more pictures."

"Do I have to work all the walls to be better?" There are so many. How did there get to be so many?

"No," he says. "It used to be thought that you have to remember every detail and experience every event, but that's old thinking. We know now that you can heal without remembering everything. Remembering everything only slows the work down. This doesn't have to take a long time. It can take two months, or even two weeks. Once you get the information you need, healing happens very fast."

"How do I get the information I need?"

"You connect with the little girl in that room."

I feel myself scowl. I don't like that idea at all. It's her memory, not mine. Why should I have to feel her pain?

"Healing happens on many levels," he tells me. "I like my patients to heal at a cellular level. You feel the pain and you push through it. Energy traps emotions in the body and makes people sick. Pushing through the pain releases the energy. It won't have power over you anymore. No more anxiety, or headaches and nightmares."

That sounds like freedom ... and like a lot of work going places I've spent my life avoiding. It means going back to something I buried thirty years ago. *Thirty years.* My head begins to pound. It all seems so impossible.

"I wish I knew a different way for you to heal, but this is the only way I know." He says it almost like an apology.

"I want to finish with this so I don't have to do it again." I think of my previous experience with therapy. It had worked for a while but the memories are still there, trapping me in my cage. "I don't want to be back here in five years with the same thing."

"You want to do some work?"

"Yes." My voice sounds small and uncertain. I don't know where the work will take me.

"Find the wall."

I relax back into my chair. My fingers twist together as I find the image. "It's a long wall."

"Move the wall to a place away from the other walls, so you can work undistracted."

"Okay."

The wall moves to a black spot. It stands white against the darkness.

"Somewhere in this wall is the farmhouse. Can you find that spot?"

There's something in the wall. I can feel it, like an entire world hidden in the thick bricks I've constructed in my mind. At the bottom, a little girl peers through a hole.

"You don't have to go back into the room," he says softly. "You can do all the work from here, get the lessons you need, let go of the past."

I like the sound of his voice. It's like warm water going through me. I want to let go. I want to be free.

The little girl on the floor in the room is tortured and as real as the dish of stones on the table. And still she is not me.

"I keep thinking about the room."

"It's easier to do this work from the walls, but it seems like you're going to do it from the memory." He pauses. "So, what about the room?"

"That girl ..." I begin. The image of her is sharp and clear. "She doesn't seem like me."

He watches me quietly.

"I don't know how I'm going to connect with that picture."

"You're already connected to it." He grabs his wrist to remind me that I do feel something in the picture, that there's a part of me that keeps me tied to it.

I scowl. I don't like his hands. *You're not supposed to touch me.* The words echo in my head and I keep the words from slipping past my lips.

"I want to change things and have a different life. I'm *trying* to change things."

"Don't be so hard on yourself," he says gently, with a tiny frown. "You've been like this for a long time. It's going to take time to change these things in your life."

But I want everything to change immediately. I don't want it to take time.

CHAPTER 7

I 've never been big on taking medication. I barely take aspirin. But now I'd taken to carrying a bottle of Excedrin around because my headaches were constant, the tension and anxiety twisting my muscles into knots. Flashbacks ambushed me during the day and it was only the Seroquel at night that was giving me any relief.

"Why," Shameful Sister asked me, "are you making it so difficult on yourself?"

Shameful Sister had entered therapy also, intent on resolving her childhood issues. She had taken the medical path, which made sense since she was in the medical field. I think it comforted her to know that there was a label for every ailment and a drug to match.

"Tell your psychiatrist to give you Zoloft for the anxiety," she told me, "and Wellbutrin. That's what I'm taking."

We found a strange link in therapy that we'd never shared in our childhood. We talked on the phone about EMDR, which she hated, and the pain of remembering. She was married with two children and had suddenly discovered that she was terribly unhappy. Worse, she saw that she had married a man just like our dad—unfaithful, self-centered and insatiable when it came to sex.

"No," I told her. "I want to do it without antidepressants and anti-anxiety meds. I don't think they're helpful in the long run. I just want to have a different life."

That was a mistake. She felt that I was judging her, and maybe I was. I didn't see how medicating our emotions could lead to a well-adjusted life. I could already see her path. She would be one of those people in therapy for decades.

But then, who was I to judge her? The truth was, neither of us was getting better.

I had taken time off work to heal, and I fell into an unproductive pattern of doing nothing except waiting for the next session. Did doctors realize the pain of starting something and not finishing it? My mind drifted and it was almost impossible for me to concentrate on any single thought. I would start to sweep the porch, only to abandon the task to get a drink of water. I would see the washer and remember I had laundry to do.

I didn't like being unproductive and needy. I liked being in charge. Getting to my therapy session seemed to be the only thing I could manage, but turning therapy into a job seemed pitiful. I felt like a fragile, damaged woman, and I couldn't help but wonder what Dr. Erickson thought of me. Did he know that I could balance my own checking account? Pay my own taxes and manage a household?

I looked at the patients in the waiting room each week and winced. Most were with a caseworker and on county assistance. They looked as if someone had to dress them each morning. I had private insurance and drove myself to the clinic. This, I told myself, made me different from them, and by different I meant better.

I didn't like knowing that about myself, but I didn't like much about me anyway. It was just one more thought to drag me down. The truth was, I was just like everyone else—a little damaged and trying to get by.

September 12

"Are we going to connect with the girl today?" Dr. Erickson asks.

"Yes." My voice is thin and weak. I have a fear of getting into the picture and not being able to find my way out. Can people get trapped in a memory? "I don't know how to, though."

"If I pin your wrist, you'll associate to it quickly."

Psychiatrists always want you to *feel* something. It isn't enough for Dr. Erickson that I've remembered. He wants me to *be* that little girl, to feel her fear and pain. Live it and release it. I would argue against the benefit of this seemingly archaic practice, but I can't get the image out of my mind. Flashbacks attack me throughout each day as the sense of helplessness and restraint intensifies.

I try to pull my hand free. Dad is stronger than I am and my efforts are useless. His fingers are probing and exploring, invading my most intimate and private area. I'm powerless to stop him. Why? Why is he doing this? Doesn't he feel my humiliation and fear? Or is it that he simply doesn't care? The little girl lies on her back with my father over her. She's crying and he's oblivious to her pain.

"You have the look of someone who's fallen into a black pit," Dr. Erickson tells me.

Why would he do that to such a small child? Didn't her pain matter? Was she only an object for his pleasure? I'm grateful the office is dimly lit. I can hide in the shadows and not feel alone.

"I want you to imagine the healing white light surrounding you," Dr. Erickson says softly. "You can take everything you need from this light. It has more love and strength than anyone can use. It's an infinite source. Take as much as you need."

It's easy to follow his voice. I move away from the little girl as the healing white light wraps around me. Fear and confusion subside. It's like a drug, this white light, and it makes me feel loved and protected.

"Your energy looks better," he says finally.

I feel better. I'm far away from the images and the little girl, but the dark places in the memory haunt me. They're living things that breathe and move. I feel them pressing against me, demanding attention. All I can think is: *I want a new life.*

I've never been more alone or sad than I am in this moment, faced with memories I can't own, confronted with elements of my life I'm unable to accept. Why did I have to look back? Will I ever be able to have the life I want?

I look down. My fingers have encircled my right wrist without me knowing it.

"I want to talk to you about safety," he says. He has masked his expression again.

I look at him in confusion. My stomach tightens, but I hold myself still and pretend nothing is wrong.

"Are you having thoughts of hurting yourself?"

Hurting myself? I feel a shield go up around me as my body tenses with offense. Is this what he thinks of me? An image comes to me: a drawn and shattered woman who can't hold down a job, who's been in and out of hospitals after suicide attempts, who has an addiction problem. She is the poster image for the abused woman.

She is not me.

"No," I say, and try to make my voice sound neutral, unoffended.

"Have you ever hurt yourself?"

He's expecting a "yes." I can see it in his eyes; the worn look he had in the hospital. I'm not his first patient, and I realize there's nothing new I can tell him.

"No, I've never hurt myself." Then, because I want him to see me for who I am, I add, "I've never wanted to hurt myself."

"What about drugs? Cocaine?"

Cocaine? No one has ever asked me if I've done cocaine or other drugs, but Dr. Erickson's question sparks first offense and then sadness; offense because I'm not a person who does drugs or drinks to excess, and sadness because he doesn't see me. To him, I'm like the hundreds who've come before me. Because isn't that what women who have been abused do? Self-medicate with drugs and alcohol, use sex as a weapon and means to gain control?

"No, I don't take drugs." It's a struggle to keep my tone polite. "I've never even *tried* any illegal drugs."

"Good," he says easily. "This work is easier when we aren't having to deal with safety issues. I was concerned, because a lot of times perps plant suggestions into children's minds. When you go back and work the memory, you can uncover a subconscious suggestion."

He looks closely at me. "Haven't you ever wondered how child molesters get away with molesting for years?"

I nod, even though I'm beginning to see how easily it can happen.

"They're masters at manipulation. A child's mind is very suggestible. A molester might plant an idea in a child's mind like, 'This is all a dream, this never happened,' or 'If you tell anybody you're going to have to kill yourself.' The child buries those suggestions with the trauma. Bring the trauma to the surface and you bring the suggestion with it. That's why I asked if your father was saying anything to you."

My father has always said lots of things. I can hear the murmur of his voice, but there are no clear words that follow. I've learned to shut my ears to his lies.

"Lots of children are abused at night in their beds and a perp will tell them it's a fantasy or a story they were told. There's an important age in child development when children have extraordinary imaginations, when fantasy and reality get crossed."

"Is that why this little girl is like Alice in Wonderland?" It hasn't occurred to me until that very moment that's who she resembles, with her pale features and proper manners. "I hated Alice in that story."

"Why is that?"

"I don't know." But I do know. To my eleven-year-old mind, there was such chaos and disorder in the story that I couldn't tolerate it. And the characters were mean. "I liked *Wizard of Oz* best."

These thoughts of my childhood turn me to pleasant memories.

"My mom used to read to us all the time. When I was real little, two, three years old, we lived on a lake in a cabin without electricity or indoor plumbing. Mom would read Robert Service or Edgar Allen Poe to us by lantern light." I smile at the memory. "We didn't have toys and there was no television, so during the day we would run around the woods and pretend we were cowboys or sailors. We only had our imaginations to keep us occupied. We'd be gone all day. I'd collect frogs and toads and snakes and put them in my pockets. Mom would get angry because I'd forget about them and they'd jump out of my shorts at night. She finally had to make a rule: empty your pockets before you come into the house."

Dr. Erickson raises his eyebrows in amusement. "Were your parents Amish or something?"

"No, just antisocial." By way of explanation, I added, "It was the sixties."

The only people I can remember my parents entertaining were clergy. We had the kind of family that drew people's attention. Eight children tend to be noticeable, even in a small Catholic community in the late sixties.

"Everybody always thought we had such a great family. You know, all of those children and everybody happy. We'd take up a whole pew when we went to church. It seems hypocritical," I say.

"It feels like you were living a lie?"

I nod. No one knew our father was molesting his daughters. I wonder now if people saw only what they wanted to see—a happy, loving family.

"Do your sisters have relationships now?"

"Yes, most are married with children."

"Did they get help to heal?"

"Some, for a while. One of my sisters doesn't like sex and another is so angry that she can't be in the same room with my father; she hates him so much. She's angry that he's never been punished. She says she's already done her healing. But she can't talk about what happened because when she does she can't have sex with her husband for a few weeks, and there are things she can't do with her husband because they remind her of the abuse." I look at him. "That's not the kind of healing I want."

"No, that's not healing. It sounds like your sister has done a good job of convincing herself. She has everything well repressed."

And still it surfaces to interfere in Angry Sister's life, I think, preventing her from having a healthy sex life, dictating her conversations and restricting her thought processes. Even the good memories of childhood have become poison fruit to her.

What I want is freedom from my memories, a life without self-imposed restrictions. I don't want to live in a tight box with limitations on what I can think and say. That's how I've lived for the past thirty years, avoiding my pain and just pretending to live. Now I don't want to simply survive; I want to thrive.

"She's older than I am," I say. "I'm the youngest girl. She was molested until she was eighteen. I don't remember being molested after the age of eleven. My father chose her ..."

... *over me.* I can't bring myself to finish the sentence.

"When he stopped molesting me, I became a non-person, like I didn't even exist. I think it was sometime after the fifth grade. He used to tell me I was a cold and unfeeling child. I remember wondering what I'd done to make him think that, to make him stop loving me."

My tone is hollow as I repeat my father's words. The lonely feeling I carried as a child weighs heavily on me. "It's a strange thing to say, but I almost wish he continued to molest me, just to know that I was loved. He chose my sisters and left me alone."

And that is one of the tragedies of child abuse: the lessons learned carve wounds so deep they become a part of who we are.

"Are you worthy of love?" he asks.

My stomach tightens and I refuse to allow my mind to consider his question. "I'd like to learn to be more compassionate."

"That wasn't the question."

I look away from him and say nothing.

CHAPTER 8

When I was a little girl, my parents fished every night. When they had caught enough we had a fish fry—tiny perch and lake trout pan-fried on the old cast-iron skillet. I didn't like fish because the bones made me choke. Mom told us that some people die from choking on fish bones, and so we had to be careful.

One evening she sent us all to the lake to wash up before bed, putting the oldest child, our sister, in charge of the four of us youngest ones. We quickly stripped out of our dirty clothes. The water was cold, even though it was summer. It never seemed to get warm and we only ever went in up to our knees, leaving us shivering when the sun went down.

"Hurry up and don't fool around," our oldest sister said. She was in middle school. She opened a book and sat on the bench near the shore.

We stood in a place on the shore where the lake bottom was clear. There were no crabs or bloodsuckers to worry about like near the dock. Our feet sank into the sandy bottom until they disappeared. If we wiggled just right, we could sink past our ankles and it would look like we had no feet. My two sisters, our little brother and I all squealed with delight as we tried to keep our balance without any feet.

"Start washing," our sister ordered from where she sat peering over the cover of her book. "And get the soap everywhere."

I liked the soap only on my tummy. I rubbed it around until the bubbles were creamy and thick.

"You have to do it this way," one of my sisters said.

The two girls rubbed the soap on my back and arms. In no time I was a mass of bubbles as their hands wandered all over my body with unrestrained enthusiasm.

"Don't get it in my eyes," I demanded and rushed to cover them.

Their hands slid over my skin easily. I reached out to soap them in turn. My younger brother joined in, and we became multiple pairs of hands, all in motion like a perfectly timed mechanism. We didn't know whose body we were touching and it didn't matter. There were no boundaries for us. We giggled and played until our oldest sister had had enough and ordered us out.

September 19

I was thinking about touch," I tell Dr. Erickson.
He looks at me, waiting.

It's partly why I came into therapy, to learn to like touch so I can have an intimate physical relationship. That's been the stumbling block, I remind myself, the cause of my isolation, and if I want this new life I'm going to have to understand touch.

"I think people touch for themselves," I say. "You know, not for the other person."

"You think it's self-serving?"

"Yes, it doesn't make sense why you would touch for somebody else's pleasure. People don't feel pleasure at being touched."

"Why is that?" His eyes brighten and I sense a trap.

"Because they don't. It's the person who's doing the touching that gets the pleasure."

I've gone round and round with my friends on this, analyzing and polling, trying to understand why anyone would want someone to touch them, and how they can possibly feel pleasure at such an intrusion. Of course, my friends say they like to be caressed and adored, so it doesn't explain anything for me.

"There are all different kinds of touch," Dr. Erickson explains. "Touch for comfort. Touch for pleasure. Touch to soothe. Touch that's tickling, stroking, scratching, playful, tender. You experienced one kind of touch and made a decision about it. That decision—that hands hurt—became your reality."

And why, I wonder, is my reality wrong?

"You say you don't like to be touched," he says. "When you assign yourself a label, it becomes you. But you didn't always hate touch. You slept with your sisters when you were little. A big puppy pile," he says, echoing my earlier words.

"Yes." All of us snuggled in the same bed, buried under heavy quilts and giggling until we fell asleep. Touch was given and received freely, and without consequences. It was as simple as breathing. I had forgotten how good touch felt, how innocent it could be.

"You have a good experience with touch," Dr. Erickson reminds me. "You told me about the boy who caressed you. You can draw lessons from that experience as well."

"I watch people," I say. "I watch how one person touches the other, thinking they're comforting them, but they aren't. They're touching for themselves, to give themselves something to do. It doesn't comfort."

He takes a deep breath and rests his arms on his knees to peer at me from an angle. "I know this goes against your beliefs, but contrary to what you believe, hands don't have agendas. Hands don't have neurons; they can't think. Hands don't hurt people. People hurt people."

Although I hate it when he tries to educate me on biology, the intellectual part of my brain kicks in against my will. I know what he's telling me is sound logic, but it doesn't feel right. Hands are instruments of harm. Hands invade. I know this to be true in every fiber of my being.

I see the little girl on the floor, struggling to free herself. I feel this so strongly in my body that my mind rejects his words. I don't believe him.

"I don't like this picture," I announce suddenly. "When is it going to go away?"

"I don't know. When you're done processing it. When you've learned what you need to."

That's not what I want to hear. His words are frustrating me.

"Something's not right with this picture. It doesn't make any sense to me." I'm thinking about how quickly things change in the picture, the blank spaces that are like vacuums. "I'm missing something." I press my memory, sending my mind into the darkness, probing.

His hand is between my legs, fingers exploring and manipulating …

"I keep thinking … that it's pleasure."

"And you reject that idea?"

"Yes."

He stands and goes to the dry-eraser board.

Arousal	Relaxation
Pleasure	Trust
Excitement	Surrender
Pain	Hopelessness

When he's finished writing, he says, "These are the things that are needed to have an orgasm. The body is hardwired. It doesn't care what's happening—Coke bottle, Cadillac, armadillo. You rub down there and your body responds."

I reject his premise immediately. My body does not react like other women's. But still I study the words, trying to fit them into my picture. Is that what happened? Did the little girl in the picture feel pleasure?

"Surrender is a type of relaxation," he says. "It's unfortunate the way the body works, because sometimes women can have an orgasm during rape when they give up and surrender."

But does that make sense? What is it that my father wanted from her? Was he looking for her pain? Or did she not respond at all? I focus on one of the words: *hopelessness.*

"That doesn't make any sense," I say quietly. "If he got what he wanted from her … it doesn't make any sense."

"What doesn't make any sense?"

"The end of the picture."

"What happens at the end of the picture?"

She's on her back, feeling panicked and trapped, with no hope of rescue.

"The girl's on the floor," I tell him. "Her hand is being held. She's upset and crying. He pushes his fingers into her." I look back at the board, staring intensely at the words as if they were going to speak to me.

Is that my lesson? Pleasure?

She lies on her back. The expression on her face is one of torment. She's a crushed and broken soul that stares into me with such haunting intensity, and if I let it, it will pierce my cool veneer of self-control and wound me more deeply than I can recover from.

She's trying to tell me something. I can see that in her *penetrating stare, in the way the image remains in the recesses of my mind.*

'Images come forward to help you get what you want.'

She's going to be difficult. I know she isn't just going to go away.

"You need to know these things," Dr. Erickson says, "but this is just distracting you so I'm going to erase it."

As he erases the words I've tattooed in my mind, I say, "I think she's afraid."

"There's a physiological response to arousal. The heart quickens, respirations increase, perspiration forms." He pauses. "Fear is a form of arousal. The body doesn't distinguish between sexual arousal and fear. There are some people who cannot become aroused unless they evoke fear. You know about people who need pain to have orgasms? Those people have confused sexual arousal with fear and pain. An important part of your healing is going to be learning how to separate fear from pleasure."

When I'm in session and my thoughts are directed to the memories and images, I've noticed that my body responds as if it were being pleasured. I can feel fear coursing through me, setting my heart to racing and tightening my muscles with anticipation, and I can feel the moisture between my legs, the gentle throb of wanting release as if I'd been indulging in an erotic fantasy rather than processing a painful and humiliating memory.

... *separate fear from pleasure.*

Have I tangled fear and pleasure, humiliation and desire? I don't want to have to feel fear to feel pleasure, but in my adult life a man has never aroused me. I know this is partly because I've never allowed a man close enough to do so, but now I wonder: can I be aroused through pleasure?

"I don't like this picture," I announce.

"You didn't like the other pictures, either."

True. "But this is different. This is longer. It's different."

"You said something interesting earlier," he says. He's folded himself back into the chair, his spine curved and relaxed.

"What's that?"

"You said she's upset and crying."

"Yes."

He nods. "Who's 'she'?"

She is the girl. *She* is the image in the memory. "The girl in the picture."

"Right, because that's not you."

"No, that's not me."

He's silent for a long moment. "How do you want to leave this today? Do you want to think about the picture some more?"

"Yes, I want to figure some things out." I want to talk to my sisters and find answers. They're older than me and remember more. I'll fill in the blank spots and then I can let the picture go.

"Try not to figure out what your father's doing, what his motivations are. Look at the dark spot from your side only."

Maybe that's what's wrong. I'm trying to figure out my father, why he did what he did. "All right," I say softly and let out a breath." He's going to do what he's going to do."

Silence.

"Hands go where hands go," he says.

I look at him with suspicion, but his face reveals nothing. Those are my words. I recognize them and it irritates me that he's repeated them. I stand. "I'll think about the picture. I'll sort some things out."

CHAPTER 9

W hen I was only three years old, I loved to play with toads. I knew where they hid: under the old leaves near the chestnut tree. I'd quickly stuff them in one of the pockets of my shorts and run down the hill to the lakeshore. I was always barefoot, but my feet barely felt the twigs and pebbles I'd trample over as I crashed through the woods. I knew my way down the embankment, but it wasn't confidence so much as sheer fearlessness that propelled my stubby legs down the hill.

My sisters and brother, all of us a year apart, were at the shore one day, hunting crabs and frogs for the ranch we had built. We didn't have toys. What toys we had gotten for Christmas were long since lost, so we made do with what we could find in the northern woods around the lake.

"We got some crabs," my sister said, and opened her small fist to show her prize.

It was a tiny crab so the pinchers didn't hurt. We didn't like to play with the bigger crabs that latched onto our fingers with their hard claws.

I saw a spotted salamander on a fallen log. My hand was quicker than the salamander and I soon had the cool lizard in a tight cage of my fingers.

"That's enough now," my sister said. She was the oldest and we followed her lead without question. "Let's take them back to the ranch."

The ranch was nothing more than a shallow circle we had dug in the sandy soil near the back of our cabin. The corral was in the middle, and a narrow sand wall offered separation for the toads, lizards, crabs and snakes we had gathered.

We dropped them into our handcrafted ranch. We pushed the tiny crabs with the tips of our fingers to get them to move. They were more fun to play with when they were moving. The fast-moving snakes and salamanders kept us busy. They were escape artists, trying to find a place to hide from our intrusive hands. We began to expand the ranch, adding water and then a moat, and soon the game had morphed into something else entirely. We added and subtracted all afternoon until we were called in for dinner.

"Let all those animals go," Dad said in a gentle voice.

That was the rule. We could play with animals, but we couldn't keep them. They had to be returned from where we had taken them. As my siblings rushed to the lake to return our captives, I went in for dinner.

"Stop," Mom commanded.

I stood at the door, barefoot and dirty after a day of playing. The cabin was smoke filled, and I smelled the sweet aroma of pancakes that filled the undersized kitchen.

"Empty your pockets," she said. "I'm tired of finding dead things in your clothes."

I'd forgotten about the toad and snake I had pocketed earlier. I quickly emptied my pockets and washed in the small basin on the counter.

The soap had bits of sand imbedded in it, which abraded my skin as I soaped up. We only ever had one bar of soap; in summer, when we went into the lake to bathe, we always tried to be careful with the soap so it didn't sink to the lake floor and get covered in sand. That was an impossible task, and inevitably one of my sisters had to rescue the soap. My older siblings hated it when we dropped the soap, because they were left to bathe with the gritty bar. Sometimes Mom bought the type of soap that floated, which was much better.

I sat down carefully in my spot at the table. The table was long and we didn't have enough chairs to go around, so Dad had made two benches. I had learned to plop down on the bench because sliding onto it put slivers in my butt.

We said grace, first, always. I bowed my head and eyed the stack of Swedish pancakes on the table. On the rare occasions we had meat at the table, there was only enough for one piece each. But pancakes I could have more of, enough to fill my tummy.

There was no formality at the table; there was no order to the way we did things in our family. Dinner was a first-come, first-serve affair, and I'd learned to be grabby, and to eat fast so I could have seconds while there were still seconds to have. Even at my young age I knew one thing about dinner in our family: when the food was gone there was no more.

We had fresh maple syrup in canning jars and we could drown our pancakes in the thin sweetness if we wanted, but I buttered the big, flat pancake instead and sprinkled cinnamon and sugar on it and rolled it up.

I didn't pay attention to the dinner conversation. I was too busy thinking about another pancake.

September 26

How do I get rid of an image in my mind?" The thought is uppermost in my mind and I blurt it out as soon as I sit down. "I've tried everything you've taught me. I've put the healing white light around it and tried to move it to another place to change the image. Nothing works."

I've been learning to work outside of the sessions, and to apply the lessons and techniques Dr. Erickson teaches to my images in an effort to move myself forward. Otherwise, I find myself waiting for the next session, feeling helpless and upset as the days pass.

"This is a memory?"

"No, not a memory, an image, something that surfaced after our talk about touch." An image I can barely acknowledge as my own. "I liked talking about touch because it's what I want to learn, but this image came in my mind the night after our session and I want to get rid of it."

I wait silently for him to help me erase these images my mind has conjured. I don't want to describe the new images that haunt me. If they're not memories—and they're not—then they come from a deeper part of me, a violent part that has no place in my life. They're disturbing and confusing, and I worry: Am I going insane?

"What's the image?" he asks.

I hesitate. It's disturbing enough to see them for myself, but to have a witness to my dementia breathes life into it. Dr. Erickson is a psychiatrist, and society has granted him a certain level of authority. My short stay in the psychiatric unit is still too vivid. I worry about what he'll think and do if I tell him.

I know that these images I'm having can't be the workings of a healthy mind, but rather the result of a tortured one. I quickly weigh the risks of revealing the disturbing image. In the end I'm left with a single concept: I have come to him for help.

"There are two," I tell him, "but I only want to tell you about one."

In the black landscape of my mind, I've segregated the images. The little girl on the floor is still crying. I can see her clearly, but I've pushed her to the back so that she's distant, her cries faint. In the forefront now, amid the blackness, is a small, shallow hole filled with severed hands.

Dr. Erickson doesn't even flinch as I share my image, but his stoic expression gives me a sense of failure.

"I've tried to send the healing white light into it," I explain quickly, "but the hole sucks it up. I tried to move it, but I can't. I've tried to cover it up and that doesn't work either."

It's a strange thing, not to have control over your own mind. If these images are my creation, then I should be able to destroy them as well; I should be able to erase them from the black palette on which they were painted. But I cannot.

"When you look at this pit, what do you feel?" he asks calmly.

Frightened, like I'm going to fall into it and be devoured. "All tight inside, like when you drop down fast on a roller coaster."

"You feel it in your stomach?"

"Mostly." There's tension between my legs, a strong sense of invasion and an overpowering need to protect myself. I can feel the hands sliding along my inner thigh, penetrating me, taking, taking ...

"Can you walk up to the pit?"

"No, it's dangerous." I can sense the danger, the anger from these hands at having been imprisoned, and anger from somewhere else, somewhere outside of the pit.

"So you have this black pit filled with all these severed hands just lying in there—"

I shake my head.

"Oh, they're alive. Okay, I'll go with that." He relaxes back in his chair. "Are these your hands?"

"No."

His ease with my dark image helps me to relax. He gives me a feeling of normality and my isolation fades by degrees. He's not going to act based on this image. I'm not going insane, at least not today.

"Are the hands all the same? Do they belong to the same person?"

Large dark hands that are severed between the wrist and elbow; fingers always moving, creeping and crawling, sneaking and taking ...

"Yes."

"Are they male hands or female hands?"

"Man hands."

"So, you disarmed him."

Is that what I did? I'd wondered where they'd come from and whom they belonged to. I know instantly they're my father's hands.

"Ask the little girl in the room if she's okay with you getting rid of these hands," Dr. Erickson says. "I want everybody on the same page so she doesn't undermine what we're doing."

I hate talking to the little girl. I don't like that she's a resident of my mind; that she's taken on a life of her own. It's impossible to get her attention. She frustrates me, and I feel helpless and angry with that. I see her lying on her back, crying and panicked. She doesn't hear me. I think she should just go away, dissolve into the ebony walls of my mind.

I move restlessly in the chair. I can feel Dr. Erickson's eyes on me as he patiently waits. "It's difficult to communicate ..."

How do I explain to him that I can't get her attention? That I don't know how to approach a crying, tormented child?

"I can't always ..."

How do I tell him that I've abandoned her to her pain and refuse to make it my own?

"I don—"

What was the question? My head pounds with tension and the back of my eyes feel ready to explode.

He's sitting quiet and still in his chair, an illustration of poise and patience.

I force myself to relax. She wants me to keep the hands. I don't know how I know this, but I do, and when I say it in my mind it feels right. She doesn't want to let them go. I can't tell him this. It will open too many questions I don't want to answer today.

"Is there anything she needs from the pit?" he prompts.

Anger. The word echoes in my mind.

"Ask her if she's okay, if the hands don't frighten her, so she doesn't have to be afraid of hands, of my hands."

I drop my gaze to the floor. He knows I'm afraid of his hands, though I've tried to hide my irrational fear from him. Suddenly I feel exposed. Can he see all my images?

"It won't make a difference to her," I say softly.

"So getting rid of the pit won't make touching okay for her?"

I shake my head. Nothing is going to make touching okay for her. As for the pit, it's a ticking bomb waiting to explode. I can feel it as I look at them: a sense of pending doom. And there's the other image I won't tell him about, the other hand that frightens me the most.

"Then she needs something else, so we'll go ahead and get rid of the pit," he says. "There's this special net I use to remove monsters and unwanted things." He begins to illustrate with his hands, making a large circle as if he's designing a net. "Will you let me take these hands in the net?"

I nod.

In the hole, the hands are never still. The silver net drops from above and captures the restless hands. Like fish in a net, they struggle against the restraints.

"The net catches the hands," he says. "That's quite a visual. They must be pretty upset. There's something called a centrifuge. It's a machine that breaks down elements, separates them into layers. What you need to take will float to the top; you can take that without knowing what it is. You just need to know that it's something you need. All the rest will return to the universe."

The net drops the hands into a big metal machine. It spins them into liquid.

"You might see layers glowing," he says quietly.

Many layers of gray, and at the top another layer that vibrates golden white.

"Take what you don't want—pain, anger, shame. Some things you may need or want." He moves his hands to scoop out the machine and then holds the imaginary refuse. "You have it, the anger and pain? You're okay to let it go?"

Don't let go of the anger! The words are a command, demanding and powerful.

"I don't want to let go of all the anger." It's for her, not me.

"No?" he asks easily. "Don't you think you can make more anger if you need it?"

"Probably." But wisdom won't let me release the anger that's not my own.

He's still holding the refuse. "Will you let the rest go?"

"Yes."

He's still holding the refuse for me. Like a mime performing, he gathers it and sends it away from where I sit.

In the expanding darkness of my mind, I see the pit of hands, undisrupted.

"The pit of hands is still there," I tell him.

"Okay." He thinks. "You can give them back to the people they belong to and we can work it from that angle."

"That's a lot of hands for one person."

He smiles. "But they're from different memories, from different times that the hands touched you. You just put them here so they can't hurt you anymore."

I only know one memory: the farmhouse. "I can give two hands back."

"Do you want to do that?"

It's already done.

"How many hands are left?"

"Six." All restlessly occupying the pit.

"Do some of these hands belong in the hotel room?"

I don't like it when he mentions the hotel room. I'm on the ceiling in that memory, far away from the bed and what's happening. I want to keep it that way.

"I don't know. I'm on the ceiling in the hotel."

"But you come down." He studies me. "You got out of that room. You're here now."

I don't know how I got out of the hotel room. I don't know what happened there, but it's a sinking feeling when I think about it, like slowly drowning. My thoughts shift back to the restless hands. "I was hoping to make all the hands go away."

"We gave it our best shot," he says lightly. "As we work your memories, the hands will go away. You'll process the information you need, and the hands won't be an issue anymore."

Process: remember, feel, release. For now they're with me.

CHAPTER 10

The family loves to tell a story of rescuing me from bees. It was actually First Brother's favorite story. I was only two years old and we were living in the cabin on the lake. The woods were our playground, and everything in there was something to explore, touch and examine.

I had developed a fascination with beehives. The large hives were suspended high in the trees. I loved the shape and sound of them, and had taken to poking them with a stick to get something to happen. That was the thing with beehives—they were a mystery. All that buzzing and activity, but no one could see what was happening inside.

"Stay away from those hives," Mom warned us.

One day I came into the house with a swollen eye.

"You were playing with that hive again, weren't you?" Mom said.

"Huh!" I said and walked away.

At least that's how the story goes.

The next year I was climbing a tree, as I often did, and fell into a hive in the hollow of a tree. I screamed as bees covered me and stung.

My older brother, then twelve years old, heard my screams and rushed to scoop me up. He ran, with me tucked in the curve of his arm, down the deer trail to the lake and dunked me in the water. My brother tells the story with much more flair and drama. I didn't remember the hive or the perilous journey to the lake, but I do remember sitting on the edge of a bed crying as my siblings held ice cubes to my stings.

My brother had gone to some nearby campers to get the ice. Over twenty beestings peppered my body. I remember all those ice cubes suspended from my siblings' fingers as they pressed them against my skin.

"It's all right," they had soothed.

I was surrounded by all those hands and felt only the ice.

October 3

"How are you doing?" Dr. Erickson asks. He stands at his desk in the tiny, cramped office, reviewing my chart as if he's seeing me for the first time.

Sometimes I think this reviewing is just a stall tactic, a psychological pause to allow me to acclimate to the office. It's disquieting enough to have him greet me in the lobby. He always comes out to get me. Even though his voice is always soft and he tries to be unobtrusive, I still feel on display. The short walk to his office feels painfully long.

"Okay," I answer softly. I promised myself not to answer that question because my answer is always a lie. "I'm worried about something."

He looks at me, chart in hand, and sits down. His expression is warm and friendly. I'm the first appointment for him today, and he's fresh and at ease. "What are you worried about?"

"Remember I told you last week that I had two images come to me after our talk about touch?"

He nods as he writes on my form. What could he be writing? I haven't said anything yet.

"I didn't want to tell you about the other image. I thought if the black pit with the hands went away, so would this. But it looks like the hands are going to be here for a while."

He looks at me.

"The other image worries me. I think I need to finish the image."

"This new image?"

"No, the image with my father, the movie in my head." That's how I've come to refer my memory; it plays like a scary movie in my mind, looping to the same scene and never moving forward.

"You changed the subject," he says smoothly, a small smile on his lips. "You use the word 'image' as a reference for several things. It confuses me."

He's confused? The images in my mind are disturbing: severed hands and knives, images of violence and anger that cannot be a part of me. Where are these images coming from, and why, suddenly, do I want so badly to hurt myself?

"So you want to work on the movie?"

"I was thinking I should fill in the blank spots."

Somehow this memory is in the center of everything, creating the dark images and thoughts, emotions that are not my own. If I can complete the memory these images will go away and I can concentrate on liking touch and learning how to be intimate.

"Do you need to fill in those blank spots to complete the movie?"

"Yes."

He takes a breath and sets down my chart. "Let me just rap at you for a while. You're a lineal thinker, but the human brain is complex. There's a right hemisphere of the brain and a left hemisphere. One side is analytical; one side is creative-slash-emotional. You're trying to make this process analytical and logical, column and data, everything adding up and balancing. You want proof and concrete evidence. What we're dealing with are emotional truths. This information isn't accepted in a court of law."

I understand what he's saying, but I still need to fill in the blank spots. The answers are there and nowhere else. I cross my legs and push myself further back into the chair.

"Can you connect with the end of the movie?" he asks.

"I don't know how."

"What's at the end?"

Dr. Erickson knows. He remembers everything I tell him. He asks just to see what I'll say.

"The little girl is lying on the floor, crying."

He watches me for a long time, and I wonder what I've said wrong. He's thinking hard about something. "What's the other image?" he asks.

"It's a hand with a knife through it," I say matter-of-factly.

He immediately writes on the chart. It's the first time I can remember him writing down something I've said. Somehow he just remembers my conversations and images, and the stories I share. Up until now he has been a comfortable and unobtrusive observer of my life, an impartial witness to my pain. Now he has made a permanent record of my image. It bothers me.

He watches me, but I can't meet his penetrating stare. I sit quietly in my skirt and heels, my hands resting politely in my lap, the perfect well-mannered lady.

"So there's this hand with a knife through it." He demonstrates a knife going through his palm.

I shake my head. "Like this." The hand is severed and a knife is pinned through the back of it.

"Like it's stuck to the floor?" he asks. "It's not going to hurt you now."

"No."

"Most people would be pretty upset about this image, a bloody hand all mangled ..." He continues to study me. "You're not upset?"

"No." I tell myself it's just an image, like a poorly constructed piece of artwork. "It worries me."

"Why does it worry you?" He tilts his head.

Because it makes me want to drive a knife through your hand, it makes me want to hurt people. It makes me want to hurt myself. "I think it's dangerous."

"Is it your hand?"

"Sometimes it's mine." I don't tell him I can feel the relief and satisfaction of driving a knife through my hand. "Sometimes it's someone else's."

Silence. The soft light in the room barely touches me and yet I cannot hide in the shadows.

"Why is it dangerous?" he asks.

"It just is. I think it's like a punishment."

"Who's being punished?"

I am. "I don't know. It's just what I feel." I'm careful not to move.

"Are you angry with someone?"

"No."

"You have a right to be angry."

"I'm not angry." I don't get angry. I've never gotten angry.

"Where do you think this image came from?" he asks.

"I don't know, but it has something to do with the end of the picture, because that's where my mind goes when I see this hand."

"To the little girl," he says with a nod. "She's been trapped in that room for a long time. Even though you don't feel her pain and anger, it exists. She lives it every day."

It's her pain, not mine. She's just a memory, a photograph of something that happened a long time ago, far away from the person I am now.

"When you connect with the girl," he explains, "you'll feel her anger and pain, and I think these images will go away."

He's tricking you.

That voice ... it's so strong it supersedes all thoughts, all reason. It's getting more difficult to ignore it.

"We can do EMDR on this," he offers. "See where the image takes you."

She lies on her back with an expression of torment and hopelessness. Her cries are unheeded, and her pain and humiliation are ignored. Her hand is no longer being restrained. At her side is a hand with a knife through it.

"I don't want to connect with her. She's dangerous."

"Is it dangerous to you?" He sits back in his chair to study me. "Do you want to put a knife in your own hand?"

Yes. It's what I want and I don't know why. I've never hurt myself before, never even thought about it, but the image is so sharp ...

in a strange way it's as though it's talking to me. Deep in my mind, I feel an urge growing.

"I don't want to tell you that I want to hurt myself, but … the thought is there."

Suddenly Dr. Erickson is beside me, sitting in a chair. His unexpected presence, so close, startles me and I flinch away from him as if he were going to strike me. He has boxed me into a corner, trapped me between the wall and his body. The room has become small and the chair I sit in seems to shrink around me.

Restless, nervous energy rises inside me as I battle the familiar feelings of being trapped and suffocated. He's too close and I feel as if he's pressing his body against mine.

My thoughts spin: Why is he here? What does he want from me?

"I'm not an angry person," I feel compelled to tell him. "My sister told me something the other week. She said that when I was nine years old, I pushed her down the stairs. I don't remember doing that, but she said I did. I don't know why I would've done something like that."

"Because you're human." A simple and complex response.

"Dr. Erickson?"

"Yes?"

"Why are you here?" I ask quietly, without looking at him.

"I thought we were doing EMDR," he says, and then adds, "I don't normally trap you in the corner. Do you want to move the chairs away from each other?"

I do. I don't like him this close and I don't like that he's blocked the only exit from the room, but the request would sound paranoid and make me seem frail.

I straighten my spine and, without looking at him, say, "No. This is all right."

"Think about the image of the hand with the knife," he says, and positions his hand for EMDR. "Think about the little girl on the floor."

The hand with the knife is beside the little girl. She's helpless and crying. The room seems to swallow her and echo her cries.

My eyes follow his hand, right to left, back and forth. I try to connect with her anger, to understand it, to ... feel it. But I can't. She's an image on the floor of my mind and as unapproachable as a frightened porcupine.

She beats her fists against the floor; even impaling his hand with a knife hasn't set her free. Her eyes are dark and haunting, beseeching ... but I don't know for what. I see you! She wears an expression of shattered hope. She has been deceived and betrayed.

What do you want from me?

He stops EMDR. I have failed.

My left hand twists sharply on my right wrist. It is she who is holding me prisoner. I want to be free, free of her and the images. My body is tense. I want to run and kick and scream, and I know that I will do nothing but sit still and proper in my chair, wanting to crawl out of my skin.

"There's this anger-release exercise I do with my patients," he says quietly. "But I have to tell you, it requires touch."

"What kind of touch?" The words are out of my mouth before I have a chance to think about them.

He stands carefully and moves the chair aside. He walks to the center of the room.

"You think about the little girl, think about what it's like at the end of the picture. You push your hands against mine, pushing out the anger."

I've curled into myself into the chair. I don't like the idea of touching him, but the thought of resisting his strength, of winning a battle appeals to me enough to override my fear. It's a need deep inside of me, like the urge to drive that knife into a hand, to feel that blessed release, some twisted satisfaction of punishing.

"How hard do I push?"

"Hard enough to push me through this window."

He's trying to trick you.

He wants me to bring him close enough to hurt me. But I know he won't hurt me. It's just the emotion the words bring forth. I push the voice aside.

He's waiting for me to answer. My body feels wrapped in cellophane. The room is too small, the air too thin.

"I've never pushed anyone before."

"I've done this exercise with grown men and I've never been hurt."

He's waiting for me, and I know he won't move until I make a decision. I don't want to touch him, but I do. Slowly, I stand and watch him. He has his palms out as if he were pushing against an invisible wall, braced and ready.

He's trying to trick you.

I twist my hands together until my knuckles crack. I desperately want to shove him, muscle against muscle, flesh against flesh. I can win this battle. I can get free.

I can't take my eyes off his hands. I hear the voice, speaking to them. *What are you going to do? I don't want you to catch me. You're not supposed to touch me.*

I see my movements in slow motion. My hands reach to mirror his. Our palms touch. In an instant, I push against him and he resists.

"Push out the anger," he instructs.

The little girl lies pinned to the floor, struggling against the hold, furious at the invasion of her body. How can he do this? Why did he do this?

"You're more angry than that," he says. "Push out how angry you're not."

Heat rises suddenly in me. My arms shake from the strain.

"Breathe," he instructs.

His fingers bite into my hands.

She pulls at the steel grip on her wrist, twisting for release. Let go! Let go!

I shove him back. Our hands break contact. I hold my breath as the room slowly forms around me.

"What happened?" he asks.

She sits with both her hands on the floor, looking at me.

"She broke free."

She is alone in the darkness, waiting.

"You look afraid," he says. "Do you want to push out fear?"

I nod. We push until the fear is gone and I feel drained. My legs are weak as I stand staring down at her.

"Are there any other emotions you want to push out? Guilt? Shame?"

Her eyes are no longer beseeching, her expression no longer tormented. She is strangely disappointed. Her victory is sorrow.

I shake my head. "There's only fear and anger." And that's gone now. I know she's free, but I wonder: Am I?

CHAPTER 11

I waited while my dad checked into the hotel room. A small television played in the sparsely furnished lobby. There was no one watching it. I eyed the rack of colorful brochures. I'd never been in a hotel. My family didn't take vacations unless it was to go up to Lake Superior to camp and hike.

"Just you and your daughter?" the man behind the counter asked.

Dad nodded.

"Do you want one bed or two?"

"Oh, I think one bed is fine."

My father had decided to take me with him on his business trip. Last time one of my sisters went, and she told me she got ice cream at a place that had more than fifteen flavors, and that Dad let her pick out whatever she wanted. She came back with a bag of candy she got from a candy store. I'd been waiting for my turn to go. I'd never been to a big city with ice cream and candy stores.

We'd driven for half the day. Dad had bought me a game to play on the long drive. We were only going to spend the night and drive back the next day after his meeting, but to me it was like a vacation I'd only ever heard other people talk about—a hotel room, dinner at a restaurant, and stopping for coffee at the Howard Johnson's along the highway.

Our room opened onto the parking lot. There was a long row of doors with cars parked in front of them. The room was small, but it had a television right at the end of the bed. We could sit in bed and watch television if we wanted.

I explored every inch of our accommodation, including the bathroom, which had tiny soaps in a dish on the counter. When I came out, I saw my dad had turned on the television and stretched out on the bed. There were no chairs in the room, so I lay down on the bed beside him, but a distance away.

"Come over here," he said.

I moved over and he positioned me between his legs. His hand had begun to caress my thigh, and his voice was soft and gentle as he spoke to me about how girls lay with boys, and that he would be okay if I found a boy I liked and wanted to lay with him this way as long as I didn't have sex with the boy.

I relaxed against his warmth and listened as he told me of his time in Japan when he was a young soldier coming back from Korea. The Japanese didn't mind men and women touching each other if they weren't married, he said. They took baths together in big bathhouses. I thought about how I took a bath in the lake with my siblings, naked and unashamed.

"Don't the nuns mind that?" I went to Catholic school and the boys weren't allowed to play with the girls. Sister Florentine told us that girls who let boys touch them were doing sin and would go to hell.

"Different religion, kiddo," he said. "The Japanese practice Buddhism."

We talked for a while about this. His hand was still caressing my thigh and I felt the moisture between my legs. I didn't know if it was because I liked what he was saying, or I just liked being along with him and away from my sisters, or if it was his hand that was causing my heart to pound. But I wanted more touching. I wanted … something more.

He kissed the side of my face. "Go take a shower."

I started the water, waiting for it to get warm. I took off my shirt. I'm not sure if Dad called me back to the bed, or if I wandered there myself, but I heard him say, "Let me help you take off your bra."

My bra was a worn hand-me-down from one of my sisters, a training bra, and the clasp in the back fell off so I had used a safety pin to hold the ends together.

"We're going to have to buy you a new bra. This one is almost nothing."

I showered with the tiny soap, and the water refreshed my mind. What was I doing? I knew I wasn't supposed to want that kind of touch from my father. I scrubbed away the moisture between my legs. This was wrong.

I changed into my pajamas. It was dark outside and my father had drawn the heavy curtain over the large window in front of the television. All the lights were off, and the television had cast the room in an eerie glow.

My dad was under the covers. I went to my side of the bed, wishing we had two beds instead of one. I curled up on the edge of the mattress and pretended to go to sleep.

"What are you doing way over there?" Dad asked playfully. "Come over here by me."

He reached out and snaked his arm around my middle, pulling me near him. I felt the heat from his body and realized that he was naked. I rolled onto my back and floated to the ceiling.

October 17

The movie changed," I tell Dr. Erickson, thinking of the little theater in my mind, the memory that plays out like movie. "It was slow in the beginning, almost stalled, then it fast-forwarded to the end. Now it's fast in the beginning, like a series of short scenes, and slow at the end."

"What about the girl?"

She's no longer frustrated and crying, but oddly still and resigned, like an animal that's been defeated. I stand near her. She lies on the floor, half-hidden by my father, but I see only her, a slight frown on her otherwise composed face. She's watching me, waiting ... always waiting.

"I can get closer to her. I stand next to her waiting. I don't know for what."

"Can you comfort her?"

I shake my head. I'm not good at comfort.

"She's been hurting a long time," he tells me. "Trapped in that room for all these years. You can rescue her from her pain. That might be a way of releasing your anger."

My mind snaps alert. "Why do you say I'm angry?"

"A hand with a knife through it ... that seems pretty angry to me. That's a powerful image."

"No. It's just an image." It's my image and it is what it is. "Anyway, it's moved away from me." I don't see it as clearly, but the urge to hurt persists. "I don't like to think about that."

"All right, we'll leave that away from you." He studies me carefully. "When children are hurt inside, holding them and comforting them goes a long way to healing the pain."

"She's dangerous."

"Is she dangerous to you now?"

"No."

While I feel the need to hurt and punish, I can control it. It's not so powerful that it drives me into action. Still, I fear her. She's the center of the images in my mind, the nucleus of my pain. Worse than that, she's become a chain hobbling my feet. "She's just so angry."

"Do you know how you fight hatred?" he says. "With love. Holding and comforting her is a good way to take away some of the power of her anger. The more afraid you're of her, the longer it's going to take to heal."

I don't like him talking about her as if she were a real person. But that's what she is in my mind: solid and unmoving, an individual girl with opinions and needs. I can't seem to move her, any more than I can make her disappear. That frightens me.

"The hotel room seems closer," I announce. "And I can't see an image of the farmhouse room without seeing an image of the hotel room. It's like they're linked somehow."

"Is it time to do the hotel room?"

No. No room. There are no lessons for me to learn. "Nothing happens in that room," I tell him.

"Something happens," he says. "You float to the ceiling."

"Yes ... but nothing happens there."

"But part of you is left behind on the bed."

"No." I don't see my body on the bed. I only see the ceiling. "I took my mind away."

His eyes sharpen. "How does your body function?"

"Bodies can function that way."

"No," he says slowly, "I'm pretty sure automatic responses are controlled by the brain."

I hate biology. I want to tell him that I really don't care how the human body functions, or that maybe I'm different from other people, but I can sense the razor-sharp responses he's honing in anticipation of that remark. I don't like to have a debate I can't win, and I know I'm going to lose any discussion about biology I have with a medical doctor.

'Pictures come forward in your mind to help you get what you want.'

My mind pulls away from the images as I feel the all too familiar sinking sensation, like the floor dropping away suddenly. The peace I'd enjoyed only days earlier vanishes. The images of the farmhouse and hotel room are back in place, solid and clear within the frame of my mind.

I feel the noise in my mind—the indistinguishable emotional chatter that distracts and conveys information. It transforms my mind into a crowded auditorium. It's getting louder and more difficult to ignore.

"I don't like that hotel room," I say softly, my thoughts drifting with the sudden cacophony. "I think something terrible happened there."

The darkness closes in on me, bringing with it a crushing feeling of being trapped and suffocated. Like being held too tightly in an embrace, the image of the hotel room evokes a strong urge to free myself, to push away the unseen hands. It's a memory tickling the edges of my consciousness, a prelude to tragedy … a secret I cannot tell.

"You're shaking something off," he tells me. "You're shaking your head, shaking something off. What is it?"

I don't realize I'm shaking my head and I take a moment to center myself and push the darkness away. "It's not time to do the hotel room," I say quietly, feeling my despair. How is it possible that I know everything, and remember nothing?

She sits alone on the hard floor, her hands supporting her weight. A small frown mars her delicate features. She no longer looks or feels like a little girl.

And that I find profoundly sad.

CHAPTER 12

I didn't like touch. It was something I had always said about myself without much thought. Only now I had to think about it.

My family didn't hug at greetings or farewells. I blamed that on my mother's German heritage. Grandpa was a big barrel-chested German with black hair and a wicked sense of humor. I couldn't expect very much of a man who idolized the Three Stooges and Archie Bunker. He was quick to laugh, though, and could always be counted on to have candy. The only time I'd seen my mother cry was the day he died.

Dad's family was worse. Dad was abandoned at the age of two during the Depression, left on a church doorstep with his four-year-old brother. A childless couple adopted him. They had wanted a girl, but Dad attached himself to his adoptive mother and wouldn't let go. That's how it was done back then. Walk into an orphanage and pick a child.

For some reason, Dad loved telling this story, but his mother never let him forget that they had wanted a girl. Grandma died before I was born. Grandpa lived a few years longer. I remember only that he brought us powdered-sugar donuts and Wrigley spearmint gum. What I didn't know as a child was that Dad's parents were strict Catholics. Grandpa was a Knight of Columbus and a strong member of the community, but Dad told me he wasn't a nice man.

My dad had an I.Q. of 163 when he graduated high school. He received a scholarship to be an astrophysicist, but Grandpa said no, he would join the family plumbing and electrical business. He loved that "Peltier & Son" sign on the storefront.

Grandpa was a simple man with few ambitions. Dad was ten times smarter than him and a natural inventor, but Grandpa took credit for most of what Dad invented. Grandpa would go to church and donate money to the community, then come home and belittle his son. I suppose this was where Dad developed his hatred of the church, seeing the hypocrisy of his own dad. Or maybe it was because his parents had sent him away to a Catholic boarding school when he was eight.

Dad drove us past the school once, years ago. It was a long brick building in the middle of a field, set back from the highway. It looked exactly like what it was—an institution—and all I could think was how lonely it must have been. Sometimes Dad could come home on the weekends, but that meant sitting silently all day on Sunday on Grandma's plastic-covered furniture while the adults talked. Children were to be seen, not heard.

Maybe that was why Dad let us run free so much, and why rules in our house were loosely designed. Our dinner table was active and noisy, and Dad never told us to sit still. My childhood had few boundaries.

By contrast, my maternal grandmother always accused us children of running around like a bunch of wild gypsies. Her words, not mine. She'd make us comb our hair before we went out to play, even though an hour later our curls would be filled with leaves.

All this could explain my family's lack of ease with physical displays of affection. Instead of a warm hug, we'd give an awkward wave as we gravitated toward the door and disappeared, as if we couldn't leave the house fast enough. Maybe it was just avoidance. Maybe none of them liked touch any more than I did.

October 24

W hat did it feel like to comfort her?" Dr. Erickson asks. He's set my file aside and is studying me with a curious expression.

"Nice," I tell him, "but sad."

"Sad?"

"Yes." She cried, and so did I. "Things are quieter with her now."

"Good," he said, nodding.

Quieter means I can think more clearly without the distraction and frustration of her image and all the demands that come with it.

"I've been thinking about the hotel room." It's been on my mind, pushing at me just like with the girl. The emotions are so much the same: fear, uncertainty. "I was thinking I'm confused about some things. I remember being nine years old when I was in the hotel. I remember that because we were at the farm. But there's a scene in the hotel room where my father is taking off my bra. I didn't wear a bra until I was eleven. So I was probably in the hotel room twice, but my mind has compressed them into one time."

He nods. "That's how the mind works. It compresses memories. It's called 'bookends'; there is a beginning and end to a story, but everything in between is compressed."

"Will I know what's in the middle?"

"Only if you need it to get to your goal."

I like the way that works. Don't dust out the corners of your mind. Keep them undisturbed. "But it's confusing being in the same place at two different times."

"Are you ready to do the hotel room today?" His eyes sparkle with anticipation.

"I don't know how to do that. I won't know where to be."

"That wasn't the question."

I know from experience that if I work the room, the images will fade. It's what I want, to quiet my mind and have a new life, to feel better and be whole. But the thought of going into that hotel room makes me cringe. What will I find there?

'You can't go forward until you go back.'

Somewhere I'm waiting for the rest of me to catch up, for all the pieces to come together to create the image of who I can be. My true self. I have to do *something*, because doing nothing means remaining in place.

"Okay," I say. "Yes."

He goes to the dry-eraser board.

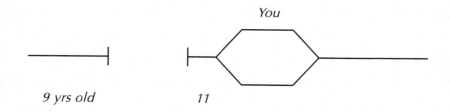

I like the diagram he draws. It gives me something to focus on and helps me sort out the confusion.

"You float to the ceiling when you're eleven years old?"

"Yes."

"Here are the bookends and the blank spot."

Still, there's something about this diagram that makes me uneasy. It tells a story that I'm not certain I want to know. And there's something here ... something I know but don't know.

"You remember the first time in the hotel room?"

I nod.

I'm lying on the bed, settled between my father's legs. He's caressing my thigh as we watch television. He tells me something about how it's okay for me to lay like this with a boy if I want to. I'm thinking how nice it is to not have my sisters near, and I'm thinking about the cup of hot chocolate he promised me.

Dr. Erickson moves the chairs to the center of the room. "Try to stay in the hotel room," he instructs. "Sometimes you can slip into other memories. I think that's what happened when we did the playground memory."

Yes, like a maze with trick passages and mirrors, my memories shift and divert around me, jumping from time and place like a poorly edited film. I sit in my chair; I'm close enough to Dr. Erickson that if I lean to the left, I will touch him. He raises his hand and my stomach tightens with fear.

He reaches out and grabs my arm in a fierce hold.

I stubbornly ignore the image and pull my body into the chair and away from his hand. He is relaxed and calm as he begins, and I follow the smooth, bilateral rhythm of his hand.

"I know I'm turning you on," my father says. "And that's okay. There's nothing wrong with that."

The sound of the television suddenly seems muffled. His hand has found a rhythm caressing my thigh as heat builds between my legs.

Dr. Erickson's hand is pale, the color of a moonbeam reflecting off snow. I hate it.

"Why don't you take a shower," my father suggests, nuzzling my ear.

I ease off him and slide to the end of the bed. His hands take off my shirt and unhook my bra.

Is Dr. Erickson's hand real? I want to touch him to know he's real and that I'm in his office.

I don't like the feel of the moisture and heat between my legs. In the shower, I shrug it away, letting the water clear the arousal. The television is still on when I return to bed. My father is beneath the covers. I slide carefully between the sheets, staying near the edge of the mattress. I close my eyes, feeling ashamed.

Did I have my hot chocolate? Or was that earlier?

His hand reaches for me and drags me across the bed. I'm on the ceiling, my nose pressed to the stained plaster.

Dr. Erickson's hand stops moving to end EMDR. "Are you getting anything new?"

Slowly, the images retreat, the emotions ebb, and I'm numb. I return my gaze to the diagram. "I want to think about this. There's something not right here. Something isn't right."

"How long do you need to think about this?"

I glance at the clock. We only have five more minutes. "Longer than we have."

"I have a cancellation this afternoon. Do you want to come back then?"

"Okay."

"I know what's wrong with the picture," I tell him when I sit down. It's late afternoon and the clinic is unusually empty. "And I know what I want."

"What's that?"

"There are too many people in the room. I want there to only be one."

He nods knowingly, with a small smile. "One of all of you, or one of them?"

I frown. I was thinking there would be only one of them in the picture. It hadn't occurred to me that I make two. "I suppose one of me."

The diagram is still on the board.

"Who is this nine-year-old?" he asks.

"She feels everything. She isn't numb like the other one."

"The eleven-year-old?"

"Yes, the one on the bed." The one I never see. "She feels nothing. She just lays there, her body numb. She's the one who stepped into my picture in the farmhouse. But she didn't exist then, she didn't exist until the hotel room. I told you she wasn't supposed to be there, remember?"

"Yes. I wasn't sure what to make of it at the time. Can you see the eleven-year-old?"

"Yes."

She's lying on the bed, unnaturally still and stoic. She's dutiful and obedient, offering no resistance. She's dead inside.

"Spirit guides can help you in finding your way inside," he tells me. "That pendant you're wearing …"

My hand goes to the tiny silver pendant. I like the feel of the smooth silver crafted into an image. "Sekhmet, daughter of Ra. She stands at the gateway of inner truth, removing the obstacles that stand in the way of finding your true self."

"I just got chills," he says, rubbing his arms with a smile. "What a perfect spirit guide for the work you're doing."

"I bought her fifteen years ago. I liked the idea of finding my true self, but I've never actually tried before."

"Spirits can be incredibly patient. Can you see Sekhmet?"

She's a goddess warrior, tall and muscular with the head of a lion and the body of a woman. She is undefeated in battle, but never uses her anger for vengeance. She's a healer and a protector of those who are not able to defend themselves. She stands naked in a black onyx temple that's open to the emptiness of space. Thick polished columns support only the air.

"Yes, she's in a temple with polished marble floors."

He takes a moment before speaking. "There's something called co-consciousness, where you share parts of yourself."

"I don't want there to be parts. I want there to be one." I don't like the images of the two girls, the nine-year-old and the eleven-year-old. I don't like how strong and present they are to me. They seem like obstacles, preventing me from moving forward.

"Can you bring the other two children to the temple with you?"

I stand on the polished floor, a girl on either side of me.

"Is there a place you can lie down in the temple?" His voice is low and satiny.

A raised pallet decorates a corner. I stand next to it with the girls.

"Is Sekhmet with you?"

Sekhmet stands at the foot of the bed.

"Lie down on the pallet with the girls on either side of you. As you lie there, imagine that each one of you is rising up into a dusty cloud above the bed, like tiny particles of gathered sand. As the cloud gets bigger and bigger, you all become less and less."

Slowly we disappear, grain by grain, like a vacuum eating up a sand painting, until there's nothing left and all three of us are floating above the bed in a vapor cloud.

"This cloud rises up, whirling together so there are no separate pieces," Dr. Erickson says. "The particles go higher and higher into space, getting larger and larger."

The universe surrounds my being. There's no beginning or ending, no years to date me, or experiences to confuse me. I am all and everything, lasting …

"When you're ready to return to the temple, you can. The cloud will come back to the bed and create one body."

I'm lying on the wide pallet, whole and new.

The office slowly forms as I leave the temple behind. My body is heavy as I draw a breath. I feel as if I'm awakening from a drugged sleep. It's difficult for my eyes to focus. The dim lighting in the office I've always enjoyed now seems like a shroud. Were there always this many lamps?

"You may notice that things look different."

My thoughts are sluggish, but I notice the silence inside. My body doesn't feel my own, as if I were a guest in it. I look down at my hands and move my fingers. Are these my hands?

"You may even feel different. These parts have been separated from you for a long time. You can feel what they feel and learn what they've learned. They're a part of you now."

They're gone. All I can think is that I can have my goal now. They're not standing in my way any longer.

I'm free.

CHAPTER 13

When I was seven, I had an imaginary friend. I called her Jennifer. She was a genie who lived in a feather I'd found. During the day I would walk around with her in my pocket and bring her out when I wanted something. I would imagine her getting up to mischief, like unlocking cars and knocking things over. When something sudden happened, like birds being flushed out of the brush, or a lamp being knocked over, I blamed it on Jennifer.

"That was Jennifer," I would say. "She's always getting into trouble."

Of course she saved me, too. She was my protector and defender. All I had to do was close my eyes and make a wish, and Jennifer would make whatever I wanted happen. I felt safe knowing she was in my pocket and could come out at any time. I only had to summon her and I had an instant friend. Only my sisters knew she existed, and they were tolerant of her as long as I didn't take it too far. At night I put Jennifer in a small jar by my bed and asked her to brush away bad dreams.

I don't know what made me want to have an imaginary friend when I had so many siblings, but Jennifer wasn't the first time my imagination had gotten the better of me. I remembered long walks with my sisters and elaborate stories I would tell them of us living on a ranch. As we walked, I used the landscape around me as inspiration and, with a few chosen words, the city sidewalk turned into a dangerous path. The trees would be bandits, cars explosives, and the street a river we couldn't cross.

I wasn't able to turn off my imagination during school hours, and spent a good portion of my time in the classroom with my mind elsewhere. I came to rely on my imagination as a kind of savior.

November 2

"What happened?" Dr. Erickson asks. He seems undisturbed by my announcement that the integration didn't last.

It unraveled hours after the event. I lay in my bed, feeling crowded inside like I wanted to escape my skin, but the images were absent from my mind, and the noise and chatter had been silenced. Integrating meant being whole, and being whole meant attaining my goal. My thoughts drifted as my body relaxed against the soft mattress, and I wondered if anything had truly changed or if it had merely been hidden.

"I liked that spirit death," I tell him. "Everything was quiet when I left your office." I like the quiet. "Later that night I was thinking of doing an experiment, to see if things had changed. I was thinking about asking one of my male friends to pull me into an embrace, to see if I would push away from him."

I can imagine it in terms of reality—the hand on my back, the masculine scent, and the undeniably male presence. It would be more than an experiment. The embrace would pull me close so that our bodies were pressed together. I would lean into his strength and stretch myself as I reached for his shoulders, relaxing into him.

I've never been able to imagine such an embrace and I know where it would lead.

"I imagined an embrace and I didn't push away, but ... something happened. I can only describe it as kicking and punching."

Tiny fists and feet punch and kick at the inside of my chest. Screams of rage fill me.

"There was this pressure inside of me, like something was trapped. I felt so much anger. I could hear it. In my fantasy, I stepped back from the man to calm everything down." *Retreating from the man in my fantasy was the only thing that quieted the noise. My surrender was their victory.*

He sits calmly, watching me. "The nine-year-old in the hotel, the one on the diagram I drew, is she the same as the one in the farmhouse?"

"Yes."

"And the eleven-year-old, the one on the bed, is she the same as the nine-year-old?"

She lies on the bed without moving. Neither sad nor angry, she is dutifully submissive. Her body is lax and unfeeling. He positions her where he wants her and she offers no resistance.

"I don't think so. She doesn't seem real to me."

"Take both of your hands and hold them out," he instructs. "Put the nine-year-old in one hand and the eleven-year-old in the other. Do they feel the same? Are they made of the same fabric?"

I want them to be. I want them to be pieces of the same imagined reality. Then I would only have to press them together to end the confusion ... to silence the voices. But I can't make them do what I want.

"They're different," I say with despair.

She's crying in frustration and rage and sorrow. Her tears and pain don't matter. She's alone in the room. She doesn't like being alone.

"They're so different." My fingers curl desperately around the imaginary objects. I don't want to be like this. This isn't the new life I wanted.

"Is she part of you?"

"No." I don't know how I know this, but it's inarguable and definite.

"Do you want to let her go?"

"I don't want her there, but ..."

"Can Sekhmet take the two of you to the place where you had your spirit death?"

The polished onyx temple is just as I left it. Feels Nothing stands obediently near Sekhmet.

"Imagine two castles facing each other," Dr. Erickson says. "Imagine a bridge connecting your world to hers. She's on one side of the bridge and you stand on the other. She's a spirit that came in from the outside," he says gently. "She helped you. You can let her go so she can help some other little girl. Do you think there are other little girls who need her help the way you did? It's okay to let her go."

My shoulders relax as my spine softens. I nod, thinking of all the other children in the world she can help.

"You can return anything you have that belongs to her, and take back anything she has that belongs to you. You don't need to know what it is; you just need to know that it belongs to you."

I take back strength and courage. I return the things I don't want any more: I return the inability to feel emotions deeply, to express them appropriately.

"Feels Everything can release some of her anger and let it flow across the bridge." He adapts my language so easily.

Feels Everything does not move. Her arms are crossed defiantly.

"Disconnect the bridge in the middle. The bridge is going to retract and fold into a wall, separating your worlds. Do the courtesy of folding the bridge into a wall on the other side."

I stand in the temple. The immense darkness of space surrounds me. I cannot see Feels Nothing any more. She's gone.

Can I get her back? What if I need her? Like an electrical jolt, fear sweeps through me. Without her to step into my place, I'll *feel* all those memories from the hotel room.

"Now you're frightened," he says quietly. "She was with you a long time, wasn't she?"

I nod. "Since I was a teenager." She taught me how to fly, how to leave my body.

"Check the castle for any holes or cracks, the ways she used to enter your world. It's a good idea to do some housekeeping, seal up any entrances. Are there any ways left that she can get in?"

I shake my head.

"Good. Did Feels Everything let go of some of her anger?"

"No."

"She's holding onto her anger?" His eyes narrow only slightly.

"She's holding onto everything." Anger, hate, pain, fear. She doesn't speak, but it's as though I can feel her words.

Dr. Erickson leans back and runs his hands through his hair. "I might have to talk to her about anger sometime later."

"How do I get rid of her?"

"You integrate with her memories. She's holding your memories."

"She doesn't want what I want. She doesn't want to be touched."

"I know."

How can I learn to like touch when she's so strong? How is it possible that I can't fantasize without feeling sick?

"She can be so ..."

"She can be so ..." Dr. Erickson repeats.

Real. "So hard to control," I tell him. "It was difficult to get to finish the movie, to get to the end and have it stop playing in my mind."

"Did you rescue her?"

"No." I can't rescue her. "It was more like acknowledgment."

"Validation."

"I don't want her there. I want her to go away." I can't make this point clearly enough. I want a new life and to put the past behind me. I want to learn to like touch and to share intimacy. I want to be a different person, and she wants none of it.

"Where's the love?" he says. "All this talk of getting rid of her and making her go away, how about some love? She's been trapped in that room for a long time, feeling pain and anger and fear."

I don't like that he speaks of her in the third person. And worse, he has taken her side.

"She's interfering with what I want," I tell him crossly. "She's standing in my way."

He takes a breath and leans forward to rest his arms on his knees. "I understand that this isn't what you want. If you just do what you want and disregard her, you're going to tear yourself apart. If you want to be healthy and whole, you're going to have to negotiate with her."

Whole. That word drifts into my mind like a narcotic, promising and seductive. *Whole* means only one of me, where I get to make the decisions for my own life. But I don't want to negotiate with her. I want her to go away, back into the recesses of my mind.

"Imagine the two of you in this room, in two separate bodies. She sits down in this chair. You have to talk to her like that, like you're sitting down to talk to a nine-year-old. You just happen to share the same body."

I want desperately for him to be wrong, but I know that he's not. She's too solid in my mind, too strong of will for her to be less than what she is: a separate part of myself.

What does that make me?

"I don't know how to be like this." She's not going to let me have what I want. I'm never going to get her to like touch. I'll always be like this: alone. "All of those images are coming from her. She's dangerous."

"Is she dangerous to you now?" His question seems casual, but I know it's intentional.

I shake my head, but I wonder: if I tell him yes, will that make him agree to get rid of her?

"You can keep her calm," he says. "You have to learn what triggers her."

"I know what triggers her." Every time I think about touch, she's like a storm inside me, pulling me apart. I hate her for this.

"No experiments," he says firmly. "Keep everything calm."

CHAPTER 14

The phone calls in between sessions helped me to find a little peace, but it was almost impossible for me to find privacy. Pleasing Sister was with me always. She couldn't drive and her mobility was dependent on me. If I wanted time to myself I had to leave my own home, which I did frequently.

The holidays were coming up and the family wanted to celebrate. I wasn't in the mood for conversation and company, and the idea of family seemed hypocritical. I spent a good portion of my days examining what my family had done to me. Knowing what I knew, how could I join them in their illusion?

My relationship with my dad over the past twenty years had been polite, but distant. I tended to rock the boat more than my siblings, pushing the boundaries and always trying to smudge the image of our perfect little family. Family gatherings could be tense, and I'd learned to hate them long ago. It was all the unspoken feelings that created the tension. The rest of us tried to pretend, but Angry Sister couldn't do that, not for long anyway, and Pleasing Sister always swooped in to fix things while I remained silent and just tried to get through it.

I recognized years ago that my personality changed when I was with my family. I became a wallflower, trying not to be noticed. Maybe it was because I competed for attention in this large family that I had rejected. Maybe I just didn't want to be part of the lie.

They knew I was going through therapy; it was hard to keep a secret like that in a large family. My sisters didn't understand why I wanted to "dig all that up again."

I tried to talk to Angry Sister again, to ask her some more questions.

"I don't want to talk to you about this anymore." She told me that the last time she had talked to me she couldn't have sex with her husband for two weeks. "Anyway, I'm over all that now," she said. "I've done my healing."

I felt strangely isolated by this. Shameful Sister wouldn't talk to me either, because it upset her too much.

"You're getting worse," Pleasing Sister told me.

It was true. I was getting worse.

November 16

The movie has stopped playing; the short film showing the little girl I identified as Feels Everything being abused. She has moved from the floor of the farmhouse and the image of the room fades from the landscape of my mind. Now she stands in the black space of my thoughts like a lost child waiting to be found.

Overlaid over this picture is the image of the hand pierced by the knife.

"I don't know what she wants," I tell Dr. Erickson. "She's just there, waiting. When I see her, everything feels tight inside, crowded, like I'm being suffocated, and I want so badly to get away."

"You feel her emotions when she's near," he says, nodding. As always, he's folded into the small chair, his legs relaxed.

"Maybe," I say softly, my thoughts drifting. But she's not the source of the endless chatter in my mind.

"Have you asked her what she wants?"

"She doesn't speak. I have to interpret her actions. It's like I can feel her words. That's how I know she's angry."

"What's she angry about?"

"I don't know."

I don't know why Feels Everything has remained when I've worked so hard at recalling the memories. I don't know why she won't go away, but I'm tired of the struggle. My head hurts all day, and there are moments of anxiety that nearly make me sick. I draw a careful breath, not allowing my weariness to show.

There's soft light where Dr. Erickson sits. If I want, he can fade from the room, dissolve into the gray shadows and be only a gentle, disembodied voice to guide me. I like it when he disappears and I no longer have to worry about his hands. Even when he's sitting away from me, as he is now, I can see his hands. He has folded one across the other, clasping his wrists in a cross grasp.

He's holding them in place. The thought rises from deep inside: he's holding them so they don't do what he doesn't want them to do.

His hand strikes out like a snake, catching my wrist and pulling me against him. His grip is unmovable and bruising. His hand moves from my wrist to my arm and shoulder, curling around to my back, digging into my flesh, and pressing me close in a rigid embrace.

She doesn't trust him and I'm in a constant battle to keep the peace.

"She doesn't like your hands," I say without looking at him. I say "she," but I'm not certain who inside hates his hands; I just know they are hated.

"Is that what she's angry about?"

"I don't know."

He studies me for long moments. "What do you want to do today?"

"I want to learn how to talk to her."

"I think that's a good idea."

If I can't talk to her, I can't understand her. If I can't understand her, she won't go away. As long as she's a separate part of myself I won't be a whole person. I'm beginning to understand what that means for me. I can't have a life where I'm inconstant conflict with myself, wanting two different things and having neither.

"I think there's something wrong with her," I say.

"Is she sick?" His expression rarely changes; it's always controlled, always masked.

I shake my head. "Not sick, but ... there's something not right with her."

"How does she look to you? Does she have normal-looking hands and teeth?"

I take a quick assessment. "Yes."

"How about her eyes? What color are they?"

"They're brown." Like mine. "She looks all right, but she doesn't feel all right. It's like when you go to a party and see a person, well dressed and laughing, looking perfectly normal, but when you stand next to them you feel ... it's like being sucked into a vacuum. They make you feel bad. That's what she's like—empty, transparent."

Although I think of her as Feels Everything, she doesn't feel everything completely. She's only anger. She's a shadow holding the emotion I myself will not own. But she's not enough, just as I'm not enough. What I've come to realize is that together we won't make a whole person. And that, too, is reason to avoid her.

"You can grow her up," he says. "Give her the experiences you have, take her from being a child into adulthood. She can be you."

"I can't just 'grow her up,'" I say, frowning. "She's only nine."

"You can do anything in your mind. You can do it all in a few minutes."

That makes no sense to me. I shake my head. I can't age her. She isn't a fantasy that I can manipulate. I can't make her do what I want; if I could, I would make her disappear.

"She's interfering in what I want. I'd like to make her go away."

There's a long moment of silence. I try not to squirm in my chair under his unblinking gaze. Finally, he speaks.

"I want to do a visual exercise with you," he says. "I'm going to move out of your line of vision so I'm not a part of this exercise. I'm going to sit next to you. Which side is okay for you?"

I deftly choose the left side, not wanting him near my right arm, not wanting him anywhere near me. I don't like him close.

He moves his chair next to me. "I see a wall," he says, spreading his arms out to demonstrate.

The wall is built of thick stones mortared together.

"On the other side is that little girl. You're pitted against one another."

She stands not far from me, watching unhappily.

"I see a key, maybe on the top, or on the bottom."

On the bottom, tucked in the corner ... a single block glowing.

"One key, and the wall will implode, like a house of cards coming down."

The wall weakens. I can feel it crack and tremble. My heart hammers for release. The tightness winds down my spine and my insides feel like a towel being rung dry. I look away. The air thins....

"Can you find the key? It can be anything you choose," he says quietly.

No!

The voice is loud and determined. The wall is too close. She's too close.

The bricks crack ...

"Right there," he points to the floor. "Can you see it? You just have to reach out and take it."

I turn away from the wall.

Stop!

The room darkens as a veil drops over me. My head spins ...

"Why are you distressed?" he asks.

You're going to change everything. I want to shout the words at him, but I keep them locked inside. On the dry-eraser board I can see it, the timeline; all laid out like a family tree. The question that took seed in my mind the day he drew that damn diagram suddenly sprouts. The puzzle pieces snap into place.

"I don't like what I see," I whisper. A band wraps around my chest. It's so difficult to breathe. My fingers twist around my wrist. I'm trapped.

"What do you see?"

"The timeline you put on the board." Weeks ago erased, but still a sharp image in my mind. I can turn my head to see where it was in the room as if it still existed.

"That frightens you?"

I nod. I feel myself falling as if the floor has suddenly opened beneath me.

"Why?" His voice is no more than a whisper.

Together we don't make a whole person. Then what are we? What am I? "I can see where she ended and I began," I tell him softly.

"The nine-year-old? Feels Everything?"

"Yes." I'm sane enough to know that I sound crazy, but the truth remains: I'm not that six-year-old running around the woods, and I'm not that little girl in the farmhouse. I'm someone completely different.

"Is she a ghost?" he asks quietly.

"No."

"Did she die?"

"Someone did." I can see it on the board, so clearly now that I wonder how I missed it earlier. This is what I have unknowingly feared: I am not real.

"Did the eleven-year-old die?" he asks. I can feel his gaze on me.

"No, the one before her, before Feels Everything."

"You don't see yourself before nine years old?"

"No."

Those images of that little girl running free are not me. My life is planned out, built on structure and safety. I'm predicable and ordinary. I'm not about anger and pain. I'm controlled in my emotions and actions. I see now that I've been this way since that day in the farmhouse. I reinvented myself, but I left parts of me behind and now these parts are clamoring to be heard, demanding their place in my life.

"This is a part of integration," he says calmly. "When you begin to realize parts you never acknowledged, it makes you feel like a liar."

Yes, my entire life has been a lie; a lie built on a lie.

"This other child, the mud-baby," he says. "Where is she?"

"Hiding someplace down deep and dark. I can't find her."

"You already have. Do you see her?"

She separates herself from the shadows. She is maybe four years old, with uncombed hair and dirty clothes. She's timid and unsure, like a child stepping onto a stage, suddenly aware of others around her.

"Yes, I see her."

"Can you hold her?"

"Yes."

She melts into me with ease, clinging to me without desperation.

"Can the two of you hold the nine-year-old?"

"No." Feels Everything is too dangerous. Her anger is toxic and I want to keep it from this child and myself.

"Can you find a nice place for this child, a place where you went as a child that was safe?"

"Yes."

In the middle of the field is a place where the buffalo grass grows. Tall wheat surrounds this soft, sculptured grass. When I lay down on the grass, no one can find me. Not even my sisters. It's like a secret playhouse.

"You sure you don't want to let Feels Everything in this place? Maybe giving her someone to play with would help ease her anger."

"No. It's better if she's not around people."

I know this only because I feel it, because thinking of Feels Everything makes my stomach and chest tighten, because seeing her image, once crying and fretful and now defiant, makes it impossible for me to believe she doesn't exist.

I want to banish her ... and the memory of what happened.

CHAPTER 15

Y ou can't."
I looked at the boy who had challenged me.

It was the fall of 1969, and a new family had moved into a house a mile down the road. The boy's mother came over every morning to have coffee with my mom, and the boy and I played together. I'm three years old, my sisters were all in school and it was just my little brother and me at home. My brother had developed a hysterical fear of snapping turtles and didn't want to leave the house without my mother.

The boy was taller than I was, but the same age as me. I wasn't used to playing with anybody other than my sisters and brothers. We'd been playing together on the lake since I was born. This boy didn't know how to play any of my games, so I invented a new one. I thought today we could jump off the well-house roof and see who could leap the farthest.

"You can't do it," the boy repeated.

"I can so jump." I did it all the time with my sisters. We would launch ourselves off the roof and into the sand below, marking our spots. "You're just scared."

"I am not," the boy said.

The well house wasn't very big and I climbed to the roof with ease, the way I'd done dozens of times before. He climbed up behind me. We both stood on the flat roof.

We didn't use the well anymore. Over the summer my dad had built a new house, with a pump right in the kitchen. I looked over the edge. It had been a while since I'd jumped off the roof and I wanted to make sure the sandy spot was still there.

"Go on," the boy said, and gave me a shove.

I lost my balance and fell off the roof. The next thing I knew I was on my mother's lap and she was holding a cloth to the side of my bleeding face. My cheek was torn open from hitting one of the green iron stakes that rested against the side of the well house.

The boy was sitting on his mother's lap, crying.

"He's just scared," she was saying.

But I didn't know what he had to be scared about. I was the one who was pushed and was bleeding. I wasn't crying; I was angry.

"I told you not to jump off the roof anymore," my mother said gently. "This is why I don't want you playing over there."

"Over there" was where the old cabin stood. Once we had abandoned the cabin for the new house, it became a kind of construction zone. Months ago I'd stepped on a nail sticking out from a board and had to get a shot at the clinic. I was supposed to wear tennis shoes, but I didn't like how tight they were on my feet. And anyway, I couldn't climb trees with shoes on.

"I didn't jump, I fell," I told my mother.

I loved to jump—out of trees, off the big cliff near the top of the driveway. I liked the feel of floating and then hitting the soft soil. I wished we had a higher roof to jump off. My sisters and I would jump off the cliff for hours, one right after another, and then we'd run back up to the top to do it again.

"You're lucky you have an eye," Mom said.

My mother said things like this all the time: don't stick your hand in those holes, a badger could chew your fingers; don't go near the wasps' nest, they'll swarm and cover you in seconds; don't feed the raccoon, it'll come into the house at night and attack your baby brother; don't go near snapping turtles, they'll latch onto your hand and bite it clean off.

I leaned against my mother as she held the cloth to stop the bleeding. I wanted my sisters to come home from school, and I wanted the boy to stop crying.

November 23

The room in the farmhouse is a distant image, a faded photograph worn and memorized after years of study. It has lost its emotional impact and become like a scene too often watched. I see only her now, standing in the black backdrop of my mind, an image haunting and persistent. She has separated from the memories, and I have separated from her.

I think more of touch and less of the memories Dr. Erickson and I are working. I concentrate on what I want, fantasizing a life with pleasurable touch, a life without emotional restrictions, a life of comfort and desire. The fantasy of this life is good, but the reality is different.

For months I've been trying to understand why I feel so afraid of Dr. Erickson's hands. Now I realize I'm asking the wrong question. It's not *why* I feel that's important, but *what* I feel.

"How are things inside?" Dr. Erickson asks. He's well rested and his usual pleasant self. He glances at my intake form. I have no idea what he's looking for.

"Crowded and tight," I tell him.

"Why is that?"

Even though he's sitting in his usual chair across the small office, I see him close to me, and that brings the unreasonable fear that he's going to hurt me.

His hand rests unmoving on the chair's arm. He's close enough to reach out and catch me. The knife is small, a dagger with a sharpened blade. It fits comfortably in my hand.

"He's going to hurt you. He's trying to trick you."

I sink the knife into the front of his hand, pinning it to the wooden arm of the chair.

"She doesn't like you," I answer without looking at him. I try to sound mature, rational. Sane. "She doesn't trust you."

"Because of my hands?"

"Yes. She thinks you're going to hurt her, but … I get the feeling that she's confusing your hands with somebody else's."

He nods. "Have I talked to you about transference?"

I shake my head, dreading a medical conversation.

"Transference is something that happens in therapy. It's actually a very important part of the therapeutic relationship. The patient can transfer emotions to the therapist. Instead of feeling angry toward your father, for instance, you transfer those feelings to me. In this case, you're transferring the girl's fear of your father's hands to a fear of my hands."

Nothing uncomplicated. The conflict inside only grows and stretches to the outside world.

"I trust you," I tell him. "But I don't like it when you're close. I don't like your hands being close to me. When you're close to me, it's hard to breathe and everything's all tight inside. I know you won't touch me. You're the kind of doctor that doesn't touch people."

These are words I've heard in my head dozens of times and I hadn't intended for them to be spoken.

He looks sheepish and thoughtful. "I want you to have the right information. I have held the hands of some of my older patients."

The idea distresses me. Why would he hold the hands of a patient? Does he think this will comfort? And who is he comforting, the patient or himself?

You're not supposed to touch me. All I can think is that he's been fooled; I know his touch doesn't comfort at all. His patients probably just tolerate his touch, uncomfortable, not knowing how to extract themselves from his grasp.

"Why don't we make an agreement," he says. "If there's a need for me to touch you, I'll ask your permission and get your consent before I do. I want you to be able to have access to the anger-release exercise so that you don't hurt yourself or someone else. Other than that, you can work with another therapist to learn to tolerate touch. There are some good massage therapists that work on that level. That way, Feels Everything won't have to worry about whether I'm going to touch. Can we agree to that?"

"Yes, I can agree to that."

All I want is to like touch, then I can enjoy intimacy and I will trust. Touch is the obstacle standing in my way, and touch is the one thing she will not let me do.

I stand before a tall, handsome man. Gentle and loving. I'm pulled into his embrace as he leans down to kiss me. A knife appears in my hand and I stab him.

"She doesn't want what I want," I tell him. "She doesn't like touch."

"She's afraid. How do you teach a fearful child? You're two cats living in the same house. One is a barn cat, all claws and hisses; the other is a house cat. What does a house cat have to do all day? Find the best spot of sun to lie in and wait to be petted. But a barn cat has learned to be fearful of touch. If you bring a barn cat into a house, it'll hide in a corner or under the furniture. It doesn't understand being petted and adored. You have to go slow with her. You have a cat?"

"Yes."

"Sit with your cat on your lap and pet it. Watch how it reacts to your touch and pay attention to how you feel when you're petting it. You have to start paying attention to how the girl is feeling when you touch or think about touch. We can identify the triggers and work the memories."

"She's so angry," I say softly. "I don't understand why she's so angry. I'm not angry."

"Have you comforted her?"

"No. She's interfering with what I want."

"So you're punishing her." His eyebrows rise.

Yes, I'm punishing her. I'll deny her what she wants from me the way she's denying me. "I can't fantasize what I want. When I try to fantasize ... my fantasies ... they turn out badly."

He's silent for a moment. "Does your lover get hurt?"

I drop my gaze to the carpet.

He lies on the bed in the aftermath of our lovemaking, sated and content. The knife is in my hand. I plunge it into his chest.

"Yes." My voice is barely a whisper. "I like fantasizing and Feel Everything is disrupting it."

"Fantasies are important. They're a way of you getting comfortable with what you want, but your fantasies are frightening the little ones inside."

"I want to fantasize what I want." At this moment, my fantasies are all I have, and she has taken them away from me. For that, I hate her. "I want to be able to have a relationship and have the things other people do, and I can't with her."

"Slow down," he says. "Slow down. It's not just you now. You have to learn to compromise. That's where all the anxiety and stress are coming from: you're in conflict with yourself."

I don't want to compromise. I want to be able to have an intimate relationship, to experience love and tenderness, and to share myself with another. And since I can't act that out, I want to have the pleasure of fantasizing it.

"Compromise. You wouldn't let a child watch an adult film," he says. "You can put her in a soundproof room, give her toys to play with, and have your fantasy. That might at least give you some relief."

It's the strangest thing he's ever suggested to me. Soundproof a room in my mind? I can't even get the voices to be silent, or make her disappear. Why does he think I can contain her?

"I don't know how to connect with her," I tell him.

"Write her a sympathetic story. Write what happened in the farmhouse from her perspective. It might help you to understand her anger."

Why can't he see how dangerous she is? Doesn't he understand that I can't get close to her without harming others or myself? She'll hurt someone soon. I can see it. I can feel it.

"Comforting her will go a long way toward easing her anger." After a moment he adds, "Ask Sekhmet if you should comfort her."

Sekhmet stands in the temple, tall and every bit the warrior goddess. I stand before her and ask the question. She nods and I see an image of the little girl and myself embracing.

"No," I tell him. "It's not a good idea."

He studies me. "I get the idea that Sekhmet gave you an answer you didn't want to hear and you changed it to what you want."

I won't look at him. My gaze flitters like a restless butterfly. "I don't think it's a good idea to hold her." And then, to justify my own lie, I say, "I'm not good at comforting."

Silence. His gaze is unnerving. "Can Sekhmet comfort you?"

The idea strikes me. "I didn't think about someone comforting me."

"I know. Have you ever been held when you're crying and are upset?"

"I don't cry." *And I don't allow people to hold me.*

"There's the process of being held together as you turn into a puddle of tears. Being held binds the edges of yourself, keeps you from falling apart. It's a way of grounding a person and allowing them to let go."

There is pleasure and comfort in the image he describes. For the first time, I want to know what it would be like to be comforted instead of being contained.

"I think Sekhmet could comfort me," I tell him.

"You can let the little girl draw," he suggests. "That's a good way to let her express herself. There's a dialogue exercise where you write with two different colors of pens; one color would be yours and the other hers. You can try writing with your left hand, your non-dominant hand."

"What will that do?"

"It's not as practiced and formulated as normal. The theory is that your subconscious reveals itself on the non-dominant side. It's very effective for most people."

"All right. I'll think about that."

My thoughts scatter and drift, and I feel the dark hunger approach, nudging the edge of my consciousness. The idea has been persistent—without form but with intent. A need I cannot define; a fear I cannot ignore. The idea drives me, and all I know is that I want to hurt.

The severed hand with the knife through it settles in my thoughts, reinforcing my urge to hurt.

"Why do people hurt themselves?" I ask him suddenly.

He stares at me for a long time, his expression masked and still. "That's a complicated question," he says finally.

"I know. That's why I asked."

"People with self-injury behavior fall into a cycle." He goes to the board. "Remember the mind map I drew, where a person stands in different places? So, here's a victim feeling powerless and guilty. A good victim doesn't get angry; instead they move over here and cut themselves. Now they feel better … for a while. But then they feel guilty about cutting themselves, so they move back over here to the victim's place, and then they cut themselves to release anger or other emotions. Then they feel better, until they feel guilty again."

He looks at me. "It's a very difficult cycle to break. People who get into these cycles spend years trying to prove something they can never prove."

I stare at him, waiting.

"That they have control. Some women who've been sexually abused become promiscuous. They use sex as a weapon of control. They have sex just to prove they can. But they're trying to prove something they never had to begin with, because they never had control."

I stare at the sketch on the board that he has drawn as a triangle, and I wonder how any of us survive our lives.

CHAPTER 16

I never sought to hurt myself. Although I suppose anyone could argue that what I'd done with my life in avoiding intimacy was harmful, in the same way that a distant mother was causing harm to her child. But that was esoteric and psychiatric, a good case study for medical students.

I had a different hurt.

Recently I'd wanted to drive a knife through my left hand. It was a strange and compelling urge that I tried not to study too closely, one of those things I wanted to put away and couldn't.

I didn't want to tell Dr. Erickson, not because it would flag me as high risk but because of what it would indicate about me. I would have become that person—the textbook abuse survivor with a tendency to self-injure. I could see the note in my medical file: Patient displays desire for violent behavior and has a strong need to harm herself. It was bad enough that I fit far too many of the criteria for PTSD.

I tried to distract myself from that image, but I knew it would feel so good to push that blade through the skin and bone until it until sank deeply into the hard wood of the table. It gave me a strange satisfaction to think about pinning my hand to the surface, a kind of Joan of Arc vengeance.

Dr. Erickson had suggested drawing, so I bought some watercolors and paper. I dipped the brush into water, reached for a color and tried not to think.

I had nothing planned as I laid brush strokes across the paper. What I painted was all red and black, flowing blood and sorrow. It did nothing to make me feel better.

I tried to keep the paintings hidden from Pleasing Sister, protecting them like any secret. I wasn't sure what painting was going to do for me, but the images coming out of my mind were distressing. I'd begun to realize just how much of my thinking was wrong.

Worse, my siblings had realized that something was wrong. Aside from letting me know that I was "getting worse," they had decided that the way to help me was to prescribe.

"You have to tell your doctor that you need different medication," one sister told me.

I didn't tell them that I'd weaned myself off the Seroquel and had no intention of requesting additional medication. Medication did nothing to cure; it simply masked. And hadn't I done that all my life on my own?

December 6

The image of the hand with the knife through it is never far from my thoughts. It's a mural on the walls of my mind. When it's near, it's an urge that is impossible to ignore and difficult to reconcile, leaving a dark impression that confuses and frustrates me.

The urge to hurt grows; the need to feel pain, to punish takes root inside. Nothing I do alleviates this desire. All I can do is watch and wait for the images to change.

"You have paintings," Dr. Erickson says with barely concealed enthusiasm. "Let's see."

I hold them tighter, pulling them against my body. I want to show them to him, but I want to keep them hidden. I haven't decided whose paintings these are and I'm embarrassed to reveal the childlike and disturbing renditions.

"Yes, I let her draw," I say softly, because only he can understand this. "They aren't very nice."

"Well, not very nice things happened to her."

Feels Everything is so angry, and now I begin to see just how angry. Will he judge me because of them? Find concern for me?

I finger the paper. He'll see the part of me I try to keep hidden from myself. But I know he's seen the darkness of the human soul, the hollow places where we dwell when we're in pain. And that knowledge comforts me because in this I know I'm not alone.

I hand him the paintings, but I want no part of them. I was but the vehicle for her expression. The brush moved across the paper as if I were in trance. I chose the colors without thought, the brush dipping into the thick liquid as if of its own accord.

I painted blue images of little girls in pools of red blood with severed hands lying next to them. Some of the hands had knives through them. Tortured images that, when I painted them, made me feel better, as if the pieces of paper had become hard evidence, a documentation of her pain.

I watch Dr. Erickson as he studies them without comment, and I search for a sign of disapproval or judgment. There is none. He is a master of control.

He holds up one of the paintings. "Tell me about this one."

At one side of the paper is a little girl kneeling before a black pit. A red background surrounds her. On the opposite side is another little girl kneeling in front of a red pit with a black background.

"I don't know," I say.

"They look like negative images, opposites."

They're not really my paintings and I refuse to explain or take responsibility for them.

He puts the painting down and watches me for a few minutes. "I'm concerned about your safety."

"Why?" I hadn't expected this. I don't like him being concerned about me.

"These drawings."

"They're just drawings." I know it's a lie, but I don't know what else to say. Silence.

I hate the silence. He always waits for me to fill it, but this time I stubbornly remain mute, trying not to move restlessly under his scrutinizing gaze. He's an expert at this, with years of experience to his advantage.

"Have you had thoughts of hurting yourself?" he asks.

"Hurting? No, I wouldn't get hurt."

"What about hurting the body?" He's clever in his word choice.

I plunge a knife into my hand, but I feel no pain. Somehow the hand is not my own and it can't be violated or hurt, any more than it can be owned.

"What do you mean?" I ask, although I know exactly what he means.

"Language is important. You say you wouldn't get hurt. What about the body you're in? Would you do something that might hurt your body?"

"No, I don't think it would be hurt."

"You don't have thoughts of wanting to die?"

"That's different from hurting." At the expression on his face, I add, "It is. I don't understand suicide attempts, making tiny cuts or taking a few pills. If I wanted to die, I would die. I'd go someplace where no one could possibly rescue me, some place far away where no family could find me."

"You've put some thought into this."

Have I?

"If you were to have thoughts of wanting to die, would you call someone for help? Call a friend or call me before you acted on it?"

I consider his question carefully, because I don't want to lie even if it would appease him. "Maybe. I don't want to die. I want to have my new life. I have lots of things to live for, lots of things I want."

"If you *were* wanting to die, I'd like you to consider talking to someone first. Can you promise me you'll call someone before you act?"

He's on this now and he won't let go. His attention is making me nervous. I finger the Sekhmet pendent and look away from him.

"I don't want to promise you something I'm not going to do, but … I'll consider it." I study him for a moment. "It's not something I want to do. I'm very motivated to have a new life."

"But it might be someone else inside of you who wants to die. Someone inside is angry," he says matter-of-factly.

"I don't know why."

He raises his eyebrows.

I scowl at him. "There's nothing to be angry about. I'm not angry."

"You have the right to be angry."

"I'm not."

"What would happen if you were angry?"

I don't get angry. I can't remember ever being angry. I've been annoyed on more than one occasion, and irritated often, but I haven't been angry. I don't even like the sound of the word. I entertain his question and imagine what would happen if I got angry.

"I think … something bad would happen," I answer. I know it the same way people know that putting their hands in fire would hurt; I don't have to do it to know it would hurt.

"Did something bad happen when you got angry as a little girl?"

"I don't remember."

"You remember something," he prods. "We don't really forget anything. Information is stored in files in our mind. Our subconscious accesses those files and makes decisions on the information every day without our conscious minds being aware of it. We talked about this before when we discussed your boss touching you. You said you didn't understand why you reacted the way you did. Do you remember how you were feeling when he was touching you?"

"Small … like a little girl." The pieces quickly snap into place. "Yes, I felt like a little girl, like I didn't have the strength to get away."

"And you didn't try."

No, I didn't try to escape my boss's assault and it has haunted me all these months, knowing that I was a victim again and powerless.

"I thought about it for those moments when his hands weren't on me. I thought about going to the bathroom, or getting a drink and leaving, but I was so afraid. I kept thinking: what will he do? I didn't know what he would do, so I didn't do anything."

"You were accessing those files that said that if you resist you would get hurt. We make decisions based on the lessons we've learned."

I'm kneeling in front of my father. His hand is between my thighs, his fingers probing. My hand pulls against his grip. I'm locked in place. Suddenly I'm on my back, the hard floor beneath me. His fingers push in …

"Do you see how these two incidences are related?" he asks. "You've done a good job of avoiding touch most of your life. When you're touched, your mind goes to those files of when you were last touched, when you were with your father. You have to update your files. That's old news. The strength difference between a man and child is enormous. You couldn't have won against him, but now you're a full-grown woman. You could do some damage if someone tried to hurt you. You can get angry and say no. If you can't say no then you won't have the freedom to say yes."

"How do I update the files?"

"Learn new lessons. Know that you can defend yourself. Know that you can enforce your 'no.' Take a self-defense class. You'll learn that you can make a man stop without anything bad happening to you."

"I don't know. I don't like to think about hurting people. I want to think about liking touch."

He says nothing for a moment; just caresses his mustache and beard with the tips of his fingers. "You asked me to help you with this, but you're pushing things away. You're pushing away the hotel room and the little girl. You don't want to do the things you need to do. You're not listening to me or to your spirit guide. I don't understand why you won't take the advice of your spirit guide. It's rude to ask her advice and then disregard it."

I drop my gaze. I don't like being scolded, any more than I like being instructed on etiquette by a psychiatrist. I want to rail back at him, but I hold my tongue because I've displeased him. And for some reason that makes me ashamed.

"Is that what I'm doing?" I ask him.

He nods. "It's not something you're doing consciously. People in therapy get very good at distracting the therapist and avoiding the subjects they find painful or difficult to deal with. That's why therapy can take so long. Years."

"That's not what I want to do," I say, almost to myself. "I'm not interested in putting your children through college. I don't want this to be a part-time job for me. I don't want to be in therapy for years, rehashing the past. I want to reach my goal and get on with my life."

"Take a look inside," he instructs me. "There's a path in front of you that leads to your goal. There are hundreds of ways to get to your goal. Let's remove the paths that might put you in the hospital, or cause harm to yourself or anyone else. Find a path that's the most efficient in reaching your goal and that serves the highest good for yourself. You don't have to know all the details; you just need to know that this is the best path. Now look at it. What's standing in the way of you reaching your goal?"

She stands in the center of the path, as immoveable as a tree. Behind her is the hotel room.

"Can you see your goal?" His voice is soft and unassuming.

"Yes."

I stand laughing, happy and carefree. There's no distrust or suspicion, none of the guardedness that has long been a part of me; I am light and free.

It's not just intimacy that I want; it's being a whole, healthy person capable of love and compassion, fearless and trusting.

"What do you need to do to reach that goal?" he asks.

"I can't have her remain separate ... and I have to finish the hotel room." But I don't know what else is in the hotel room because I only see the little girl on the bed and nothing more.

"How long will you need to get to this goal? A week? A month? A year? Two years? Seven?"

"Seven?" I'll be old by then. It's already the end of the year and I feel no closer to my goal than when I left the psych unit.

"It can be as long or as short as you want."

"April," I say. I think about April and spring and launching into the dating world and new beginnings. April is a good month, a good time to finish and begin. "I want to be done by April."

CHAPTER 17

It was the summer of 1984. Shameful Sister had joined the navy a year earlier, and I had just turned seventeen and graduated high school. I had taken the train across country to the Bethesda Naval Base, where my sister was stationed. It was my first trip away from home without my family.

One of my sister's friends on the base had a rented apartment, so we didn't have to stay in the small dorm room my sister shared with another girl, who, my sister complained, borrowed her underwear and cried at night. The apartment was large, with a small kitchen.

My sister and her boyfriend were cooking, and although I tried to help they kept pushing me into the living room with Ernesto. Ernesto was a seaman first class. It was couples night and my sister had set me up with a date.

I felt out of place among the military people, who had all seen more of the country than I had. It was strange to see my sister in this new role as a woman who drank and had boyfriends and could take care of herself, a long way from the shy teenager who had flirted with the boys and could only talk about being a medic in the navy.

I sat on the couch with Ernesto at my side. He had a thin mustache. He was a Filipino, and although he was only a year older than me, he had worldliness about him, a sexual maturity that put me on guard.

We'd been sent out three times for things they needed for dinner: mushrooms, eggs, milk. I was glad to be sitting instead of moving in and out of Ernesto's Corvette, trying to find things to say. I wasn't used to dating and making conversation with men, but I pretended to be relaxed and tried to keep the conversation going so he wouldn't know I had no experience.

"You're really pretty," he said smoothly.

I smiled softly and looked away. I didn't feel pretty. I felt very plain and small. My hair was never in the right style, and I didn't know what kind of makeup to wear so I used blue eye shadow because that's what everybody was wearing. I didn't wear perfume or jewelry. I was nothing like the other young women I'd seen on base, confident and assertive.

Dinner was served with wine, something we never had at home. Neither of our parents drank, not even on holidays. My sister whispered in my ear to be careful with the wine. Ernesto wanted to fill my glass again, but I let it sit untouched.

My sister and her boyfriend did the dishes and didn't let me help. I sat back on the couch with Ernesto, making small talk about things I pretended to know. I didn't want him to think this was my first date. I wanted him to think I knew what I was doing. I didn't want him to see that I was nervous about where his hands were and what they were doing.

His arm moved around my shoulder. Somewhere in the conversation, his arm slipped to my waist. I could feel his hand by the side of my breast. His thumb caressed the swell of my breast and I felt my heart pound with excitement. He was gentle and unrushed. I liked that he wasn't demanding, but seductive and kind.

They had rented porno movies for the night. I'd never seen a porno movie and didn't know what to expect, but the woman who rented the apartment knew all the names of the cast. I looked around the living room. My sister and her boyfriend were on the floor on a blanket. The woman and her boyfriend were in a chair, snuggled together. And I was on the couch with Ernesto's hand on my breast.

He was on duty at six o'clock in the morning. He'd mentioned this several times to me and I could feel his impatience and uncertainty about the night. I wondered where he was going to sleep. Here in the apartment, in the spare bedroom, or was he going home ... alone?

The woman who rented the apartment smiled at us. "There's a spare bedroom if anyone needs it."

Ernesto gave me an approving look. I tried to focus on the television, which was offering no relief in distracting my date. I liked his hand on my breast and the softness of his lips on my neck, but I didn't want to go into the bedroom with him. I didn't know what would happen there, but I knew it would feel like falling off a cliff, like everything would be out of control and I wouldn't be able to slow things down. I picked up a sense of impatience from Ernesto, although he'd given me no indication he would be that way.

I watched the other woman and her boyfriend. Their hands are all over each other. She was reaching down low. I could hear his husky laugh as he said something to her that made her laugh. They touched easily and without bounds. I liked how certain of herself she was.

"It's going to be hard for you to sleep tonight," Ernest whispered, "with everybody in a room together and you all alone."

"I'm okay. I'm really tired tonight."

"Are you sure?"

"Yes. I'm going to go to bed early. I'm tired from traveling."

My sister's boyfriend laughed softly. "You need your sleep, Ernie."

We watched some more television. It was dark outside, and I was falling asleep on the couch with Ernesto's hand on the side of my breast.

"Come outside with me," he whispered, and tugged on my hand.

I followed him to the door.

"You have to stay in the apartment," my sister called.

He waited just outside the living-room door. I didn't know why he wanted to say goodnight in the hall, until he pulled me near and kissed me. His lips were soft on mine. I put my hand on his chest to keep control of him. I didn't like to be caught and held tightly.

"Are you sure you don't want to come home with me tonight?"

"Yes, I'm sure," I said softly. I would have liked more touching, but he wanted something else. He wanted to go into the bedroom.

"You break my heart," he said playfully, and walked away.

December 16

I'm sad," I tell Dr. Erickson.

My paintings have become more disturbing, more violent. I paint images of little girls without left arms, their limbs dripping blood.

"Anger directed inside turns to sadness and depression," he says. "Have you held the little girl who's angry?"

"Yes." There's a hint of defiance in my tone. I'm still stinging from our last conversation about pushing things away. "Last week you said I was pushing things away. I don't want to do that. I'm listening to everything you have to say. I'm going to try harder to do the things I need to do. So I held her, but she doesn't respond at all. She just lies there, as if I'm not even there."

"It's important that you give her love, but it has to be genuine," he says quietly. "You can't fool the people inside. They'll know if you're not being honest."

"I'm honest. I didn't mind holding her."

"Good."

It hasn't made the difference he seems to think it would. Suddenly, I'm having strong visions of cutting off my left arm, strange thoughts that it doesn't belong to me. It's the inside chatter that's so distracting.

My arm doesn't belong to me. I'm not supposed to have it.

"You can step into one another," he suggests, "and be the same person in the same space. That might help you to understand how she feels. You know, walk in someone else's skin."

"She's angry," I say, although I'm not certain anymore whose anger it is. It's easiest to assign it to her. Her anger frightens me.

I hold the knife in my right hand and drive it into my thigh, sinking the blade into my flesh.

Why do I want to hurt? Why do people hurt themselves? I glance at him, sitting patiently at the other end of the office, and contemplate what the criteria is for a seventy-two-hour hold in the local psychiatric unit and if I'm about to meet it.

I've been seeing Dr. Erickson for several months now, and have come to trust him with my secrets and fears, despite the objections from inside, and the unreasonable fear of his hands that I can't quite process as my own. As the urge to hurt myself intensifies, I reach for the one person who has not judged me.

"I have such … an overwhelming urge to … drive a knife into my leg. It's not what I want to do. I don't want to hurt myself, but … the urge is so strong."

"Have you hurt yourself?"

"No," I say quietly, staring at the carpet. It's difficult to meet his penetrating gaze. He makes it impossible for me to hide.

"Can you keep yourself safe?"

"Yes … I think so."

"Do you need to do the anger-release exercise?"

"No." I don't feel anger.

"We'll want to do that before you're in crisis. It's easier to manage that way." He studies me. "Are you still drawing?"

"Yes. The pictures are still violent." I don't want to show him the pictures of the little girls without arms; I don't want to tell him my thoughts of cutting off my arm.

"What's going on inside?"

She's kneeling in the darkness, stabbing her leg with a knife.

"We can do EMDR," he says, after hearing my description. "See if the image changes."

He's brought a special wand to use for EMDR instead of using his hand. It's a piece of dowel, with a small ball attached to one end. I move my chair and he sits a few feet away. I like the space the new device offers; I can concentrate on my images and not on what his hands are doing.

"Think about the little girl stabbing her leg ..."

I stand in front of her in the darkness. She's kneeling, and she calmly drives a knife through her leg. It's a repetitive motion that evokes no pain or emotion in either of us.

"Stay with this image," he says. "There's information here."

"Not all touch is bad," I tell her. "We can have what other people have. It can be nice."

I fold into an embrace with a man. He presses me close as my arms wrap around him ...

She stands and, in a fit of rage and frustration, runs the knife blade across her arms, cutting the flesh open.

I turn away in disappointment and sorrow, wanting the images to stop. I can't even fantasize pleasure or present the girl with a nice picture to enjoy. Her anger dominates everything.

Dr. Erickson tries to get me to follow the wand and continue, but I remain turned away. "What are you seeing?" he says.

"She's cutting her arms and making them bleed."

"What is she releasing?"

"I don't know." The images distress me. More violence I don't want. I haven't done anything wrong. Why is she punishing me?

"Is she releasing rage? Fear? Shame?"

He often mentions the word "shame." I don't know why.

"Anger maybe. I'm missing something. She's like a child throwing a tantrum."

He raises the wand again and my eyes automatically follow the lateral pattern.

"I missed something," I say again softly, as I follow the wand.

"What did you miss?"

"I don't know, but it feels like that kind of frustration you have when someone doesn't understand what you're saying."

He stops and I focus on the tiny spiral designs on the carpet.

"You don't have to hurt yourself or others to express anger," he says.

"I know."

"I'm talking to that part of yourself who's angry, the part who's painting the pictures and cutting her arms. There are other ways of expressing anger. We did one of them when we pushed against each other. You can buy dishes and throw them against the wall. That's a great way of releasing anger."

"I'm not angry."

He takes a breath. "I know you're not angry. *She* has your anger. You can't keep ignoring it. She's trying to tell you something. You're making things very difficult inside for yourself."

Heaviness settles in me. My efforts to move ahead seem futile. Always I return to her, the prison guard at the gate. How will my life change when part of me refuses to change? How will I be able to love when all she knows is hate?

"I want things to change," I say softly. "I want to be able to have people touch me and feel pleasure the way I imagine it. I want to be able to fantasize and experience that desire."

"Can you feel desire?"

"Yes, I feel desire. When I've gone on dates I've wanted the man to touch me, and I've thought about what kissing would be like. I can be aroused."

"Do you masturbate?" he asks casually.

My thoughts stagger as I struggle for an answer while attempting to compose myself. I don't want to appear flustered, but I am. Without warning my Catholic upbringing surfaces, bringing embarrassment and shame. I quickly remind myself that this man is a physician and a psychiatrist, and most likely has heard it all.

It was just a matter of time before we got to this subject. Freud notwithstanding, every psychology class addresses sexuality and the human mind. I knew there was no way I would be able to see a psychiatrist without delving into my sexuality. I've been lucky to go this many months without the subject coming up, and now I find myself wondering if I can lie convincingly, and then just as quickly dismiss the idea. I know it would be more alarming for a psychiatrist if I claimed that I didn't masturbate than to admit that I do.

"Yes," I answer.

"Are you orgasmic?" he asks. He tosses the question out onto the floor like the proverbial gauntlet.

All I can think to say is, "That's a good question." Finally I say, "No. Well, no, I don't think so. I'm not sure." And then, as if to defend myself, I add, "I feel pleasure and ... a kind of ... tightness, but it's too much ... I back away. It's too much."

"You've never gone over the edge, let yourself go?"

"No." Of that I'm certain.

He stands and goes to his desk. "There's a book that's helpful to women who have difficulty in reaching orgasm. It's a little dated, but it's still the best book out there. It might help you."

He gives me a piece of paper with the book title written on it. I smile as I read it: *For Yourself.*

CHAPTER 18

How could I hide from my mind? All around me were holiday festivities: brightly lit garlands, and the fragrance of evergreen and cinnamon. It was torture to go to the stores and be surrounded by holiday shoppers and their exuberant cheerfulness, as if they had no idea that little children were being sexually assaulted.

I looked at fathers with their daughters and cringed, wondering if the children were being molested. It was impossible to tell by sight alone; after all, didn't I look happy once?

The holidays were quickly becoming my least favorite time of year. I couldn't get excited about family gatherings. Everything seemed obligatory, and I wanted only to stay home and remove myself from them.

"Are you going to celebrate Christmas or what?" Second Brother asked. It sounded like a challenge, not a question.

I could hear his frustration at my unwillingness to participate in the charade. Part of me wanted to capitulate to his needs. After all, he didn't do anything wrong. He only wanted me to be the person I was, the agreeable and compliant sister. But the other part of me was angry because he wouldn't let me change.

"You used to be fun," he said. "You used to come over for dinner and play games."

That was true. I couldn't explain to him why I didn't want to be around family anymore. Why nothing seemed to make me happy. Why everything I'd ever known about myself was false.

Couldn't he see how manufactured we'd all become?

December 21

The sadness inside has retreated a little, but not entirely. It lingers now like a persistent haze on a summer's day, distorting the background but not masking it. As always, a change has brought a change of images. I don't need to close my eyes to see the image of her kneeling in the darkness, calmly stabbing her thigh in the same way that someone might unconsciously tap a pencil on a tabletop.

While I feel the sadness, I don't feel the anger. I watch as the image of her stabbing her leg changes to one of her stabbing her arm. I struggle with the new image, and try to find a way to coexist, moving myself further from the distressing image that still brings with it the desire to harm.

The saw blade slices through my left arm, severing it from me.

I focus instead on a different impulse.

For weeks now I've had an urge to play with paper dolls. I've dismissed it, refusing to surrender to the inner-child craze that's been sweeping the women of my generation and, more importantly, refusing to feed the idea that I have a child within me that has needs and desires of its own. Still, the urge to play has been so great that I reason it can't harm anything, except maybe my ego. What I've discovered, by succumbing to the playtime urge, is something else altogether.

"I brought some paper dolls to play with," I tell him sheepishly.

"You let her play." It's not a question.

We've spoken of her need to play, the sudden desire to play the games I'd loved as a child, my desire to cuddle a stuffed animal.

"How is playing?"

"Nice … sometimes."

I like dressing the dolls. It's like being catapulted back in time, where suddenly I'm eight years old again, pressing the tabs of the colored paper outfits in place and admiring the stylish beauties with gentle pleasure. But the feelings I experience playing dress-up are not at all gentle.

"There's this strong feeling that comes over me when I play, like I don't want anyone else to touch the dolls, like I want to protect them."

"You hold them very close when you say that," he observes, demonstrating my body language. "They're mine, gimmee."

His description is not flattering. Never mind that I'm thirty-eight years old and shouldn't be playing with dolls, but now I'm a selfish thirty-eight-year-old playing with dolls. I was taught to share my toys. With older sisters, I never had the luxury of having my own toys. Toys were community property and that was the way we liked it. So I'm wondering where this sudden desire to hoard the dolls comes from.

"Play therapy is very important," Dr. Erickson says. "If you want, you can bring the dolls to therapy. I can watch you play and tell you what I think."

Dr. Erickson reaches for one of the paper dolls. He holds it as carefully as I do, pretending to play.

Boys aren't supposed to touch girls. My stomach and chest tightens as I feel the now familiar anxiety squeeze at me. I imagine what it would be like if I were to play with him.

I'm watching him and what he does with the doll. I feel a pushing from the inside, like an energy pushing to get out. He's not supposed to touch them!

The battle inside is so forceful. *I* don't mind if Dr. Erickson plays with them, but something inside does mind. It minds very much.

157

Suddenly, I snatch the doll and tear it up into tiny pieces … and breathe a sigh of relief.

"I don't know," I tell him quietly. "I'll think about that."

"How are things inside? Still sad?"

"Yes. She's stopped stabbing her thigh. She's stabbing her hand now."

"Which hand?"

"The left one. That's all she does."

She's sitting in the darkness with her knees tucked under her. Her left hand lies on an invisible platform. She drives a knife into it, over and over …

"Does she want to hurt the dolls?"

"Yes. She doesn't like that they have two arms."

The dolls aren't supposed to have a left arm. I'm not supposed to have two arms. It's how I see things in my mind, and the image is so strong and the impulse so powerful that it's all I can do to keep from tearing off the tiny paper arm and making the doll right.

"Why can't they have two arms?"

"I don't know. They just don't look right with two arms."

"Which arm does she want to remove?"

"The left one." It's how I draw pictures, with the left arm missing.

It's not mine. It belongs to somebody else.

The voice is clear and calm, the way one would speak having a polite conversation.

She looks at Dr. Erickson in his familiar place in the office. "You have blue eyes. They are kind and gentle." She softens, her hand poised on the knife that's buried deep in her left hand. "You can have it if you want. It doesn't belong to me."

"If thy hand offends thee, cut it off," he says simply.

The hand has offended?

"What did that hand do?" he asks.

"Nothing." It's not my arm. It belongs to somebody else. Not me.

"When you were in the farmhouse, kneeling with your father, where were your hands?"

"On him."

"All the time?"

My right hand is pinned to the floor and I'm helpless to stop his hand from exploring me.

"Where is your left hand?" he asks.

"It's … I don't know. I don't see my left hand."

"Is it supporting you?"

"No. I'm on my knees. I don't need support."

"Where is it? What's it doing?"

I search the memory, but can find no answer. "I don't know. It's not doing anything." I look at him. "I don't like that she wants to take the arms off the dolls."

"Let her destroy or alter the dolls if she wants. It's important to let her express her emotions."

Only a psychiatrist would suggest something so absurd. It's *me* he's talking about. It would be *my* hand that destroys the dolls, just as it's *my* hand that draws the pictures … and *my* hand that wants to hurt me.

It's not my arm. I don't have two arms. How can I be two people at the same time? How can I accept her and stay safe?

"We can do the pushing exercise when you need it," he offers. "You said it helped the last time."

How can I push with only one arm? "Yes, it helped, but it's not what I want now," I lie. "I'll try letting her play with the dolls the way she wants."

Maybe removing the arms from the little paper dolls will satisfy my urge enough so that I don't remove my own arm. But I'm craving it desperately, the way a drowning person craves oxygen. It's a force that's driving me, and I don't know how much longer I can keep myself safe.

CHAPTER 19

The miter saw in the basement held a morbid fascination for me. I could see the sharp blade coming down on my left arm and severing it. I curled my fingers around the handle and imagined the satisfaction I would feel at removing my arm. All I had to do was bring the blade down. I'd cut wood before and knew the feel of the machine vibrating in my hand, the quickness and ease with which the blade cut. That could be my arm, finally removed from me. Finally gone.

I rested my head against the cold metal and released a sob. Some part of me was holding back, but I had to fight the impulse.

Pleasing Sister knew something was wrong. Despite our current situation, we had a strong connection. She knew me too well and sensed something was amiss, maybe because I'd retreated into my own little world. Therapy was a kind of a secret society with exclusive membership. Maybe she'd seen more than I thought she had.

We didn't talk therapy. What was there to say? I went off every Tuesday to my appointment, made my secret call from my room every Saturday, and in between we survived.

I resented her ebbs and flows. I moved from wanting to take care of her, to being angry she would never leave. She, on the other hand, had remained silent. Until …

"Everything going good in therapy?" she asked one day.

Because of her medical background she didn't have a high opinion of psychiatrists. To be fair, I hadn't met anyone who did have a high opinion of psychiatrists. "Psychiatrists are damaged people," someone told me when I mentioned I was in therapy. Sadly, I'd hear the sentiment again over the next year.

"Yes," I told Pleasing Sister. "I like Dr. Erickson."

She nodded and walked away.

I hadn't told her that we couldn't live together anymore.

January 3

I failed. During the long break since the last session I almost succumb to the overpowering need to take off my arm. The insistent pressure squeezes and squeezes until my entire body feels like a twisted piece of dried meat. Cut off my arm and everything will be better, no more visions, no more urges. It will be finished. Done.

I need to do it, the way an addict needs a fix, but some part of me resists the idea.

At a late hour on Christmas Eve, I find the knife in my hand, and I have nowhere to turn.

If I can't actually cut off my arm, I still feel the need to take the knife and drive it into my hand, right through the tiny bones to match the image that's been haunting me. But I only draw the blade across the flesh and watch as blood weeps from it.

On the patient-evaluation form, I had left the box by the self-cutting category blank. I didn't want to lie, but I didn't want to tell the truth either. The act itself is all too common for women with my past.

Women like me, who have been sexually abused as children, are often self-destructive, and exhibit inappropriate sexual behavior. We're expected to be addicted to drugs or dependent on alcohol to get through our lives.

We're expected to have co-dependent relationships and to self-medicate. We're not expected to make good choices in our lives, to have thriving careers or healthy relationships.

The fact that I have now joined the millions of women who self-injure only saddens me more; I have become predictable.

Put them together. Open the door.

The instructions come from far away, and yet the voice is close. It's not the voice of the little girl, carrying abstract conversations and disconnected thoughts, but a celestial voice that quiets everything inside like a mother reassuring her child.

I don't know what door I'm to open. I don't see a door in my mind. But I know who the voice means when it says "put them together." They are the two little girls I've locked in my mind—anger and sadness. I cannot keep them apart any longer.

The scar is visible, but the weak lighting in the office offers me protection from Dr. Erickson's penetrating gaze.

"I'm trying to connect to the room," I tell him. "I spent some time this week in the hotel room, lying on the bed, trying to be her. I've felt all this anger rising up from some place deep inside. I thought if I could connect to the room the anger would go away. But I can't be her. I'm trying, but it's just not working."

It's what he's been telling me these past months: associate with the feelings, make the memory mine, integrate with her.

"Where do you feel the anger in your body?" he asks.

"In my pelvis." The strange queasiness is always there, low in my belly, like an invisible hand tightening on my insides.

"If you look inside, is there something there?"

"Yes." I know it without looking because I feel it, a dark place with a little girl at the bottom. It's how I see things on the inside, from the top down.

"Is this the girl with the knife?"

"No." I can see that girl. She's where I left her, still stabbing her hand. It's become a familiar scene that numbs me.

"A different girl?"

"Well, I don't like to think of it that way. Maybe it's just a sense of things."

"Because you don't want there to be another girl? Keep the inventory down to a minimum?" he says with a small smile.

"Yes. I only want there to be these two girls." But somehow I know there are more.

He nods. "Do you want to rescue this girl from the pit in your pelvis?"

I think about going into that dark place, descending into the deep pit in search of the presence I feel, and the idea frightens me. I get the sense that something is lying down there, waiting, and that awakening this feeling would be like awakening a volcano.

Talk to the hands, they know.

I look at Dr. Erickson's hands. He's always so careful with them, keeping them still on the arms of the chair, or folding them into each other as if they're holding themselves. Or is it that he's restraining them?

"I don't want to go there," I say in answer to his question. I can't keep my eyes from his hands. Everything inside of me is focused on them.

You're not supposed to touch me.

"Okay." He watches me closely. "What about the other girl? Is she still stabbing her hand?"

"Yes, that's all she ever does; all day. She's the source of the anger." *And my need to hurt myself.*

"Look at that little girl. Does she look okay to you? Does she look normal? Have normal teeth and normal hands?"

She sits in front of me, calmly stabbing the back of her hand. There's no blood from the wounds, as if the blade were penetrating dead flesh. Her expression is stoic, but not cold. And then I see it. Her eyes ... they're black.

"Like doll's eyes?" he suggests.

"She's so transparent, like there's something missing from her. She's so angry." I don't know why she's so angry. I don't know why she wants to hurt me. "She's so dangerous."

"Sometimes people are affected by 'rage monsters.' It's kind of like insanity. We can take that monster and remove it from her, and that might quiet things down inside. Do you want to do that?"

I nod. Maybe that would help to keep me from cutting myself again. Any relief would be welcome.

"First you need to put her in a bubble of healing white light. This bubble has special walls where she can't get hurt, and she can't get out. She might kick and make a fuss being put in there, but that's okay. Let her kick and scream if she wants."

She doesn't struggle. The healing white light is around her, and she seems more intrigued by it than outraged.

"We have to have a place to put the monster once we remove it, so we're going to have a tube-ex system," Dr. Erickson says. "It's going to take the monster from her and put it into a protective bubble within the bubble she's in. That monster inside the special bubble goes into the tube-ex and goes way out into the universe. I'll tell you what to do with it once we get that far. Sometimes the monster hides in the back of her neck, and you can unbutton that spot at the back of her neck. Look at her and see if you can find where the monster's hiding."

I try to think of the monster in the back of her neck as he's suggesting, but my eyes go to her belly. I feel a strong presence there inside her.

"So you want to be very calm. Monsters love it when you get angry. They eat that up. You have to be very matter of fact about this. It's like removing a tic from a child. Make sure the monster stays inside the inner bubble. Do you have the monster?"

It doesn't look like a monster, more like a blob of glowing light that kicks and scratches.

"How does the little girl look? Sometimes when you remove monsters the afflicted person sags and looks almost dead."

"No, she's fine."

"Good. You have the monster contained?"

"Yes."

"See if it has anything of hers before you send it away. You can put the squeeze on monsters, and anything they have that doesn't belong to them will fall out. You don't need to know what it is. You just need to know it belongs to her."

The bubble twists around the monster, squeezing it like a rag being wrung out. Something drops out. I see it as a green glowing piece.

"Give that piece back to the little girl," he tells me. "Now you can send the monster into the tube-ex. This will go out into the universe, to the source. That's the place where all the negative energy of the monster will be transformed into positive energy and sent back into the universe to do good."

She stands calmly in the bubble of healing white light, looking at me with quiet expectation.

"You can let the little girl out of the bubble," he says. "How are things inside now?"

"Quiet. I feel better. I don't feel that pressure."

Now if I could only get her to stop talking to his hands.

CHAPTER 20

There were brief respites from the darkness and confusion. I liked to test my boundaries and had begun to think about masturbation, something I hadn't been able to do since entering therapy.

A dear friend gave me a vibrator for my thirtieth birthday; according to the packaging, it was a "hand vibrator." It was small and sleek. She called and asked if I liked it.

"Yes. It's nice, but I really don't have any hand pain."

There was silence on the other end of the phone. "Darling, it's not for your hand."

And thus began my education into the fine art of masturbation. As practiced as I had become over the years, I had never been able to orgasm. I always pulled back. Now I wanted to incorporate my fantasies into the practice and that had become more difficult.

It wasn't that I was without desire; the difficulty was reconciling the confusion inside to be able to enjoy it. So I had arranged my fantasies into modestly descriptive scenes and found a window of pleasure to practice masturbation. I had my first orgasm, losing myself to the waves of pleasure that pulsed from within. There was still fear of letting go, and as my body succumbed to the stimulation with an almost violent response, I wondered if that was normal.

As I reached orgasm, was it fear I was responding to or desire?

In those moments, I disappeared from the sadness and hopelessness that had shrouded my life. In that narrow gap of space I forgot that time was running out.

January 11

*T*alk to the hands, they know.

These words are uttered repeatedly, cluttering my thoughts as I sit in my usual chair in Dr. Erickson's office. I have visions of him sitting next to me, catching me and holding me in place. These visions have become so frequent that it's impossible for me to think of our sessions together and not have them interfere, inserting themselves into my reality.

The visions are not memories, and I can't categorize them as fantasies, but they're so vivid they seem real, almost like a memory, or a premonition.

This is not the working of my rational, logical brain, the financial manager who pays the bills on time and balances the checking account; the person who comes to therapy every week looking for answers. It's that separate part of me that thinks on another plane, the part I've trapped in the past.

"You wrote the words 'teach me,'" he says, examining the folder that holds my paintings.

"Yes," I say. Thoughts come into my mind after I paint, and sometimes I write them on the folder. "I'm supposed to teach her something."

"And you wrote 'free her.'"

"Yes … someone's trapped, I can feel that. I always want to be free."

"You drew a picture of a little girl in a cage. Is she the one you're supposed to free?"

"I don't know." I put her in that cage to keep her in place and keep her from hurting, but I'm the one who feels caged. "I have a sense of rooms colliding, merging. I'm in the farmhouse and the hotel room. I'm being held down. I have the strongest need to get free ... but I don't know how."

"You sit like that often," he says quietly.

I look down at my legs, wondering what he's talking about.

"With your left hand holding your right wrist."

"I do?" I remove my fingers from my wrist and rest them on the arms of the chair.

"Yes."

Father's strong fingers are wrapped securely around my tiny wrist, pinning my hand to the floor.

"It's the only thing I feel in that memory," I mutter. "Those fingers on my wrist. I don't like to be held down like that."

"When people have a physical sensation that links them to a memory, it can keep them connected to that memory. In your case, it's keeping you from finishing the room."

"But I tried to connect to the memory. It didn't work."

He studies me for a moment. "I think I know a way for you to get free. If I hold onto your wrist, you'll associate with the memory, only this time you'll be able to get free. *Both* of you can pull free."

I stare at his hands. *You're not supposed to touch me.* I remind myself that I can choose who touches me and for what purpose. I tell myself that Dr. Erickson has never touched me without asking permission. He's given me no reason to distrust him, but I feel the chaos inside at the suggestion, the fear and helplessness.

"How would we do that?" I ask. I like to know the rules. I like to know how things are going to happen before they happen. I run through every scenario in my mind of what might or might not occur, analyzing the possibilities and calculating the risks and rewards.

"I hold your wrist the same way your father did and you pull free."

His hand is on my wrist and pulls me close. His other hand reaches for my arm and, like a piece of fabric pulled into the spokes of a machine, he soon traps me.

"How hard are you going to hold me?"

"Hard enough for you to struggle to get free."

You're trying to trick me. Why do you want to touch me? "I want to think about this," I say distantly. My thoughts spin and collide, creating a maelstrom of emotions. "I have a lot of thoughts in my head ... and I want to think about this."

I don't like the thought of him touching me, any more than I like the idea of connecting to that memory, of being in that room again, of feeling what she's feeling. Dr. Erickson would be holding me in place, trapping me. What if I can't get out of the memory? I don't want to feel what she's feeling.

"You're in control here," he reminds me calmly. "It's important for you to remember that. This decision is yours."

My fingers play on my left hand, pinching the skin. It's a habit I've developed lately, an obsession I have with my left arm.

The saw blade slices through my arm just below the elbow, a clean, painless cut that severs my arm. I am free.

"I'd just pull free?" I ask.

He nods.

I wonder what I'd be pulling free from—the hand between my legs, or the hand restraining me?

"I don't like the rooms colliding together." My voice is soft and distant. "I don't like things all unorganized. There's something there in these rooms I don't like."

"What is there that you don't like?"

There's no blood when the blade cuts through my arm, as if it's slicing through soft wood.

"A secret ... it feels like a secret." My fingers pinch the skin of my left hand. "She doesn't think she has a left arm." I hesitate. I haven't told him of this vision. I've been waiting for it to disappear, but now I want to tell him in the hope he'll understand the need. "I've been having these visions of cutting my arm off. It's like an urge, like a craving for something; it's always there."

He's quiet for a long moment. I hold my breath. "This is the same arm she stabs all the time," he says finally. "Stabbing is a metaphor for masturbation, penetration … rape."

I don't like that word: *rape*. It tightens things inside and I feel like a boiling pot about to burst. "There's a sense of protecting it," I say, "keeping it from people. She doesn't want me to have it."

Suddenly, his eyes sharpen. "Is that where the secret is? Did you hide the secret in your arm?"

"I didn't."

"Memories and emotions can be stored in the body as encapsulated energy. That's what makes people sick—unprocessed emotions, feelings they don't want to deal with. Release that memory and the energy is released with it." He stares at me. "If you have your arm then you have the secret, but if you get rid of your arm then you get rid of the secret. There's a twisted logic here, but it's not the solution."

"I don't know," I say softly. "I just know I'm not supposed to have an arm. It doesn't belong to me."

"To whom does it belong?"

You can have it if you want. You can take it. "I don't know. Not me."

Silence. He studies me with a strange mix of compassion and intrigue. "Do you want to find your left arm?" he asks. "Find the emotions it's hiding?"

I consider his question. I answer the only way I know how. "I want to be free."

He looks at me, and I know he's wondering how badly I want to be free.

"I'll think about that," I say. It's a stalling tactic, and I know he sees through it. My thoughts shift from the hated arm to other information that's been confusing me.

"Question?" he prompts.

"Yes." I won't look at him. It's not a subject I'm comfortable with, but I want an answer. I need an answer. I study the fabric of my jeans, running my fingers over it. The silence stretches until I realize he's not going to fill it.

"So ... I had an orgasm." Once the words are out, it is easier for my thoughts to follow. I feel a calm infuse me. "It was nice. It was very nice. It was like this pressure building and this flush of heat. My whole body was galvanized, my back arched ... I kicked the cat off the bed."

"Sounds like a good one."

I release a breath, suddenly relieved. "I was worried about that." Worried I was experiencing violence rather than pleasure. But I'm normal. "I wasn't sure ... my girlfriends weren't very clear on this."

"Did you explain it to them with as much description?"

Was I too descriptive? "Yes, but they were vague about it, so I didn't know." Another thought comes to mind. "Is that what sex is like?"

He's silent for a time. "Sex is different. There's another person there."

True, but ... "Why does that matter?"

"People worry about how they look, what the other person is thinking. Remember what I put on the board about orgasm? The conditions that need to be met?"

"Yes."

"Relaxation and arousal. A lot of people think too much during sex, and it interferes with their ability to relax."

"Why do people care what they look like?" This is a strange concept to me. "They're having sex with this person, that's something as intimate as I can think of. I'm comfortable with my body. I wouldn't worry about that."

I'm convinced it's due to undressing in front of my sisters. With eight children and one bathroom, privacy was a luxury we couldn't afford.

"That's good," he says casually, and stands.

The session has ended.

CHAPTER 21

New Year's Eve had always affected me strongly. It had been like that since I could remember. A new year meant a fresh start, starting over, a clean slate. But nothing was new for me now. Everything was old—my life had become about the past, not the future.

Pleasing Sister and I had always celebrated New Year's Eve with flare. We'd set up a cornucopia of delicacies out and open a bottle of Asti. We'd go over what we didn't want to drag into the next year and write out all our goals. There was something about the promise and hope of the uncharted days ahead, as if anything could happen.

We had celebrated the new millennium in style, hosting a family reunion in our newly built home, toasting the new century with champagne and making a family time capsule. All my siblings had contributed. The house had filled with laughter and celebration as uncles, nieces, nephews and spouses came together.

It was difficult for me to remember that happy time as I looked around the house now and let New Year's pass without a moment's thought. There seemed to be nothing exciting in my future. I felt my life was accelerating to a close, and at the same time I was in a race to put the pieces of myself together, to heal as a whole person before time ran out, before I acted on the images that tormented me. I existed in a narrow window of space that was neither the past nor the future, running on the universe's treadmill and going nowhere.

But maybe that was just the nature of therapy, I told myself. I was a planner. I wanted to know what was going to happen and when. I had set the deadline of April to be finished with therapy and I worried that I wasn't going to make it. Another failure.

I knew I did not want to be in therapy for years. I had to get my life back, I had to move on, to make the changes I wanted to make, to go back to work, to date, and maybe even to marry. I wanted to have a life of my own. But I was still with my sister, I was still battling images and desires, and nothing was changing.

January 18

I want to do something today," I tell Dr. Erickson. "I want you to pull on my arm. I want to be free."

Thoughts of sawing off my arm are constant. It has become a plan, and I'm unable to go near the miter saw for fear that I'll attempt to recreate the vision. I battle with conflicting beliefs: *It will not hurt. You cannot do it.*

My only hope is that by pulling free of Dr. Erickson, maybe this strange need inside of me will go away.

"All right," he says quietly. "But recreating this situation could be very intense for you. Some emotions might come up that you haven't thought of before."

"Like what?" I ask, frowning.

"I'm not sure, but I want you to be aware that you could experience some emotions that aren't in the memory. The memory right now is dissociated, it's not personal."

"Okay." It's all I can think of to say. I'm not sure what to expect. I begin to resist the idea.

"There are some things I want to talk to you about first," he says. "I want to make sure that the little girl is okay with this and that she understands what we're doing. I don't want to hurt you and I don't want to be hurt, either."

"She won't hurt you," I say quietly. "If you were playing with the dolls, then I'd worry, but … she's afraid of your hands."

He nods.

"She's worried you're going to do more than just grab my wrist."

"I'll only grab your wrist. My only interest is in you getting free."

They're not going to do anything. They're bad hands. My insides are taut and twisted with conflicting emotions. Suddenly the room is too small, my chair too restricting.

"I know that's what you want, but what about your hands? She's not sure you have control of your hands."

He looks down at his hands with an unreadable expression. "They're my hands. They'll listen to what I tell them."

The girl stares at his hands and tells them, "You can only touch my wrist and nothing else. You can't take whatever you want. You have to ask permission."

I trust Dr. Erickson; she does not. While I fear the exercise and what it will mean for me, she is intrigued. It's a test for him, to see if he does what he says he'll do. She likes tests.

"Okay," I say quietly.

"Okay what?"

"Okay, I want to do the exercise."

"There's one other thing. If you leave the room during this exercise, don't leave the building without talking to me first, okay?"

I have no idea why he thinks I would leave the room, and these precautions are doing nothing to alleviate my fears. Still, I say, "Okay."

He sits quietly with his arms resting on his knees. He reminds me of a priest sitting down to talk to a parishioner. There's a warmth to him that spreads across the room.

"What do you think is the best way to do this," he says, "standing or sitting?"

"I was sitting with my father, so I want to sit."

"Do you want to give me your arm, or do you want me to grab it?"

Offering my arm for capture seems like surrender, and too much like giving permission. I don't want to surrender. I want to fight. "You should grab it."

"You want to come out into the middle of the room?"

I move my chair so that I'm not trapped against the wall. He moves his chair closer and I begin to feel like an experiment he's about to explore. My heart pounds. He's going to touch me the way my father touched me. He's going to catch me and be mean. I don't want him to be mean. I move my arm away from him.

"When are you going to let go?" I ask, keeping my arm from him.

"When you pull free. I'm going to make it difficult for you, so you have to try to get free."

Try to get free. Those words are like an epitaph. What if I can't get free? What if I can't get out of the memory? Who will come to rescue me?

I stare at his hands. They're so close and he hasn't moved. He won't until I give him permission to begin. I desperately want out of the room. I want to run as far and as fast as I can, run away from the memory and that damned room where everything stopped.

Blood rushes in my ears.

The voice comes again, celestial, maternal. *Push the door open.* Is it the door to the rooms? Is it a door out? I've been running away from this room for thirty years. I want to stop running. I want to be free. But I don't want him touching me. I don't want to feel what happened in that room.

What will happen when he touches me? Could I do the memory and not feel?

He waits silently and patiently. It's difficult to breathe. I don't want to do this. I don't want to feel what the girl is feeling. I want to be free. I'm tired of feeling trapped, but I don't want him to touch me.

Before I can think any more, I rest my arm on the chair arm. I don't look at Dr. Erickson, but I see his hands. They're pale, a doctor's hands.

"I want you to think about the room." He speaks in his soft, hypnotic voice and it penetrates my fear and uncertainty. "Think about sitting with your father ..."

The cold floor ... on my knees ... the hand between my legs ...

Dr. Erickson grabs my wrist with a strength that surprises me.

Strong fingers are wrapped securely around my wrist, forcing it to the floor. The hand between my legs is probing ... searching ...

"You're not pulling," Dr. Erickson says.

I can hear his voice from far away, but the words are not for me.

"At least tighten your shoulder. I don't want to dislocate your arm."

I can't pull free. I'm not strong enough to struggle against his immovable strength. The fingers explore ...

Dr. Erickson has released me. Or I've pulled free. I'm not certain which. My body is numb and heavy, as if I've been drugged. My mind is swaddled in thick cotton, my senses dulled. One thought penetrates the fog: I don't like his fingers on me.

"That's a lot of energy." He's a little breathless and looks as if he's been playing a game of tug of war.

I don't feel the energy. I sit calm and rested, wondering why he's so tired. That was strange. When Dr. Erickson put his hands on me the entire room disappeared, like a gray curtain falling on top of me. Did he know that I stopped breathing when he touched me? Does he know that he wasn't in the room anymore?

He studies me like an art critic trying to authenticate a painting. "What did you learn?"

"I don't like the feel of your hands."

"Okay," he says calmly.

They didn't feel normal to me, even though I don't know what normal is.

"Do you remember pulling?" he asks quietly.

I shake my head. Part of me is still in the room with my father, still trying to pull free ... and still failing.

"You want to do this again?" he asks.

I want to pull free.

"Let's try it standing," he suggests. "There's more room."

I stand numbly by as he moves the chairs out of the way. He grabs my arm. I feel as if he's swallowed my entire body.

Father's fingers have half of his weight pressing my hand to the floor. Large fingers probe between my legs as I feel rage rising like a tide within me. I scream silently in anger and frustration. Inside, I'm kicking and struggling, venting my rage against the hands that have so thoroughly trapped me. On my back, I still hear the screams in my head, though I know I haven't uttered a sound. Rage fades to sorrow as the first tears slip down my cheeks. Somewhere, I have lost myself.

"Why aren't you pulling free?" Dr. Erickson asks.

I don't know how.

"You're free," he says gently. "Look."

The room is shadowy and subtle, a surreal place that has not quite taken shape. I'm in both rooms ... and I'm in neither.

"Look," Dr. Erickson repeats.

Slowly, my gaze follows. His hand hovers above mine. My arm is stretched out in the space between us, suspended in the air. I stare at his hand that remains poised six inches above mine.

"Why aren't you getting free?"

It's a trick. I can still feel his hands on me, the imprint of his fingers on my warm skin.

I move my arm back and he catches it again, laughing cruelly as he twists and pulls my arm.

Dr. Erickson's hand remains suspended above mine. Very slowly, as if I were performing a delicate and dangerous task, I pull my arm in. Once it's safely close to me, I scratch at the imprints his touch has left, erasing them from my skin.

"Something interesting happens," he tells me. "When I stop pulling, so do you."

"I do?"

He nods. "Until we stopped pulling altogether and I let go. You kept your arm in place. You choose to remain trapped."

I can't get free. But I *am* free.

Did my father let go and I kept myself passive and obedient? Were all of my wailing and threats and raging bravado just meaningless emotions thrown into the empty air? Did she even *want* to get away?

Nothing had changed. I was still trapped. "I want to push," I tell him.

"Want to push out anger?"

I nod.

He holds both of his hands up, palms facing me.

He's trying to trick me. I press my palms to his. Immediately, his fingers close around mine like a steel trap. In an instant, he pulls me close and wraps his arms around my body, holding me in place.

I like the pushing exercise. Something about the resistance appeals to me. I like the feel of my muscles straining against his strength. I like that I can make him move. It's like an emotional domino effect—one emotion toppling the next until there are no more to feel. I want to push out the anger I feel deep inside, buried beneath thick layers of denial. I want to push out the fingers my father has inside me. I want to punish.

I want it more than I'm afraid of Dr. Erickson and what his hands will do.

He's tricking me. I ignore the voice and match my palms to his.

I feel the fingers inside of me and I push against the invasion. No! Get out! I don't want it! Every muscle and nerve, every cell and fiber within me converges to expel the invading fingers.

Why did you do this to me?

I cannot push out the fingers. I am helpless.

Dr. Erickson watches me as I stand in front of him. My hands are still held in the position of pushing against him, but we're no longer touching. My arms tremble with fatigue as a single drop of sweat trickles down my side.

I'm incapable of winning against a memory. The fingers will always be there. I will always be trapped.

"You need to push some more?"

Without answering, I press my palms to his.

My anger is like water boiling in a pot. At first it gently simmers with an occasional rising bubble, then it builds to a frantic boil that steams and erupts from the container. The anger within me wants to erupt. Anger created from injustice, from helplessness and fear, from sorrow.

I feel the anger in the center of my being, a dark force with a frightening presence. I cannot move it.

Something is standing in front of me like a barrier or shield.

I can feel like I can feel Dr. Erickson's fingers still on my wrist.

I stop pushing against him, distraught. I want the dominos to topple. I want it to be like it was before, a release that will lighten me. But I cannot get the anger to move.

"What's wrong?"

"There's ... something here," I tell him, waving my hand in front of my body. "Something ... dark standing in the way. I can't push the anger out. There's something here."

"Something's blocking the anger?"

I nod. I don't know how else to explain it. I only know it exists.

"Can you see what it is?"

"I don't see it. I only feel it. It feels ... male."

"Is it from you?"

"I don't know."

"Can you make contact with this male presence? Find out what it wants?"

The familiar tightness grows in me, the twisting inside that makes the world so small and crowded, like my body is wrapped in cellophane. I've learned to pay attention to the tightness, to listen to the panic inside.

"It's dangerous. I don't want to do that. Everything inside is ... afraid."

He stares at me silently.

"It's like a dark shadow. I want to think about this. I'll think about this."

CHAPTER 22

When I was two or three years old, I was fearless. I was the one leading my two sisters and younger brother to explore the woods, to climb trees, to see what was in the hole in the ground. It would drive Mom crazy.

"It won't be so fun when a badger chews your arm off," she would say.

Scare tactics never worked with me, and besides, I didn't know what a badger was. You would think that Mom would have had us on a short leash, the way she worried. If you could image seven children running wild in the woods of Wisconsin in 1969, you could see how maybe my mom had given up trying to keep control of us all. We'd run all day until she'd call us in for supper.

She had only one rule: Don't go to the other side of the lake.

I spent many days before I started school plotting how to get to the other side of the lake. I had this idea that it was a magical forest and that was why Mom wanted us to stay away. Instead of a magical forest, I had to settle for whatever I could find.

My older siblings had dug a fort. It was just a deep hole in the ground, but to me it was perfect. It was just up the hill from where the tiny cabin sat. Mom had a garden in the clearing on top of that hill, and two of my older siblings had dug the fort deep into the ground at the edge of the trees. I'd watch as my siblings poked their heads out of the pit and spied on Mom as she tended her garden.

Then they discovered that the fort it made a great retreat, and they played war in it, tossing balls of mud into the pit to persuade whoever was in there to get out.

I didn't play war. Us younger kids weren't supposed to play in the pit. It was for the older kids, but we went in anyway, when they were at school, and played captive. Sometimes we gathered ferns and flowers and took them in with us as little treasures. It was like our private world, dug deep into the earth. It was so deep, we had to use a branch to crawl out, or sometimes we'd climb on each other's shoulders.

I liked that pit. I liked sitting alone with the rough-dug earth around me, and the blue sky above. If I sat quietly, I could pretend that nothing else existed, as if the earth had swallowed me.

January 25

S omeone's in pain," I say softly. Somewhere down deep in the darkness. If I let my mind take the journey, I can see them—children lying at the bottom, hurt and crying. "It makes me sad."

"Tell me about the sadness," Dr. Erickson says easily.

He's always easy about everything, as if we were old friends sitting down for a pleasant conversation. The dim lighting in the office offers comfort, as always. I sit in my chair where the pale light barely touches and hope my anxiousness doesn't show.

"It's ... sadness." I struggle to put words to the emotions I don't understand. "It's heavy and dark ... children crying and ... hurt ... some place down far ... dark."

They're lying at the bottom of the blackness, four children that appear to have been dropped onto a black canvas, separate but connected. They're shadows with form and substance, living presences that appear so much like reflection of my memories.

"Are they in a pit?"

"They're some place. I just know they're there." I twist my fingers together as if anchoring my body in place. I have an urge to flee the room. Like an animal sensing a trap, I'm hyper-vigilant, acutely aware of how far Dr. Erickson sits from me. "They make me sad."

"When things change it can bring sadness." He studies me closely. "Do you want to rescue these children?"

I shake my head.

"You did great work last week."

Did I? "I've been worried about something," I say. "Last week I thought I didn't feel anything. You know, like I'd shut off my emotions and was just concentrating on pulling. I didn't understand when you were talking to me. I couldn't understand what you were saying. I couldn't … connect the words."

He nods. "Trauma time. You were someplace else."

"She didn't get free." I can still see her pinned to the floor, crying. I look at him. "Did I pull free?"

"Yes," he says carefully. "It took you a while, but you pulled free." Pause. "What else did we do last week?"

"I pushed."

Push open the door. The voice is calm and instructive, a gentle directive given with confidence and care. I would ignore it, but I see a door in my mind. When I paint, doors are painted in black, and they're always closed like a threshold waiting to be crossed.

"I want to pull again," I say suddenly.

"All right."

Dr. Erickson stands and I move my chair to the center of the room. Immediately, my chest constricts, like an invisible band is being pulled across me, squeezing and tightening. I draw my right arm close to my body. I don't like the feel of his hands. I don't like feeling what she feels.

The saw blade slices through my left arm, severing it neatly and painlessly.

The image only disturbs me because it's an urging, a prompting demonstration of what I must do, and I don't understand why I have to cut off my arm. I only know that things will be better if I do it.

I rest my right arm on the chair edge. I don't want to think about cutting off my arm. I want to pull free.

Without warning, Dr. Erickson grabs my wrist.

I'm on the floor and on a bed, the two images superimposed. Lying on my back with my father's hand between my legs. I strain against the strong fingers that hold me in place.

"You're not pulling."

"Yes, I am."

His fingers are immovable. They're cutting into my bruised flesh.

"No, you're not. Look."

I stare down at my arm. My hand lays limply over the chair rest, my wrist relaxed. "I was pulling ..." I'm never going to get free. I'm always going to be trapped. Anger and frustration rise in me. "I want to do it again."

This time I watch as Dr. Erickson's fingers circle my wrist. I don't like him touching me. I don't like his hands on me. I watch as he pulls my arm without resistance. I don't feel his hand on me. It's as if he's wearing gloves. There's no warmth, no emotion ... no connection.

I focus my attention on my arm, tightening the muscles, pulling at the shoulder. The tendons stretch, the skin pinches. Slowly, my arm pulls against his firm grip. It takes a concentrated effort to pull free, but at last my hand slips past his fingers.

Dr. Erickson is staring at me with a barely concealed expression of amusement. "Two out of three?"

The next time we stand, clearing the room.

"I'm going to use both hands so I don't bruise you." He grabs my wrist with a zealousness that freezes me.

In an instant it's another hand, larger and stronger. But this time I remain connected to reality. Although the office doesn't disappear, it dissolves slightly. I know that as I struggle against him, the girl is also struggling to get free.

Pull! I strain against Dr. Erickson's grip as his fingers bite into the delicate skin on my wrist. Slowly, I feel his fingers slip along my hand and then tighten in a last effort to keep me in his grasp.

"That was better," he says. "You didn't wait as long before you started to pull, but you still have a freeze response."

"It's difficult to get my mind to connect to my body. It takes me a moment to think about what to do."

He nods, understanding. "In dangerous situations the body has a freeze-or-fight response, like a rabbit that remains still in the mouth of a dog."

"Is that response dangerous?"

"Yes, it can be. It can also save your life. When you were a little girl, freezing probably saved you from something worse. As an adult, you want to be able to fight to get free."

"Fighting against a strength that's too much could get you hurt." I'm thinking about offering a small resistance and being crushed.

"There's a physical difference in strength between a male and a female, but there are still weapons you can use."

Sometimes fighting makes the difference, and sometimes it's the worst thing a person can do. But I want the choice to do either.

"How do I get my body to fight?"

"Practice. There's something called exposure therapy. The more you're exposed to having your arm pulled, the less emotional impact it will have on you, until you can pull away at the first sign of danger."

"Do people pull away automatically when someone grabs their arm?"

"Most people do, yes."

People who haven't been wounded. People whose bodies work normally.

"Let me show you something." He offers his wrist to me. "Grab my wrist."

I hesitate, but then slowly and cautiously circle my fingers around his wrist.

"Now pull."

I pull his wrist toward me, but he keeps his arm in place, not pulling against me. I ease up on the pulling, and with the speed of a striking snake he tugs his arm free. The unexpected speed startles me. My fingers still feel his wrist.

He's smiling gently.

"How did you do that?"

"You lightened your grip," he says. "When someone least expects it, that's when you make your move." He grabs my arm again with both hands. "How can you get free?"

It's difficult to think when he's touching me. My brain seizes in a collision of ideas and images, all of them frantic to be free. I don't like the feel of his hands on me, and I don't think it's fair that he gets to use two hands.

He tugs gently as if to get my attention. My stomach convulses as nausea rises.

"I can step back," I say, trying to find the words that will make him let go.

"Yes, that might throw the man off balance. What about this?" With both of his hands on my wrist, he raises his foot to touch my left arm. "What about that?"

He's not letting go and I'm not pulling. His hands have shackled my wrist and I don't understand what he wants from me.

"I could kick him," I say reluctantly.

"Yes, that would work."

I don't like the feel of his hands. I don't like to be held. He's just standing there, holding me. "I want you to let go now."

"Pull free," he says simply.

I do. As soon as I find release, I begin to scratch at my wrist, scratching at the imprint of his hands. I can feel Dr. Erickson as if he were still holding onto me. The shadow is standing in front of me, and I know for all of my pulling that I have not found freedom.

The door is firmly shut and I'm still a prisoner.

CHAPTER 23

Where did my brothers fit into all of this? First Brother left home for the air force when I was barely nine years old. He flunked out of high school with a genius IQ, so it was either the military or homelessness. He was the mirror of Dad—intelligent, creative and unable to complete anything. I always said that First Brother could build a rocket with a toaster and string. He, like Dad, could make anything work.

I have a memory of First Brother coming home from leave and taking me, Shameful Sister, Angry Sister and Second Brother out to the gravel pits to watch for UFOs. It was 1975 and every conspiracy theory about UFOs was alive and well on the farm where we lived. The gravel pits were deserted and the night sky seemed to have fallen on us. We watched for hours as First Brother entertained us with facts and theories. The what-will-we-do-if-a-UFO-appears conversations went on until midnight.

We felt safe with him, and we would have followed him anywhere. He only stayed for a week, but it was a week of fun and unpredictable adventures. Like an apparition, he appeared and then disappeared. First Brother never knew that while he was learning in the air force his sisters were being molested.

Second Brother is a year younger than I am. He was lumped with the three of us younger girls by virtue of his age, and everyone thought he was one, too, with his mop of curls that were always too long.

As we got older, he separated from us, no longer interested in things girls were interested in. Suddenly he liked fishing and hunting, and spent more and more time by himself. He only seemed to enjoy the company of one or two people, and spent most of his time at home reading. Even when we walked to the bus stop, he always trailed behind. I often wondered he felt left out of our little girls' group.

Dad focused on his daughters. We were the ones who got the trips and presents and special walks. Dad never spent time with Second Bother, and he told me much later, after I had told him about what Dad did, that he grew up thinking he was unloved.

Third Brother is six years younger than I am. He came along after we'd moved from the house on the lake. To us girls, he was a new toy to be played with. We'd shake the bassinet to get him to cry and take turns feeding him. Like a living doll, he got all our attention and love. And then he was left behind when we all moved out.

Unlike First and Second Brother, he was a natural salesman. In that he was like Dad, who could sell bikinis to Eskimos.

I was the one to tell our brothers that Dad had molested us. It was one of those things that percolates and comes to a boil, because a person can keep a secret only so long. It was a burden I did not want, and finally, a few years ago, it all came to a head.

I had discovered that Dad was downloading pictures of children and I realized that nothing had changed. Our silence hadn't bought anything. We had even modified our language; while we sisters could speak of, it was always understood that we could never share it with our brothers—until I did.

Our brothers' anger surprised me. They demanded to know details that neither my sisters nor I were willing to provide. Not only did I have to endure my brothers' anger, but that of my sisters as well. Our big secret had made its first debut, but without much success.

They demanded to know why they had never been told. Each one worked rapidly through their anger, sadness, anger, and finally acceptance. Somewhere in there also was guilt. I didn't understand their emotion. After all, nothing had happened to them.

"I could have protected you," Second Brother said.

No, I thought, you couldn't have.

February 1

S adness is inside me, like a heavy anchor I'm dragging with every step. It weighs on me, making it difficult to rise out of bed in the morning, to draw a full breath, to go about my day as if I have purpose. It's February and the April deadline for completion of my therapy approaches. My sense of time running out is increasing, and I'm tired. I don't know where I'm going.

I hate my body. It doesn't work right; it's all disconnected and fragmented. I want to be like other people, and feel touch without needing to disappear within, to have my body respond to my wishes instead of remaining separate from my thoughts.

I don't want to be here. Like a litany, I say it over and over, wanting to be in some other body, a body that works right, a body that will give me what I want.

When the sadness comes, my goal is far away. How am I going to experience intimacy when I can't get my mind to stay with my body?

There are the visions—the waking dreams—that plague me, as well.

I stand on the roof, looking down six stories to the concrete sidewalk below. I hold a doll in my arms and carefully drop her over the edge. The doll lies on the sidewalk.

Follow her.

The instructions are clear, the image persistent.

I jump off the roof, my body falling … falling …

Again and again the scene plays in my mind, like an unforgettable vignette in a movie I can't scrub from my memory. I don't know what it means.

"Why do you want to jump?" Dr. Erickson asks me. If he's alarmed by my vision, he doesn't show it.

"I'm supposed to follow her." Follow the doll down to the sidewalk. He watches me silently. "Do you want to die?"

"No."

"Does somebody inside want to die?"

That's a question I've never thought to ask. I want to leave my body, but that's different from wanting to die. Although I have a sense of my life coming to an end, of time running out, I don't think about dying.

"I'm not sure. I don't think so."

"What happens after you jump?"

My body hits the sidewalk. I feel the impact of the concrete on my chest and the side of my face. I lie next to the doll … then I get up and walk away.

"Do you think you can get up and walk away after falling that far?" he asks.

I can't argue with the images in my mind, any more than I can alter them. I get up and walk away in the image; it's the only reality I know. Frowning, try to I think of an alternative answer.

"It's not a trick question," he says, as my silence continues.

"Well, I never know with you." My quip is out of my mouth before I realize that I've spoken. Before he has a chance to annoy me further, I answer: "Yes."

"That's an alarming disconnect."

Disconnect? There's no disconnect. Even though his words say differently, I don't hear any kind of distress in his tone. He sits unmoving, with practiced ease, his chin resting on his fingers like a professor deep in thought. I wonder what it would take to shake his well-practiced manner.

"No," I answer, refuting his statement. Jumping off a building is something I need to do, not something I want to do. I tell myself that difference separates me from the patients waiting in the lobby.

I feel his gaze on me and I make every attempt to appear impervious to his scrutiny. I know what I know. What Dr. Erickson doesn't see is the perfection of the vision. It wouldn't be dying. It would be living.

"Do you have a breaking point?" he asks.

"What do you mean?" My voice sounds as though I'm hypnotized. It's difficult to pull myself away from the visions of falling. I study them with the intensity of a scholar studying scripture.

"A breaking point," he says, "something that would make you want to die."

Visions of falling fade away as I concentrate on his question. I've never thought of a breaking point. I don't think in terms of ending. Not like that. I ponder the question. I can't summon a scenario that would fit his description. What would make me want to die?

I run through a quick list: cancer, blindness, paralysis, poverty, heartbreak, loneliness.

"I can't think of anything that would make me want to die," I say slowly, reviewing the list. "I can overcome a lot of things." I am strong. I'm a survivor.

"Do you still have visions of cutting off your arm?" he asks.

"Yes."

The visions are stronger than ever. I'm constantly inundated with images of sawing off my arm. During the day, my fingers caress my arm in response to the thoughts I refuse to label as voices: *It's not mine. You can't take it. I'm not supposed to have it.* While the voices puzzle and mystify me, the image gives me a strange sense of relief.

"It's because I don't want it. I think it would better if my arm weren't there." That I know for certain. The images and urges would disappear with the arm. I wouldn't have to see it or think about it anymore. I would have peace.

Dr. Erickson sits next to me and takes my left wrist and pulls. My arm comes off, right below the elbow, where I always see it severed. He smiles and holds my arm near.

"Images of cutting off your arm are a distraction," he reminds me. "Pay attention to where your thoughts are when you have those visions, and we can find out what it's trying to distract you from." He pauses. "What do you feel when you think about cutting off your arm?"

"Frustration." I don't know why I have to get rid of it, why this has become so important to me, and I don't understand my contradictory thoughts. "I have a strong need to protect it, to keep it from you, but at the same time I don't want it. It would be better if it weren't here."

"Why would it be better?" he asks, frowning.

"Because"—my fingers pinch the tender muscles of my left arm—"then I wouldn't have to worry about it anymore. I wouldn't have to think about it." I would be free.

"Frustration and confusion," he says. "Isn't that how you felt when you were with your father?"

"Yes," I say slowly. But this is different.

"You were frustrated and confused, feeling that you were doing something incorrect, not pleasing him. Do you see how the information is all the same?"

You can't take it. I can give it to you, but you can't take it.

She's innocent and genuine in her offer. So persistent, so intractable, and nothing Dr. Erickson says will sway her. She doesn't want the arm. Inside, I can see the little girl sitting on her knees with her legs splayed out, fingering her left arm and chattering words I'll never let him hear.

The conversation has turned my attention inside, to the black painted walls of my mind.

She sits methodically stabbing her arm with a knife. Single-minded and deliberate in her actions, She's too focused to be distracted, too dedicated to allow emotion to interfere.

Another girl, a replica image of the other, sits fingering her arm, innocently chattering a steady stream of fragmented thoughts in a manner only a child could deliver. She is the one who wants the arm cut away, pleading and persistent, the way a child might plead for a toy.

And then there is the door. It opens to darkness. It's where Sekhmet stands now, a centurion at the gate.

None of these images touch one another. None knows about the existence of the others.

"I'm thinking about the door," I say softly. I'm watching it from where I sit. "It's open."

"Do you want to go inside?"

"I did before." I've learned how to take time and wonder through the images. It's a way of moving things forward. "I thought maybe there would be a room there, a place I was supposed to go."

"There's not a room?"

"No. It's just a door. When I walk through it, I fall into darkness."

"What's at the bottom?"

"I don't know."

"You could test the journey; take an excursion in your mind without actually going to the bottom."

"Yes, maybe. I'll work on that this week." I'll find out what's at the bottom.

CHAPTER 24

I told Pleasing Sister that I wanted to live alone. It wasn't as simple as I would have liked. I couldn't just remove her. She wasn't a tenant to be evicted. She had helped to build the house and had put money into it. By all rights, it was half hers. I suggested we build her another house on the property, but that didn't sit well with her.

"You can't have it both ways," she told me. "You can't have me here and not here."

I realized that was exactly what I was trying to do. How convenient for me to have her near for company occasionally, and yet separate for my independence.

After a few weeks, we decided to sell the house and split the equity.

"I'm not asking for anything I haven't earned," she said.

She was sad and I didn't blame her. It wasn't her choice to give up the home she loved. We hadn't built the house to sell it. We'd built our dream house. We'd talked about retirement and me working from home. We'd planted a prairie and an apple orchard, and done the things people do who believe that nothing will end.

"Now that you don't need me," she told me, "you're just going to toss me aside. I'm worth more than that."

Her anger surprised me. She was Pleasing Sister, the mediator and fixer who never wanted anyone to be unhappy. She had accommodated me my entire life, deferring to me even more frequently in the past years since she'd been disabled. I knew our relationship was unequal, with her overcompensating because I was the financial support.

She had her own issues of worth. Was it ironic that she had been Dad's favorite? I'd never been the favorite. My uncles bet I'd be in jail by the time I was sixteen. I guess I had a reputation for bucking the rules. But what could you expect from a little girl who ran barefoot through the woods with little to no supervision, and whose favorite game was jumping out of trees?

It was only later that I became fearful. Thankfully, I never fulfilled my uncles' prediction. I was the bookworm in school, disappearing into the works of Carroll, Keats and Poe. What else was a girl who was afraid of boys to do?

February 8

I *step through the door that I've been watching for weeks now, barely noticing Sekhmet, who has moved aside to allow me to enter. I fall without fear, down and down, through darkness and space. And then I see them, at the bottom.*

"Who is there?" Dr. Erickson asks.

"Four girls."

Shadowy figures—more replicas—wait in the darkness, but I can see them clearly. Some of them I've drawn as soft figures sketched in pencil. Others are only too familiar.

One girl lies prone and still. I see her as dead.

Another girl is on her knees, partially draped over a table.

One is on her knees, very still, her face hidden in her hands.

The last girl stands away from the others, a knife in her hand.

"Is that the same girl who is stabbing her arm?" Dr. Erickson asks.

"No." I can see the girl stabbing her arm. She's not down deep. "She's stopped stabbing her arm. She's driven the knife into it and stuck it to the table."

"Do you comfort her?"

"Sometimes, but it doesn't stop her from stabbing her arm. She makes me sad."

"You're merging with her."

She'll become less and less and I'll become more and more. Is that what's happening?

"These others are different," I say. "Not really people at all."

"Can you rescue them from the pit?"

"Why?"

He raises his eyebrows. "Give them a nicer place to hang around than the bottom of a pit. Ask Sekhmet if that's what you should do."

I ask Sekhmet about rescuing the girls, but she doesn't respond. She remains as a disciplined guard at the door. I look at the door and imagine what it would be like to rescue them from the darkness when I feel the gnawing in my belly, intense and sharp.

"I don't think I should," I say.

"What does Sekhmet say?"

"She doesn't say anything, but I don't think I should. It doesn't feel right. Things are tight inside when I think about that."

"Okay, so that's for another time. You must need to do something else before you can rescue them."

Why do I have to rescue them at all? Why does my mind keep producing these images? It's so strange to have to deal with them, and yet I know that if I ignore them they won't simply disappear.

"Ask Sekhmet what's next on your path to healing," he instructs.

The saw blade slices through my left arm.

"I don't know," I say softly. My right hand is drawn to my left arm, touching and fingering the flesh. "I'm thinking about something else."

"What are you thinking about?"

"Cutting off my arm."

Dr. Erickson grips my left wrist and tugs firmly. My arm slips off just below the elbow.

"Will that still make you feel relieved?"

"Yes." I feel a huge sense of relief, a burden lifted. I imagine this is how addicts feel hungering for a fix. They resist the driving need until their muscles are strung tightly and every cell and nerve in their bodies screams out to be satisfied. "She doesn't want it there. I don't like to think about it. It's better if I pretend it's not there. When she notices it, that's when I think about cutting it off."

"Your arm is hiding a secret," he says softly. "You think that if you get rid of your arm you won't have to deal with the secret. But the secret isn't going to go away with the arm. This is a distraction, a way of your mind keeping you from thinking about something else. Pay attention to where your thoughts are when you get the urge to cut off your arm. That's a clue."

It's not mine. I don't want it. "I don't want to keep it."

"Cutting off your arm isn't the solution," he insists quietly. "It won't solve the problem that you think it will. Your problems will still be there, and you'll be missing an arm."

"I could give it away."

"That's an insane remark so I'll ignore it."

It's not insane at all.

He continues. "Imagine your life without an arm. Imagine getting dressed or making dinner, holding someone with only one arm."

I can give it to you, but you can't take it.

It's difficult to pull myself away from the intrusive thoughts and listen to what he's saying. He's reasoning with me, trying to convince me of the importance of keeping my arm, but he doesn't understand that none of that matters.

I don't want this arm. I can't keep it. Still, I think about what I want so desperately, embracing a man, touching him … I will need both arms and hands to caress him.

Hands take.

"Yes, sometimes hands take," he says.

I glance at him, uncertain if I spoke the words aloud or if he had somehow read my thoughts. My fingers keep in constant contact with my left arm, fascinated and obsessed.

"When you touch someone, aren't you taking, too?" he asks.

The notion stills my fingers and my thoughts focus on touch. "No." When I touch, I don't take. I wouldn't take from people.

"No? Lovers take from one another all the time. When you touch him, aren't you touching for your pleasure?"

My thoughts jumble and spin. I imagine what my lover's skin feels like on the tips of my fingers, the warm flesh and hard muscles relaxed beneath it. Why am I touching him?

"There's nothing better than a greedy lover," he says casually.

"But ..." I don't want to take. But I feel pleasure at touching him. Does that mean I'm taking? Is he liking my touch, the way my cat likes my touch, stretching out under my attention? I can imagine touch pleasing, but I can also imagine touch violating.

"I don't know how to say it to make it be that way," I say. "You know, like an affirmation that will change my thoughts on touch."

I've been practicing affirmations to change my beliefs: *I'm confident and capable. I'm generous. I'm worthy of love.* Maybe an affirmation on touch will help me think of it more positively.

"Touch isn't one thing or another. It's not all taking or all giving," he tells me.

That's the first thing he's said to me in months that actually makes sense.

"Didn't you tell me that when you were little you felt curiosity when you touched your father?"

"Yes, there was curiosity." I know that without having a clear memory of it, and it makes me sad that I was curious about how my father's body felt.

Sometimes things are taken and sometimes things are given. The voice sounds quietly in my head.

"Sekhmet says that sometimes things are taken and sometimes things are given," I tell him.

"Yes, they are," he agrees.

I refuse to explore the idea further, knowing it will take me into a memory I'm not yet ready to acknowledge. My thoughts don't stray too far from the arm I've disowned.

"I don't understand why I have all these thoughts."

"It's a puzzle. We have to put the pieces in place. All of this is information. That's what you keep telling me when you talk about your arm, that it's just information."

"I do?" Not only do I not remember telling him that, but I also don't understand what it means.

"Yes, you do." He grabs my chart, which signals an end to the session. "It'll all come together."

Then I remember what I wanted to tell him. "Oh, I thought about something last week," I tell him. "You asked me about my breaking point. I couldn't think of one, but I remembered something. When I was a teenager, I had a breaking point. It's one of those things that you know for certain that's inarguable. I always thought that if I was raped I wouldn't survive."

He stares at me from behind his impassive mask.

"I forgot about that," I say. "I was just a teenager. I believed it until I was in my twenties and then I forgot about it. Of course, as an adult I'd like to think I don't have a breaking point."

"Wouldn't we all."

CHAPTER 25

Going to school opened up a new world for me. My sisters were in other grades and so I was forced to make friends with my homeroom classmates. Having friends meant experiencing how other families functioned. On the occasional after-school visits with friends, I quickly saw the disparities.

My friends were either only children or had a single sibling. They had their own rooms, which were filled with toys surrounding pink canopy beds and matching lacey linens. Their houses were quiet, orderly and ridiculously clean. Bathroom doors were closed when in use. I hadn't had the luxury of using a bathroom in private until I moved out when I was nineteen.

And then there was the food, which seemed to be plentiful and unrestricted.

One of my friends had a snack drawer. After school, she got cookies or chips out of the drawer, and we each got a bottle of Pepsi.

My family never had snacks after school. Food consumption was tightly controlled. We had to wait for dinner, unless Mom had made bread or her famous pie-crust cookies.

To see a drawer dedicated to sweets made me envious. I couldn't believe all those cookies and chips were just sitting there. In our house, a rare bag of store-bought cookies wouldn't last an hour, and soda was something we never had. We were a Kool-Aid family, and even that was rationed.

I learned to hide food when I was two. I frequently got into trouble for stealing my baby brother's bottle. I'd take his bottle and sneak under the bed, siphoning the contents before handing it back to him empty.

While I enjoyed visiting my friends after school, I rarely slept over. When I was seven years old I was invited to my first sleepover. I'd never been away from my family and I was afraid of leaving them, even for a night. I cried the night before I was supposed to go. I got out of bed and went into the living room where Mom was sitting.

"What's wrong, Dumpling?" she asked.

"Mommy, I don't want to go to the sleepover tomorrow."

"You don't have to," she said, and pulled me into her lap. "You can stay here."

She held me for a while and I relaxed in her arms, my head against her shoulder. No matter what was happening in the world, no place made me feel safer than my mom's arms. Still, I felt bad about not going. I didn't understand why I couldn't do such a simple thing. Other kids slept over all the time. They seemed to have fun and be relaxed about it. I was anxious and fearful when I faced my friend's disappointment the next day.

It was another year and another school before I accepted a sleepover invitation. My friend's family had different rules. Mom let us watch Night Stalker on Friday nights, but my friend's parents thought it too scary. We played Hungry Hippo instead. I got bored in three minutes and wanted to go home. I spent that night lying in bed, silently crying.

I missed my sisters, and I discovered that the house of an only child was eerily quiet and lonely. There was just the two of us in her room. Lights out, no talking. Her mom hadn't kissed her goodnight or said prayers with her, and her dad was buried behind some paper he'd been reading. He looked up once to utter a brief "night" and I didn't see him again until morning. I wondered if my friend had done something to make him angry.

I never did another sleepover.

February 15

I like the sense of falling, but I'm afraid of the vision, afraid of the dolls that fall from the top of the building to the sidewalk below, the ones I'm supposed to follow. It's a moving picture in my mind, a short scene constructed from need or desire. I watch the vision as it plays, fascinated and intrigued, fearful and excited.

The image of the hand with the knife in it has moved away, almost faded, but the other images remain.

"Something changed," I tell Dr. Erickson. "The girl doesn't have her arm. It's not connected to her. I tried to take it from her, but it was anchored in place with a knife. She pointed toward the door."

"The door that Sekhmet is guarding?"

"Yes."

I've learned to work in this spiritual plane outside of our sessions. I take an hour or so a day and meditate, stepping into this altered reality that's a little like walking into an Alice in Wonderland-type story, only I'm the author, trying to make the story go the way I want it to go. It's strange to me that I have no control over these scenes, as if I'm merely a character in a tightly structured play. I'm as much at the mercy of these girls as they are at mine.

"Did you bring the children up from the pit?" Dr. Erickson asks.

"No, Sekhmet wouldn't let me through the door."

I haven't told him that I've been thinking about that dead girl at the bottom. I want to know why she died. And then I get an idea, a thought that's so clear and so loud in my head that it drowns out all other thoughts: murder. Someone killed her.

But I don't want to talk about that today. My fingers press lightly into my left arm. Visions of Dr. Erickson pulling off my arm play repetitively in my head like a film with a skip that I can't get past. I know I must do something to move forward or condemn myself to living with the fear and confusion about my arm, battling thoughts of removing it, struggling with the voice in my head that wants to give it away. Even pretending it doesn't exist isn't working any more.

"Are we going to find your arm today?" he asks. His tone says he already knows the answer. Though he remains relaxed in his chair, there's something about him that reminds me of a cat about to pounce on a mouse.

My fingers pinch gently into my flesh. I have a difficult time making eye contact with him, but I'm acutely aware of where he's looking and what he's doing. At this moment, he's waiting for me.

He reaches for my left arm as I sit holding my breath. His fingers curl carefully around my wrist and pause. I watch his hand, more curious than expecting. He tugs. The bone separates and the skin stretches until the thin membrane tears. He holds my arm, pulling it close to his body like a hard-won prize.

My gaze bounces off Dr. Erickson. I know my mind has manifested this vision out of fear and some need that I haven't yet identified. I know that my arm won't come off, just as I know that Dr. Erickson doesn't want to take it, but that's exactly what will happen if he pulls my arm. I can't argue with the certainty of the vision and I can't tell him what I'm thinking. I'm sane enough to know that it sounds crazy.

I stare at his hands. *You can't take it. I can give it to you if you want, but you can't take it.*

I recall the last time we pulled. After the intensity of being thrust into the memory and my struggle to free myself, the trapped feeling I'd been battling for weeks had disappeared. Psychiatrists call it processing. I'd read about it on an academic level, but never fully understood the method of pushing through the emotions and then releasing them. It's a roadmap out of the depression and behaviors that shape a person's life.

Body memories; secrets stored in parts of me; fragmented emotions and memories—all of it wanting release, and me wanting to be whole. The mind wants to heal; it wants to be whole. All of my ideas and visions, no matter how irrational in context, are being conjured in an effort to move me forward, to heal.

Your conscious isn't going to do anything to hurt you.

Only I can hurt me.

The trick is to get your consciousness out of the way and let your subconscious do the healing.

"Okay, yes," I say softly in response to his question. "We're going to find my arm today." My own voice can't convince me of the soundness of this idea. My body is tightly wound, my insides squeezed by an invisible force. "Maybe then I won't want to take it off."

He nods in agreement. "This is a distraction, a method your mind has invented to keep you from knowing the truth. There are parts of you inside that don't want this new life you're trying to bring about. Their experience with intimacy was not pleasant. They're letting you know that they don't want things to change. In a way they're protecting you."

"I don't like these visions." I don't want it. It's not mine.

"How are things inside?" he asks.

"Waiting."

She sits fingering her arm, listening and watching him. Finally she won't have the arm to think about any more.

"How do you want to do this?" he asks. "Do you want to hand me your arm and have me pull, or do you want me to grab it?"

Neither option sounds appealing, but there's something powerful about having him grab my arm that will give me the most movement. "Grab it."

"Do you want to stand for this exercise?"

"I want to sit." I don't like standing; he has an advantage over me.

We negotiate the guidelines and rearrange the chairs. As before, he sits close to me, poised at the edge of his chair as if I were a frightened rabbit and he the keeper.

I suddenly move my left arm away from the chair's arm, pulling it close to me and guarding it with my right hand. What will it be like when he pulls? What will happen to the vision and the fear? What if my arm comes off?

I wonder how many people live in this space of confusion, allowing their minds to control their actions by manifesting irrational notions: the plane will crash, you'll never find another man to love you the way he does, you'll drop the baby and kill it.

It would be so easy to stay in this narrow gap where I've been living. I would have a good life, safe and secure. I would have a career and my successes, but would I be happy? What would I be missing that I've hidden and protected? Is the truth too horrible to know?

'Your conscious isn't going to do anything to hurt you.'

Dr. Erickson waits patiently, watching me from his too-close position. He knows the truth. I can feel that about him, and my rational brain knows he's guiding me to the freedom I crave, to the new life I want for myself. I'm being offered a choice, to retreat into a life of safety and comfort, or to trust myself and change.

I slide my arm onto the chair's edge. With both of his hands, he grabs my wrist.

He pulls and the bone separates. My skin stretches and tears like rotted flesh. He holds my arm, balancing it with both hands, and admires it.

You can't take it like that. I'm not giving it to you.

Hands go where hands go.

Boys aren't supposed to play with girls.

It's not mine.

Let go. You can't have it. It's not yours.

Let go.

My fingers slip out of his grasp. The office slowly materializes around me, but I can only see Dr. Erickson's hands resting comfortably in his lap. My arm is heavy and tired, numb. My body is weighted and exhausted, as if I've been swimming through layers of mud.

"Is that your arm?" he asks softly.

Yes, I have an arm.

"Is that why you're pinching it? To know it's there?"

I look down at my arm and the tiny dents I've made in my skin. Where did those come from? I move my right hand away and curl my fingers around the wooden arm of the chair, anchoring it in place. I don't feel my left arm. It lies on the chair like a dead thing.

What happened? Something happened and I missed it. I search inside for anger and fear, but all is still and soundless. The voices have silenced and I feel like an empty shell, hollow and numb. Suddenly, my body trembles and I can't make it stop. My stomach is tight and convulsing, as though I'm warding off the cold.

"Are you trying to feel your arm?" Dr. Erickson is in a different chair, no longer close but off to my right side near the door. "You're cutting your thumbnail into your finger. Is that so you can feel it?"

I stare at my left thumb and will it to stop its motion. My gaze travels to the bookcase and the many magazines. I'm in the office. My arm didn't come off. Strangely, I'm uncertain if it's mine. I don't know where I went or how I got back. I only know I can't stop trembling.

Is this what my life has come to? Is this what I am, a shattered and wounded person who has fallen prey to her own tortured visions? Will I always be unable to touch without falling apart? Tears sting my eyes and I'm as angry about the weakness of my tears as I am with the betrayal of my body.

"I didn't like that exercise." My voice is thin and I try to hide my fear.

"I know that was difficult."

It's as though I've been sleepwalking and everyone tells me what I did that I don't remember. Except that there is some part of me that does remember, because what I've learned these past months is that the body never forgets. Will it always be this way, I wonder? Will I never be like other people and touch freely without concern?

"I don't like the way my body reacts to touch." I don't know why I speak the words.

"Isn't that why you're in therapy?" His tone is easy and unassuming.

I hate it when he states the obvious. I'm certain it's a rehearsed response he reserves for his patients to distract them from internalizing, but it sounds more condescending. *Of course there's something wrong with you, that's why you're here.*

"I want everything back the way it was," I say softly.

Something is changing inside and I don't know what it is, but I can feel the shift of energy and thought, a slight deviation from the orderly chaos. It's like walking into a dark alley when the hairs rise on the back of your neck and you know you've just made a huge mistake. Everything inside of you says turn around, you fool, and go back.

"You want to undo everything?" he asks quietly.

I nod. "I don't, but I do."

Because at least the place I was in was familiar—hated and confusing, sometimes dangerous, but still familiar.

"Do you want to do this again? I hate to have all this work undone." He sits watching me silently for a moment before adding, "Sometimes, if you don't solidify the work, you have to start from the beginning again. Is that something you want to do?" He knows the answer to his own question. He poses it in a psychological way, giving me the illusion of choice.

I don't want to begin again, any more than I want to continue forward. I teeter between saying yes and saying no, carefully weighing the consequences of my decision. What I want more than anything is freedom—

freedom from the confines of the tiny office, and freedom from the trappings of my own mind.

I realize, suddenly, no one has ever gotten free by doing nothing. "Okay," I say.

"Okay what?"

"Okay, I want to pull again." My voice is soft and uncertain with just the right undertones of determination. I sound like Oliver Twist: *Please, sir, I want some more.*

He watches me for a moment then looks around the office. "I can find something to help ground you." He fishes out a piece of molded glass from his drawer.

The cobalt blue glass is smooth and cool in my hand. My fingers curl around it. The glass will be my lifeline to the office, a piece of the outside world to anchor me.

He takes the chair on my left side. Without ceremony, he grabs me, wrapping all of his fingers around my forearm in a living shackle.

He's changing everything. The voice is heartbreaking, a child with a broken toy.

I watch as Dr. Erickson pulls on my arm. The tendons in my shoulder stretch, but still I offer no resistance. My arm isn't coming off, and that has made me stumble mentally. If he can't take it, does that mean I have to keep it?

Pull!

My shoulder pops slightly, though I can barely feel his fingers on my skin.

Pull!

I begin to resist, pulling my arm from his grasp. His fingers tighten, but slowly, by degrees, I pull free.

"That was better," he says breathlessly. "Should we go again?"

This time we stand. It takes me a moment to realize he's grabbed me. My body is thrust into paralysis at the first contact and my mind goes numb.

And then comes the voice: *Pull!*

It takes an effort to pull free. He's determined to make it difficult for me, to create an emotionally charged atmosphere, but I wish he wouldn't try so hard. As I pull free, I move my arm away from him, tucking it behind me slightly. In a surprise move, he reaches around me to capture my arm.

I pull free again, but this time I hold my arm up to my chest, pressed close to my body. I watch as his hand carefully approaches and, using only the tips of his fingers, he touches my wrist, as if he's trying not to touch me at all. I'm the observer as he gently takes my wrist and pulls it toward his body.

I pull back immediately, twisting my wrist to slip free of his grasp and return my arm to my chest.

Slowly, so slowly that I can see the designs in the ring he wears, he approaches my wrist and takes it as before. As he pulls my arm toward his body, I pull free.

"You know you don't have to let me take your arm," he says, but his fingers are on my wrist again.

We do this until my mind and body are connected and in synch, and I'm finally able to defend myself from his touch.

CHAPTER 26

Finally I was completely off Seroquel. I had slept through the night without dreams and I basked in the simple pleasure of uninterrupted, natural sleep. I was exercising during the day to give my body something to do. The workout helped me to sleep and was a great way to expend the energy my disturbing thoughts seemed to have created. But it wasn't enough.

I took a meditation class to quiet my mind. It helped with the anxiety, which was lessening in frequency but increasing in intensity. I didn't know what to do about the nagging desire to hurt myself, to stab at my arm.

Psychiatrists seem to think that any change is good. To go from depression to rage is a change and therefore good. It seemed to please Dr. Erickson when my emotions and images changed, because he saw it as movement in the process of healing. I wasn't so sure.

My emotions changed daily from hopelessness to fear to frustration. I navigated from wanting to cut off my arm, to wanting to stab it, to a strong desire to jump off the house roof. How could this be healing?

I felt that all my life I'd been pretending to be what I believed others wanted me to be. I'd disappointed Pleasing Sister and angered my family by going into therapy. No one in the family wanted to look at what had happened. No one wanted anything to be wrong. If I was having problems, did that mean they were going to have issues as well? After all, I'd seemed all right to them, but I still ended up in the psych ward.

But it wasn't just the therapy that angered them.

How can you just leave her, they asked of my announcement to leave Pleasing Sister. She has no one.

Interestingly enough, neither did I. But that's how it was in the family. They saw Pleasing Sister as someone to be taken care of, and as long as I was doing it they didn't have to. Pleasing Sister had been sick a lot in her life, with surgeries and knee infections. There had been a deathbed watch when she was only eighteen, the first time she'd gotten an infection. I knew it was difficult for everyone to let go of that image.

But I knew she'd be okay. Pleasing Sister was capable of taking care of herself. I wasn't leaving her destitute. She had her disability check, which guaranteed her a paycheck for the rest of her life.

She's on a limited income, they retorted when I pointed this out.

So is everyone who works a job, I thought. I said nothing to them, but it angered me. Did they think it was okay for me to dedicate my life to satisfying another? Were they all right with me staying broken and unfulfilled? Didn't I get to have the life I wanted?

February 22

Things never quite go the way I want, not in life and not in therapy. The visions of cutting off my arm have stopped, only to be replaced by thoughts of stabbing it. There's an idea brewing in the depths of my mind, simmering in anger and frustration at my arm's very existence: *Get rid of the sickness in your arm.* I want to poke holes in it and lance the flesh, to release the illness that festers there.

I don't know what to do with my thoughts, or how to find peace in the ever-conflicting landscape of my mind, so I make a decision that offers a momentary truce.

I detach my left arm; sever the bone beneath my flesh. I no longer need to be concerned. It doesn't belong to me.

"Things aren't the way I wanted them," I tell Dr. Erickson. "Things are changing."

"Are you still having thoughts of cutting off your arm?"

He sits in his usual chair, at ease with the familiar subject. What, I wonder, would it take to shatter that professional reserve?

"No, but ... it's not the way I thought."

He stares at me for a long while before saying, "That's a little vague."

I'm fingering my left hand again, pinching at the skin. "You've changed things." *You've made it impossible for me to continue; you've created a no-win situation.*

He waits patiently, saying nothing, leaving me to fill the silence.

"I have it and I don't want it. It can be given away but not taken. And I don't know how to keep it."

Immediately he stands and goes to the dry-eraser board. He writes down my words. "Words are important," he says. "What is *it*?"

I stare at the words on the board. "What do you mean? I'm talking about my arm."

"Are you?" He stands patiently by the board, watching me. "Those are three things."

Three things. Three ...

"Everything has been three lately," I tell him. "Three stones, three dolls I play with, three cootie bugs. I have to separate everything into threes. There are three girls in my mind, too."

Three girls without left arms stand in the temple darkness. Shimmering, heavy liquid flows beneath their feet, creating a river that pools into a shallow center, like a puddle of quicksilver.

"I'm way off at the edge," I tell him, "away from them."

"Where's Sekhmet?"

"Guarding the door." As always. "I'm on the edge of the temple. It drops off into nothing."

"Who are these three girls without arms?" he asks. "You have it and you don't want it. What do you have that you don't want?"

"Innocence." The word is out of my mouth before I have an opportunity retract it.

He writes it on the board. "What's the opposite of innocence?"

"Lust."

"You have innocence and you don't want it. You can't give it away and you don't know how to keep it."

The eerie truth of his words seeps into my bones. I've always been embarrassed by my virginity, my lack of sexual experience.

It was difficult enough to acknowledge my inexperience when I was twenty-six and again at thirty, but now at thirty-eight it seems like an albatross around my neck. I'm working with Dr. Erickson so that I can permit myself a sexual, intimate relationship, but I didn't realize until now that it would mean going to a man without any experience, having to stumble through like an awkward adolescent.

I begin the old dance of accepting who I am. Is it that simple? Amputate my arm and I amputate a part of myself I no longer want to own; the ultimate act of self-denial.

"What else?" he prompts. "Three girls, three *its*. What else do you have that you don't want?"

You can be a whole person. But that would be integrating anger and shame. "Wholeness," I say, knowing that it's something I want and something I fear.

"And the opposite of wholeness is …

Three girls without left arms, four children buried in a pit, an angry girl stabbing her arm. "Mutilation."

"What's the third thing that third girl represents?"

A long time ago, Dr. Erickson asked me if I believed myself worthy of love. I had responded that I wanted to be more compassionate, because even in that state of mental disrepair I could see that something was missing.

My father used to call me "cold and unfeeling," and I told myself it was because I was strong and he was weak. I built a wall around myself to keep out the hurt and never realized that it was also keeping the love out. That wall has gotten so thick and strong that I'm not certain I could even recognize love.

"Love," I say, and try not to be embarrassed by my own need.

"What's the opposite of love?"

"Hate."

There they were on the board, the words that were the girls inside me, my obsession with three, the reasons I want to amputate my arm.

Innocence/Lust
Wholeness/Mutilation
Love/Hate

"You can make these three girls a part of yourself," he says. "Integrate with them."

I stare at the board. Dr. Erickson has unknowingly diagramed my life, with all its lacks and conflicts. I see how complicated I have made myself, how set apart I am from the simplest emotions and desires.

"Everything is so opposite with me, so extreme, all hot and cold, black and white. I like balance, and there isn't any there."

"If you have both love and hate, aren't you balanced?" he asks.

"Yes," I say cautiously.

"Can you take all three of these things and make them your own? Can you make them a part of you and accept them? Have a spirit death?"

I want to say yes, because that's the fastest way to get what I want, but it doesn't feel right. "I want to think about them. I can't just take them inside without understanding them."

"Can you take in one of them?"

"Maybe." I study the board.

"Which one is the least emotional?"

"Love/Hate."

"What do you need to do to take Love/Hate and make her a part of you?"

"I don't know." I'm not certain why they aren't a part of me. I don't know how they became separated from my person, segmented out from my daily life. I want to love, but when I say it to myself it gives me a feeling of being the fool. There's something about love that says pain.

"What happens if you love?" he asks quietly, studying me carefully.

My thoughts stall. I try to conjure an image of love … and fail. I bite my lip and move restlessly in the chair.

"Do you love your sisters?" he asks.

"Yes."

"So you have love inside of you already."

I do, very deep and very strong; buried so deep I can hardly recognize it. But it exists, waiting to emerge without fear of rejection, without fear of repercussions. That's what being whole and healed is, isn't it?

"Okay," I say softly, staring at the words. "Yes."

"You don't have to have hate," he says. "Some people experience only love."

My stomach twists. What kind of a person would only know love? A perfect person with perfect parents and the perfect childhood, a person who would be about love and forgiveness, a person without any wounds. A person not like me, who has had someone punch a hole in her world and introduce her to hate. Am I supposed to be all love to be loved? Can't I have hate in me and still love?

"You can't have love without hate," I tell him.

"Oh?" His expression shifts to disbelief.

"No. You can't truly appreciate love without experiencing hate. It's like a person standing in the sun all the time; they don't really appreciate it because they've never done without it. But someone who has been living in a cave without the warmth of the sun, when they step out into the light, they feel it so much more intensely because they've been deprived of it. That's what love and hate are like; they have to be inside the same person. Not the relationship, but the person."

I've always felt that those with wounds inside made the best people, that they loved a little deeper, treasured their relationships a little more, and learned to appreciate the smallest things in life. But this is only, I'm discovering, when those wounds heal. A person with raw, open wounds is fragmented, living in a limited reality of their own making.

"And you have both love and hate inside you?" he asks, tilting his head.

"I don't like to say I have hate, but I know I must. I see the images and the violence. That has to come from anger and hate."

He nods. "Having hate inside makes you human. We all have those emotions inside of us. It's when we disown them and pretend they aren't there that it causes us trouble. Once you learn to make these emotions your own, the images will go away. You won't need them anymore. You'll be a whole person."

A heavy feeling settles inside of me. I can feel it pull me down like an anchor. It's too late for me to be that perfect person who only knows love. I already know hate and I can never be all kindness and forgiveness.

She stabs at the arm, letting it bleed. It's a release, like letting the air out of a balloon. She watches with relief as the blood flows.

"I want to open up my arm," I say very softly, looking away. The image comes with an urge, a strong desire to do myself harm.

"You want to make it bleed?"

I nod, unable to look at him.

"People who cut themselves do so to release emotions they aren't able to process. There are other ways of releasing your emotions without hurting yourself. As you know, there are several emotional-release exercises. We did one of them, the pushing exercise. You can throw dishes against a wall, punch a pillow, scream."

I scream a lot in my head, but the idea of screaming aloud makes me uncomfortable. I wouldn't like to hear the sound of my scream, the rage and fear.

"You did brilliant work last week," he says. "You took a giant step toward making that arm your own, but in this work things usually get worse before they get better. There's still a secret you haven't discovered. Is that what you want to release, the secret?"

"I don't think about the secret. I don't know what it is. I only think about my arm."

He leans in slightly and lowers his voice to a conspiratorial tone. "Your arm is holding the secret. Someone inside of you knows the secret and is trying to hide it from you. Remember, this is a distraction."

"I don't like things to be this complicated." I release a heavy breath.

"People are complicated."

I hate it when his answers are so obvious. Doesn't he understand that I don't want to be different?

"If I want to be whole in my mind and have a whole life, have intimacy and relationships, then why is it complicated like this? Why can't I just know the secret?"

"That's the right question. Why can't you know the secret?" He watches me for long moments, his expression guarded. "Ask Sekhmet if you can know the secret."

Sekhmet stands at the door.

"She doesn't say anything."

His fingers brush his beard. "Ask her if I can tell you the secret."

Let him help. The celestial voice, calm and knowing.

"She says, 'Let him help.'"

He sits unmoving, studying me with his inscrutable expression. "Can you know the secret?"

"She only says, 'Let him help.'"

The silence grows as I wait for him to speak. In the soft lighting of the room, I'm nervous.

"What was your breaking point as a teenager?" he asks finally. "When you were seventeen or eighteen years old?"

My thoughts darken. I can see the smoky veil descending.

"What is it you thought you couldn't survive?"

I remember our conversation. I know what I said, but at the moment I resent him for making me remember. *Rape.* The word swims in my head, stirring up old fears. I immediately push the emotions away, never allowing them to settle. I feel my face become paler as the room grows cold.

"It's what I thought at the time," I explain. "That if I were raped I wouldn't survive."

He continues to study me and I will not offer him help.

"It's possible for you to not know the secret and heal," he says. "You can still have your goal."

Can I?

CHAPTER 27

He had on only a pair of jeans and he was standing a few feet from me, smiling and playful. I twisted my fingers nervously in the fabric of my skirt. I was sitting on a blanket on the floor in the bedroom. He was beautiful in his confidence and gentleness. I remained still as he sat beside me and kissed me lightly.

I liked the feeling of being in his arms. I liked the smell of him and the way his hands rested gently on me, patient and undemanding. His moves were unhurried. His hand slid beneath my skirt, trailing along my thigh. He hooked his fingers under the edge of my panties and, with a gentle tug, slipped the delicate garment off.

My hands were still twisted in my skirt. I parted my legs as his hand moved closer, his fingers teasing, caressing. The pressure built rapidly. I sank my fingers into the blanket to ground me as I rode the tides of pleasure, gasping for air. I was both relieved and saddened when I reached orgasm, reaching for his strength.

He was not quite naked in front of me, but I could see his penis in all its male strength, and I reached for him, wanting to make him as happy as he had made me. My fingers closed around him ... and became still with uncertainty.

Should I go fast? Should I move slowly? How much pressure? What did he like? What was the right way to please him?

He pulled me near. I could feel his wanting. I felt his need and frustration, his desire and his love. I wanted more than anything to please and be pleased, but I didn't know what to do. My fingers slipped from him and I shifted my focus to kissing him, building the passion again.

He pressed against me and the pressure between my legs tickled the inside of me, creating a restlessness that bordered on frustration.

I wanted to have sex. I didn't want penetration.

I want to have that blessed release. I didn't want him to orgasm.

He was too big. I was too small.

He was too fast. I was too slow.

The sweet ache between my legs was almost gentle. My instincts urged me to open myself to him, but a larger part of me rebelled. Fear—cold and powerful—prevented my surrender. I could sense pain and displeasure as certainly as I could sense desire.

He nuzzled my neck, pleading and gentle.

The cold block of fear was firmly in place. Tears rolled down my cheeks. I wanted to please him and feel the pleasure I had imagined. I wanted to experience the release of the pressure building between my legs. I wanted to ride that tide with him.

But he could not penetrate me.

March 1

Peace is flowing like a river. The short verse of the song plays in my head, overlapping the images and, for the time being, drowning out the urges to hurt. There's something calming about the song. I imagine stepping into the flow of the river, letting go, being swept away and knowing that everything is all right. It's a pleasant thought, although when the words pop into my mind I immediately see the black polished temple floor and the girls who are waiting.

Identical replicas, the three girls stand calmly, unconcerned about their missing left arms. The quicksilver liquid flows from beneath their feet, moving like a living organism across the smooth marble. Then there are only two of the three one-armed girls. Almost two. One of the girls—Love/Hate—is fading. I can barely see her.

I understand more of love and hate, and after much contemplation and numerous discussions with my friends, I accept that I can love, and have hated, and that this doesn't take away from the person I want to be.

Emotions are neither good nor bad. They are simply emotions. They are what they are, and if I'm to heal and be the person I want to be, then I must accept who I am and not try to be someone I'm not.

Like most people, I look to others to find the elements I want in my own life. But instead of emulating these loving, nurturing people, I've resented them, thinking they were good and I was bad.

I cannot expunge the wounds from my past; I can only heal them.

I cannot deny my pain, but I am discovering that I don't have to allow it to define me.

"I keep thinking that you want connection," I tell Dr. Erickson. I'm reluctant to confess this to him, but the thought has disturbed me and I'm concerned it'll interfere with our work and me getting what I want. "It's a thought that keeps running through my mind." *He wants connection. He wants to connect with me. I don't want connection.*

"There are all kinds of connection," Dr. Erickson says. "People make connections every day. There's emotional connection and physical connection. What kind of connection do you mean?"

"Physical." I try not to squirm under his gaze.

"By physical do you mean sexual?"

The hand on my arm is gentle and restricting. I'm held in place by the lightest touch, standing naked in front of my father.

"Yes ... I think so."

"You do know that I don't want a sexual connection with you." He says as a statement and not a question. There's no judgment in his tone.

I'm surprised at his bold statement and immediately wonder what I've said to make him think I thought he wanted sex. Of course he doesn't want that kind of a connection with me. The idea never occurred to me, and I'm a little offended.

"I know," I say.

Father's fingers are wrapped securely around my wrist. He tugs and the center of my belly tightens. My heart beats rapidly and the first sensations of a flush warm me while my muscles loosen beneath my skin.

Fear and pleasure. I don't know how to tell the difference.

"You said, 'He wants connection.'" Dr. Erickson says. "Who is 'he'?"

"My father," I answer simply. "My father wants connection."

Father's hands are on my arm, gentle and playful. They move along my body until I'm encircled in his arms, trapped and powerless. He is wanting. I can feel his excitement and desire, the plan he has orchestrated so carefully and meticulously, calculating every move to achieve his ultimate goal.

"What do you mean by connection?" Dr. Erickson asks.

Father's hands are everywhere. There are no boundaries he obeys. He's hungry and wanting.

"Invasion."

"What is invasion?"

His fingers slide between my legs, searching ... probing...

"Intrusion."

"Rape?" he asks quietly.

"No, that's not rape." I feel my irritation at his insistence and make no effort to hide it. He knows I don't like the word.

He watches me, wearing the unreadable mask. "What's your definition of rape?"

"Forced sex." My mouth is suddenly dry.

"Rape can be penetration by a penis, an object or digits." He wiggles his fingers, though his demeanor is clinical, his tone professional. "Is it penetration? Is that what you mean by connection?"

"No." It's a trick question and I'm immediately on guard. "Penetration means penis."

Silence.

"Which word is more emotionally charged—invasion, penetration or rape?"

"Rape" is more emotionally charged and sends my thoughts spinning and twisting, but I won't use the word and I won't allow him to use it. It's not something that applies to me.

"Invasion," I say, knowing my answer is a lie, that it's transparent and he can see through it easily. I can read this much in the practiced professional mask he wears. He's too disciplined, and that gives him away.

"He wants connection; he wants invasion," he says easily. "When do you feel that?"

"When you pull my arm." My fingers play on the skin of my left arm, gently pinching and pulling the soft flesh. My head begins to pound.

Dr. Erickson grabs my wrist and pulls. The bone, now severed beneath layers of tissue and muscle, separates. My flesh breaks under the strain and my arm slips free.

"Are the three one-armed girls still in the temple?" he asks.

"Yes ... well, there's almost two now. One of them is fading."

"Which one?"

"Love/Hate."

"Are you ready to make her a part of yourself?"

"Yes, but I don't know how."

"You can melt into the liquid that's hers and reform as one," he says. "Or you can drink the liquid. It's appropriate at times to create a ritual—light a candle and some incense—create the atmosphere to solidify the emotions you're consuming."

I'm not big on rituals, despite my overly organized life, but I like the idea. Maybe that's what has been missing in my healing: a sense of spirituality. I'm not paying enough attention to the signs, and I'm not giving the appropriate amount of respect to the healing process.

"Okay. I can do that."

"What about the other two? Which one of the two is easier for you?"

I don't want to talk about either, so I let my mind choose. "Innocence/Lust."

"What's innocence?"

"Being pure, untouched, naive."

"What's lust?"

"Desire."

Silence.

"What else?" he prompts.

"Hunger."

He studies me quietly. "Lust can also be greedy and wanting."

"Yes." I suppose.

"A greedy lover is a good lover," he repeats. "A lover who takes care of his or her own pleasure allows the other to feel more. In a sexual union, both parties are joined equally. There's an equal give and take, a sharing of pleasure without boundaries."

"I don't mind lust," I tell him. "I have desire in me, and lust is good as long as it's consensual and no one gets hurt. It's innocence I don't like."

His eyebrows rise in obvious surprise.

"I know you think I'd have a problem with lust, but I don't. I think sexual relationships are healthy. Probably too many people don't think of them that way, but … I can imagine being lustful and uninhibited with my lover, but I don't like being innocent."

He frowns. "Why not?"

Heavy sadness pulls me down. I can feel it weigh my insides and drag me into the darkness where all my inadequacies and failings reside, my stumbling attempts to get close to a man, my inability to please, my lack of knowledge and experience that turn my efforts into failures.

"I … I don't want it."

"Why not?"

My lover sits next to me. He's intelligent and gentle. We kiss and touch with the easiness of longtime friends. There's no fear or hesitation in my exploring touches. My mind shifts. I wrap my fingers eagerly around his aroused penis, excited and wanting to please. As soon as my fingers make contact, I hesitate. Uncertainty halts my actions and he's left frustrated and annoyed.

I keep my vision private.

"Men don't want women without experience," I tell him.

"There are a billion men on this planet. You're talking about one."

"*I* don't want it."

"But you have it," he says simply. "Are you going to lie? Is that how you want to build your relationship?"

"No, but I want things to be different. I want something to offer him. Men look for that in women."

His face suddenly lightens. "You're afraid you'll be undesirable to men."

"Yes. Men want women who are experienced."

"What a gift to give him," he says gently. "What an honor for him to be chosen."

What a burden to press on him. What a strain to slow the relationship. I look at Dr. Erickson, trying to decipher his meaning. Is he being sincere or is this a psychological ploy?

"You're going to have to tell me why men find virginity so attractive." I throw down the challenge, expecting him to flounder.

"Because they can teach you. They won't be self-conscious about their performance. You won't have anyone to compare them with."

"And?"

He pauses as if indecisive or unable to find a viable reason. "They can be the first."

"That's all?"

"That's huge to the male psyche," he says. "Men want to be first, the adventurer, the best, the strongest. Every little boy wants to be an astronaut or explorer."

It makes no sense to my female psyche. "You'll have to do better."

He stares at me with a pained expression.

"I won't have anything to share in the relationship," I tell him out of frustration. "I want to give and receive."

"You are capable to giving men what they want."

"I don't know what men want." My voice has risen.

"That's the point."

I fight the impulse to scream. "I went into therapy so I can contribute to a relationship. I have nothing to give, no experience the way a man wants. I'm inadequate."

"You have your innocence to give."

"I don't want it."

"Then why don't you get rid of it?" he says in a very cavalier way. "Find a man and have meaningless sex and you won't have to worry."

"Do you think I haven't thought of that in the past ten years?"

I've done more than just think of it; I've made several attempts. All of them failed, leaving me fearful and frustrated. It's not a lack of desire. I've always been a sexual creature, exploring and curious. It was only after my adolescence that touching became too intense and fearful for me, a building terror that has since taken on a life of its own.

I have desire and lust, but I also have fear and uncertainty that are not at all adult. In many ways, I'm the little girl wanting the light on in the closet to keep the monster away. I know what I fear.

"I don't want to talk to you about this anymore," I tell him. "You're not understanding."

Sex is the monster that pursues me. And everything male that comes with it.

CHAPTER 28

D r. Erickson recommended reiki and acupuncture. I tried them all. They were gentle therapies, not like what we did in session. It seemed as if nothing was happening during reiki or acupuncture. I just lay on the table and closed my eyes. The practitioner balanced my energy, which was supposed to make a difference. Images and thoughts did arise, but I wasn't looking for movement. I was looking to be healed.

Still, I decided to learn to do reiki on myself. I was studying affirmations and wanted to give it a try. One hour in the afternoon and an hour in the evening while doing reiki. I was trying to reprogram my brain to change my behaviors and somehow find a way out of the mess I'd made of my life. I'd studied on this and had added it to treatment, hoping it would change my life.

My parents' fiftieth wedding anniversary was approaching and the family was conversing more than usual around this. All the siblings had given them a party, with balloons and the much-dreaded family slide show. I stood back in the room and watched as pictures of us all were projected onto the wall, and the room filled with laughter and stories of recollections. We looked so happy in the slides.

Mom and Dad met through a priest. Dad had just gotten out of the Korean War and the priest of his church asked if he wanted to meet a nice girl. His priest talked to Mom's priest. That was dating in 1953.

They didn't really care for each other on the first date. Dad said he only agreed to a second date because he didn't want to insult the priests who had set them up. By the third date they knew they were going to be married.

My mom loves telling the story of how Dad spent the entire wedding reception in the kitchen with the help, chain-smoking Parliaments and trying not to be noticed.

For their fiftieth I gave them a cruise to the Caribbean. Pleasing Sister and I would go with them. This was what I did—gave gifts I didn't want to give, built houses where I didn't want to live, worked a job I didn't want to do. I wasn't sure what had driven me to give them a cruise. Maybe I was buying their love. Maybe I wanted to be seen as the good daughter who gave her parents cruises and took them out to dinner. I was the pretender.

A few months earlier, Dad had asked why I was going to therapy. I stared at him for a full minute, trying to sort through my thoughts. He looked genuinely concerned and bewildered. If I was the pretender in the family, Dad was the master from whom I had learned.

"Because of what you did," I said calmly.

He blinked. "Oh." After a moment, he asked, "What did I do?"

Are you kidding me? Are you playing with me? I had realized only recently how manipulative Dad was, how effortlessly he got people do what he wanted. He liked to be treated like a child, to be cared for and tended to. I thought this was just subterfuge, yet another ploy to get sympathy.

"You molested me," I said.

This seemed to bewilder him even more. "I didn't mean to hurt you," he said.

I nodded and walked away.

March 8

Fear builds inside of me, growing out of my childish perceptions, and is fed by the disturbing images that reside in my mind. I battle with the concept of innocence, fighting a strong desire to extract the self-assigned label. Even as I wage battle, I know I'm losing the part of myself that has given me such comfort, the part that is content to play the role of survivor and shroud itself in a protective cloak of isolation. That part knows that acceptance of my solitary life means safety.

What I'm striving to do is create a life outside of the safe iron wall. But that means reconciling the feud over my innocence and accepting my inexperience, something I cannot bring myself to face.

Dominating my contradictory thoughts are the vivid images that I can no longer push away.

"I was thinking about something," I begin softly. My fingers are once again gently pinching the skin of my left arm, a habit I can't seem to break.

You can't take it. It's not yours. I can give it away, but you can't take it.

The continuous chatter of illogical thoughts is wearing today. While I'm no longer haunted by images of sawing off my arm, the short movie scene of Dr. Erickson pulling off my arm continues, causing growing distress. I can bypass the images and convince myself it's a means of distraction, but I'm still left with an overpowering thought: he wants to take something from me.

"I'm still having thoughts about my arm."

The quiet fills the room. Dr. Erickson sits relaxed and at ease in his chair. "Are you having visions of cutting it off?" he asks finally.

"No, but it doesn't feel like mine."

I don't want it. You can have it.

"Do you want to find your arm?"

She sits on her knees with her legs sprawled at odd angles, pinching her left arm and chattering to herself.

What I want is for the chatter to stop, but I can't tell Dr. Erickson about the thoughts crowding my mind, or of the little girl who wants to give him her arm. It takes great strength to keep the words from escaping. I'm always on guard with him, careful not to let my inside thoughts be known, cautious about what I reveal.

"Yes," I answer faintly, without looking at him, but then show no interest in following through. My thoughts retreat from the office and begin searching inside.

"Do you want to come out from the wall?"

His words are distant and take a moment to penetrate my mental fog. I move my chair into the center of the room and he takes a chair nearby. I immediately move my arm away from him, guarding it with my right hand.

You can't take it. It's not yours to take. You can't take whatever you want.

Uncertainty fills me and I feel an overwhelming need to protect myself, to keep him from taking from me.

He's trying to trick you.

Dr. Erickson grabs my wrist and pulls, and my arm slips free.

"Wait," I say, even though Dr. Erickson has made no attempt to move. My voice is thin with distress and I cradle my left arm close to me. I'm looking at his hands, watching diligently. "What are you going to do?"

"I'm going to help you find your arm."

A high-pitched buzzing reverberates in my ears. My vision darkens as the air slowly leaves the room. I'm flushed and cold.

"We've done this exercise before," he says soothingly, calmly. "My only interest is in helping you connect with your arm."

His gentle presence permeates the room, penetrating my fear enough to encourage me to move. To retreat now means failure and the long process of beginning again, and another week of fragmented chatter and mounting fear. I know it won't be any less frightening later, that my mind has constructed this elaborate ruse to keep my life in stasis. But still I can't erase the disturbing image or the fear it evokes.

Dr. Erickson's fingers clasp around my wrist in a locking grip. He pulls, without malice, and my arm separates from me.

Isn't that what I want? To be rid of it? No, it's what she wants. The buzzing is hypnotic and oddly calming, drowning out my indecisiveness. I can feel Dr. Erickson near, although I don't see him. The edges of my vision darken.

"Are you afraid your arm will come off?" he asks quietly.

I nod. Maybe it was because he understood my fear and saw the images in my head, or maybe it was because he didn't judge me, but something prompted me to relinquish my arm. In a mesmeric haze, I rest my arm on the chair's arm, curious as to what he will do.

Gently and slowly, with the kind of deliberateness reserved for surgeons, he clasps my wrist and carefully raises my arm. My stomach tightens and I hold my breath. "It's still attached," he says plainly, examining my arm.

I stare at the smooth skin on my arm. Of course it looks attached. The flesh is not severed, only the bone hidden beneath it. A sharp tug and it will come free.

"I'll perform some minor surgery," he says and, without releasing my arm, begins to suture my arm just below my elbow. He draws the suture into my flesh without touching it, making big loops with the needle and thread. In and out, around my arm until he completes the circle. He cuts the thread with his teeth and sets back to examine his handiwork.

"Let that thread dissolve into your skin, into your muscles," he says in a tone that mimics conspiracy. "All the way into the marrow of your bones."

The thread sinks into my skin, down into the muscles, past nerves, finding the severed bone.

"Now it's all sewn together," he says, giving my arm a gentle shake. "It can't come off." Then, without warning, he tugs my arm.

I stop breathing, waiting for the images of my arm separating, but they never come. Thoughts and images stop inside and for a time all is black and quiet.

Pull!

I don't feel his hands on me, but I can see them. They are all I see; his fingers wrapped around my narrow wrist. Why don't I feel him?

Very slowly, and with great effort, I begin to pull away from him. I feel pressure on my bones. My stomach tightens and twists as I resist his strength. His fingers slip to my hand and tighten as I pull free of his grasp. Again, I wait for the images and chatter. Again, all is still and silent. The image of the little girl wanting to give her arm away is no longer there. And my arm?

"I want to do this again," I say.

After I pull free, the silence remains. For the first time in months, I relax. It's mine, and no one can take it.

"How are things inside?" he asks.

"Okay," I say. "Quiet."

"What about the little girl stabbing her arm? Is she still there?"

"Yes, but she's not stabbing her arm. She's stabbing her thigh." It's all become so routine now that I can't find any oddity in it, and I've long since given up trying to understand the images. I look at him. "But I feel better." At least the voices have quieted.

"How does your arm feel?"

My arm is attached and feels heavy, but my thoughts are no longer focused on it or its removal. Suddenly, it's no more significant than a book on a table. "Fine. I don't want to give it away."

"Good." He moves back to his usual seat.

But I remain in place, deep in thought. Time passes, and then I realize I must do something.

I return my chair to a safe distance against the wall, and let my thoughts settle away from the exercise and images. Dr. Erickson watches me. The silence in my head is a relief, but the removed chatter and clutter has revealed a new concern that I'm too uncomfortable to broach.

I sit in my chair with my fingers tapping nervously on the wooden arms and doing everything imaginable to avoid Dr. Erickson's eyes, which never waver from me.

A fear has been building, although I only recognized it recently. Not fear of taking or confusion of ownership, but fear of the future, of my reality. Once identified, I haven't been able to bring myself to voice my concern, but I so desperately want an answer I know Dr. Erickson can provide, a solution to my dilemma.

"Something is bothering you," he says.

"Yes." I drag the word out without looking at him. I don't want to tell him my thoughts, which seem childish, but I haven't found an answer to my fear and I have no other person to turn to for help. At least I know that he won't judge or mock me, and there's a certain safety in confessing here, within the confines of therapy.

I open my mouth to speak then close it suddenly. The tapping increases and I find myself studying the faded stain on the chair's arm. "I'm ... there was this ..." I'm stammering like an adolescent. I struggle to string together, not only a comprehensive statement, but also an intelligent and mature one. How am I going to say this without sounding juvenile?

"Take your time," he says easily. "Go inside, to that place you go to talk about these things. You have a place."

I do have a place. It's warm and dark. It's a good place to curl into, unaware and unassuming. My fingers still and the room fades. As I speak, Dr. Erickson disappears into the shadows of the room.

"I was out with my girlfriends the other night. We went into one of those fantasy stores, you know, the ones with those … with sexual paraphernalia. We went down an aisle with these—I don't like this word, but I don't know what else to call it—dildos."

I'm not a prude. I know adults lead sex lives where experimentation plays a large part in sharing experiences. My friends have healthy, respectful sex lives that don't involve devaluing or demeaning acts. So when we entered the store in search of fun toys to celebrate the return of one of my friend's military husbands, I adopted a mature and nonchalant attitude.

I failed on the nonchalant.

"I was looking at them, and they didn't seem right to me." My hands move restlessly, trying to find a place to rest. "They didn't look right to me. But my friend said no, that's what they look like. I was still thinking they didn't look right, they didn't look real." I rush to explain. "I don't know why I didn't think of this before. I never thought about it before, that they would be like that. And now that I've seen them, they don't look right."

He sits silently for a moment. "You think this—we'll call it a toy—was too big?"

"Yes. I don't know why I didn't think of it. I don't usually go into those stores and I have no reason to think about … size. But when I saw them, they looked too big."

"The average erect male penis is about six and half inches long," he explains. "Was that the size of the toy you were looking at?"

"Yes, I think … my friends said they were average."

I remember staring at the toy in utter terror. Of all my sexual fantasies I've indulged in over the years, I can't remember thinking in terms of size and length. Sure, my fantasy figure had a penis, but it didn't look anything on the scale of the synthetic replica I saw in the store. I suddenly began to understand the full scope of male power.

"That concerns you?" he asks congenially. "The size?"

"Yes." I hear an edge to my voice and make an effort to tone down my defensiveness. "Because ... because ..." It's too big! I exhale with exasperation, feeling my shoulders and spine sag. "I ... can't imagine that fitting."

Silence.

"A woman's body is incredibly adaptable," he says quietly. "It can accommodate a man's size."

I stare at him, scowling. "I know my body."

"The female genitalia is basically a muscle, and like any muscle it can be stretched with conditioning. Women have babies. They are a very substantial size."

"I'm not having a baby."

I look away. I don't like being thirty-eight years old and having the conversation of a ten-year-old. I know that what he's telling me is true, and I know with the same conviction that it's not. "I didn't think of it before. I only thought about touching. This is different. This feels different."

"Have you ever watched a porno movie?" he asks suddenly.

"Yes, when I was eighteen."

"The men in those movies are usually ... well endowed."

I remember watching the movie in the female dorm at the naval base in Bethesda on my trip to visit my sister. My first taste of pornography, and it went by in a blur of shouts and laughter, leaving me bewildered and slightly numb. Of course the Long Island Iced Tea I'd consumed did nothing to clarify things.

"I remember seeing people having sex, but ... that was them, not me. It's different for them. Now I'm thinking about my body and ... it's different."

"You saw your father's penis."

My hands are wrapped around father's stiff penis.

"Yes, but ... there's no ... size in my mind. I don't know how big he is." It doesn't have anything to do with me. "I don't think men should be that big."

"One of the ways you can overcome your fear is to get comfortable with the object that frightens you. You can purchase a toy and get familiar with it, the size and shape. Are you still masturbating?"

"No," I say sadly.

"How are your fantasies?"

My scowl deepens. "Okay."

"Does your lover still get hurt?"

"No, there isn't that any more. I like the fantasy. It's nice, but it's not very complete."

He stares at me, waiting.

"It's boring to you," I say, moving restlessly in my chair. I'm ever thankful for the dim lighting. The silence fills the room and I know I've lost this battle. My words are rushed and unembroidered. "He masturbates me and then I masturbate him and then we have sex. Only not really. I mean we do, but it's not very complete."

"Why isn't it complete?"

"I don't know, it just isn't. I don't fantasize him ... penetrating me. I don't like to think about that part, but I can imagine sex, you know, after that part. It's just ... different." I try to keep my body still in the chair, but every nerve is singing.

Silence.

"Is your lover a man or a woman?" he asks.

"A man."

"Are you sure?"

"Yes."

He studies me for a moment. "Have you thought about being with a woman?"

"Yes. I thought about that about ten years ago. I wondered if I was a lesbian because I could never be with a man, but women don't thrill me. It's not that I have an aversion to homosexuality. If I did, then I'd wonder what I was hiding, but I don't. It would be easier if I were homosexual. Women, I'm not afraid of."

His steady gaze makes me uncomfortable. There's nowhere for me to hide from his scrutiny, and there are no words that I can find to make this conversation rational or my fears justified.

"Have you been around horses?" I ask.

"No, not really."

"They're big beautiful creatures, and you're drawn to their beauty and gentleness. You can't help but pet their soft noses that blow warm breath on you. And then you run your hands along their necks and shoulders, feeling all that muscle and power beneath your fingers, but the horse just stands still and you forget how strong and powerful they are. Until they shift their weight. All of a sudden your entire body is pressed against the fence and you can't move that animal for anything. You realize how completely powerless you are. No amount of pushing and yelling gets that horse to move. And they just stand there perfectly relaxed, oblivious to the fact that they've pinned you against the fence. All they did was shift their weight. That's how men are. They're like horses with all that power. They're all beautiful and strong, but when they shift their weight, you can't move them."

"I think you're romanticizing," he says. "The strength difference between a child and a grown man may seem like the difference between a person and horse, but you're an adult woman. You're not powerless."

That's what I must keep reminding myself: I'm not powerless.

CHAPTER 29

I amazed myself with my ability to pretend.

The cruise was nice. I loved the ocean and the fresh air and the immensity of it all. Mom and Dad had a separate cabin. Dad had always done his own thing. He and Mom were awake before dawn each morning and had coffee on deck.

Pleasing Sister was always awake before me. She had pointedly suggested that I take medication with me and I agreed. The Seroquel calmed my emotions somewhat and it was easier to pretend that everything was all right, that I wasn't in therapy because Dad had molested me, and that I couldn't seem to have intimacy with anyone, and that I now wanted to hurt myself.

While Dad was content to sit at a table on deck and lose himself in the fantasies of his mind, Mom sought the company of her children, as she had always done. She was always waiting eagerly for us to wake and begin the day.

One morning I sat at the table and inhaled the fresh ocean air, watching Dad, examining the emotions that rose in me. He hadn't been a good provider. In my teens, I noticed that my friends' fathers worked hard to support their families. Their fathers always seemed to be off working, while mine was locked up in his room, working on a novel that never seemed to be complete.

We rented house after house because he would get too far behind on the rent and we'd be evicted. Dad never worried about tomorrow. He lived in the moment, taking care of his own needs first. I often thought that fatherhood had been too much for him, even though he and Mom had told us on numerous occasions that they had wanted eight children. Maybe that was true, since Dad had been abandoned as a baby and then become an only child.

In theory, a large family sounded good, but the reality was that they were a lot of work and responsibility. My dad wasn't big on responsibility.

Even now, he wasn't working and Mom paid the bills. He hadn't worked since he'd gotten a bleeding ulcer back in 1974. I had to get a job when I was fifteen, and half of my check went to help support the family. I had to buy my clothes out of the other half. Dad would come around on payday with his hand out, and then go to lunch while Mom tried to figure out how to feed the family with what he gave her.

My dad is complicated.

"I remember the day my father died," he told me once. "When they lowered him into the ground I thought, I'm finally free."

What would I think when they lowered my father into the ground?

March 19

I'm feeling profoundly sad and I don't know why. Is it because I see my goal slipping away as the complexities of my mind slow my healing process? Or am I sad for the girl who waits in darkness, stabbing her leg in rhythmic motions?

I rest my head in Sekhmet's lap and cry, trying not to think. Darkness covers me, bringing with it a need to hurt, to end my life. I seesaw between hope and hopelessness, between joy and despair, one moment believing I can change and the next knowing I cannot.

Wholeness/Mutilation and Innocence/Lust stand near the water at the temple. I'm perched on the edge, wanting to fall into the empty darkness. I try to fall, leaning my body over the edge, but some type of force field keeps me from my goal. I'm unable to fall.

Sekhmet stands at the door to the pit, and this time she lets me enter. I take the healing white light with me, using it as a rope to lower myself into the narrow tunnel and to protect myself.

They wait at the bottom in the same places where I left them. Sadness languishes with her head resting on one arm, while Shame remains on her knees, her face buried in her hands. Anger still holds a knife posed to make a killing thrust. She stands near the back of the pit, pressed to the cold darkness, away from the others. In the center is Dead Girl.

I stand at the bottom, surrounded by the healing white light. Without direction or reason, I reach for Sadness. She comes to me easily, wrapping her tiny arms around my waist. I pull her to me, curling over her to offer her the protection of my body.

"It's all right," I say. "You don't have to stay here any longer."

With my free arm, I pull in Dead Girl. Her light body hangs limply from my arm. Shame follows. I look at Anger. She will not come to me and I will not reach for her.

I make my ascension as the healing white light carries us to the door.

"Why didn't you bring up the girl with the knife?" Dr. Erickson asks when I finish.

His office has become so familiar to me, and I find comfort in our routine, in the places we sit each week as we begin our work. It has become work for me, a job of sorts that I must complete.

"I think it's best if she stays there," I tell him.

He's silent for a moment. "Did you integrate with the three girls you rescued?"

"No."

"Where are they?"

"They're sitting by the door with Sekhmet."

"Just sitting?"

"Yes, they're waiting."

I kneel in front of Sadness and hold her. Out from the darkness of the pit, the girls seem content to wait in the protection of Sekhmet's shadow. The door is only a short distance from where the girl sits stabbing her thigh, and all these images are below the temple that rests high in the openness of space.

Dr. Erickson studies me quietly and I wonder what he sees, what he's thinking. "How've you been doing?" he asks.

"I've been sad." I focus on the wall opposite me and avoid looking at him. "I don't know why."

Silence.

"I've been doing some research," I confess.

"Research?" His eyes sharpen.

Our discussion of penises ignited my analytical brain and launched me into a fact-finding fury. My girlfriends have been too vague in answering my questions, while Dr. Erickson has been too descriptive, and I can't discipline my mind to accept either explanation. My frustration at the conflicting information is quelled only by my insatiable curiosity. How big is a man's penis?

"I went to this website."

I focus on the arm of the chair because it's less painful than meeting Dr. Erickson's penetrating gaze. I don't want to have this conversation, which will only reinforce my inexperience and ignorance, but I don't know how to sort through the confusion that's cultivating my growing fear.

"It showed pictures of men when they're aroused and when they're not. I wanted to see what it looked like normal, before it was aroused."

Because the adult sex store doesn't sell toys or photographs of men relaxed, I began to wonder if I would fear a flaccid penis. The website was far from scientific, but the photographs displayed average men.

"I was thinking you were wrong about the size," I tell him.

"What did you discover? Was I accurate about the size?"

"Yes." My thoughts turn inward and I feel myself retreating. I can see the web page in my mind—disembodied penises lined in neat rows on my computer screen. "I don't like the look of men aroused."

It's the sound of my words and not the context that concerns me. Sitting with my feet curled beneath me in a chair that now seems too big, I couldn't feel more like a child, pouting and fretful, seeking reassurance from a parent.

"It's not that I don't think it's beautiful. I do. I want to touch and know how he feels, but … not close to me. I only like it when it's away from me."

And that makes me sad. I want to feel the rush of pleasure; the tiny thrill that women feel as a man approaches them, their bodies like tuning forks, vibrating with anticipation. I want the easiness of pressing into someone and feeling the warmth of their skin, and the freedom of fearing nothing.

"In your fantasy, the man has a penis," he reminds me.

"Yes. That's different." Though I've said it, I don't quite understand how it is different. "In my fantasy, he's sitting. I don't think it's so bad when he's sitting, but when he's standing ... It's different when he's standing. It's like a weapon ... threatening ... dangerous."

He stands a good distance from me, naked and aroused. My body tightens with fear.

"I don't want him to come close to me."

"This website wasn't pornographic, was it?" he asks. "Was it just for study?"

"Yes. That was the point of the website, to show average men."

"So you saw what a man looks like and that hasn't helped ease your fears"

"I still think it's too big."

"A woman's body is made to accommodate a man." His tone is considerate and gentle. "Have you had a pelvic exam?"

"No."

"What about a pap smear?"

"No."

"You've never had a pap smear?" There's a slight frown on his face.

"No. I told you, I don't like doctors." In fact, I've made a career out of avoiding them, despite the urging of friends to submit to a pap smear.

"I was going to say that the specula used in the exam is no bigger than a man's penis." He thinks. "The wall of the cervix is covered with a membrane and thousands of blood vessels. When a woman is sexually aroused, blood flows down to the vaginal walls, engorging them. So the walls close in and tighten around a man's penis, and that's not only pleasurable for him but for her as well."

I listen stoically. I hate it when he talks like a doctor, as if I cared about the biological functions of the human body, as if any of this applied to me.

"The vagina is very stretchy. Think about it, a baby passes through there," he tells me again.

"That's other people, not me," I insist. He never understands this. "I haven't had sex and babies. I know my own body."

He narrows his gaze. "What will happen if you have sex?"

Something bad will happen. I ignore the voice, even though I want to utter the words aloud because some part of me believes them, and that frightens me

"I …" I expel a deep breath and gather my thoughts, feeling the rise of frustration close around my throat. "I …"

I can't make the words come out. They are the fear that anchors me, the chains that bind me to my solitary life, and yet I know I can't contain them any longer. To hold them inside in the protection only a secret can offer is to give them power.

I bow my head and shrink a little in my chair. "I don't think it will fit. It's too big. It will be too much. It'll be …"

My body fills and stretches, my breath choking in my throat. I feel myself splitting … dying.

"… suffocating and … I won't be able to move or breathe."

Pain and fear and powerlessness: crushing me. I look back at my fantasies like a well-graphed timeline, seeing for the first time how incomplete they've been, how immature and romanticized. I've been a blind woman dreaming of color. Though the desire is there, my fantasy has been incorrect. Now that I've seen the real size, I cannot fantasize sex, but the fact that I don't want a penis anywhere near me is another matter altogether. The magic and pleasure of fantasizing are gone, and I feel like a child who has just been told that there's no Santa Clause. This too, is my sadness.

"When people have phobias …" he begins gently.

Phobias? People who are paralyzed with fear and can't leave their house have phobias. People who freak out when the elevator doors slide shut, or phase out when confronted with a snake have phobias. The term is clinical and makes my fear more important than I want it to be. I don't want to hear about phobias.

He's staring at me. Waiting. "A good way to overcome a phobia is by exposure.

We talked about familiarizing yourself with a penis," he says. "Have you purchased a toy?"

"Yes."

I took my girlfriend and asked her to pick a realistic-looking one from the display shelf. No simple task, as the choices ranged from neon color to alien lifeform. I wanted nothing that required batteries or glowed in the dark.

But the experience of the sex store was nothing short of an assault on my emotions and left me in no mood to explore my new purchase. The toy has stayed in the brown bag under my bed since.

"That's a good way for you to know that you can accommodate a man. If you can handle the toy you'll have the confidence to know that you can handle a man."

It isn't my confidence I'm worried about; it's getting to the mental place where I can enjoy sex and anticipate it with excitement and pleasure. Dr. Erickson speaks of these things as if he's teaching me to breathe, and I can't make him understand how daunting the idea of sex is to me. It's always been my blockade, and I fear now more than ever that I'll never know the freedom others take for granted.

"When I fantasize, it's nice when he and I are together," I say softly. "It's important that he knows I have desire and that I want to be pleasured. I can touch him and he touches me. But then he wants to have sex and … I can't. So I start to cry."

"Why do you cry?"

"I'm sad because I can't have sex with him and he's wanting."

"There must be something with the X chromosome," he says matter-of-factly. "I run into this all the time with women. They take responsibility for the man's erection. They get upset that he has an erection and feel they have to do something about it. A man may make you feel you're responsible for his erection, but the only person responsible is *him. He's* the one that got excited."

Is it as simple as that? Do women buy into the sales pitch that men sell? Or is it that we're taught obedience and servitude at such a young age that we've never evolved beyond it?

What I know for certain is that this is a portion of my sadness: my inability to please.

My deadline approaches for completion, the date I've set to achieve my goal, and I've never felt further from it.

How am I going to have sex if I can't even fantasize it?

CHAPTER 30

I was seventeen years old when I fell in love with Jim. He was twenty-four, and a dark-haired Irishman with blue eyes and dark brown hair. He worked at the same place I did. I was a pre-cook and he was the head cook. There was something about Jim that was dangerous, unpredictable and sexy. When he smiled, his eyes shined and he had this mischievous expression, as if he knew something about me that I didn't.

We flirted, but he seemed to treat me like a little sister he indulged and not the woman I wanted him to see me as. He dated the waitresses, who then told me how great he was in bed, and that infuriated me. None of them lasted very long and I convinced myself they weren't right for him.

His sexual experience intrigued me. He was easy about his body and the things he'd done. After work on Saturday night, a bunch of us from work would go to his house and play poker. I did anything I could to get close to him. He was nice to me, but never took it beyond that.

One night we had gathered at another house for a small party. I'd had a few drinks, and two boys I didn't know approached me. Apparently, I'd been talking about being a virgin rather loudly and this had drawn attention. The boys wanted to take me for a ride and I said yes.

Without warning, Jim pushed me roughly into a chair and pointed his finger at me. "You're not going anywhere."

The boys promptly left and I sat loose-boned and high, watching the party blurry-eyed and despondent. Maybe, I thought, Jim secretly loved me. I waited with hope, but was devastated to learn, a few months later, that he was moving out town.

Work threw him a goodbye party. I put a good face on my despair. Pride goeth before a fall. But during the party I had the chance to be alone with him. We were sitting in a booth and I decided to ask him what' I'd always wanted to know.

"Jim, why didn't you ever date me?"

"I would have ruined your life," he said gently.

"Yeah, but think how much fun we could've had."

He smiled at me and shook his head.

I was eighteen years old and I wanted him to confess his love for me, to ask me to go with him. But instead he got up to ask someone else to dance, leaving me alone in the booth.

March 23

I have a sense of something ending, a powerful feeling of things drawing to a close, and I'm uncertain if it's an event or my life that's ending. I just know that I'm running out of time. Each day, time slips past and I move closer to an ending, take another step forward to a conclusion that will finally free me.

There's no joy in this sense of ending, and no contentment in finding a connection with my memories. I'd been promised a way out of my cage, and instead I was delivered a riddle. I want to come to my lover with the ease of an experienced woman, but I can't get experience until I have a lover, and I can't get a lover until I have experience.

My fear of men has transformed into a fear of penises, and that seems like an overpowering obstacle that I don't know how to begin to overcome. I start to think I'll always be crippled by this fear, condemned to feel desire and never experience it. Worse, I see that even if I do discipline myself to overcome this fear, no man will want me with my inexperience and timidity.

It's this realization that anchors my sadness and ushers me to surrender the fight. I try to find solace in my fantasies, but they, too, fail me.

"How are you doing?" Dr. Erickson asks easily as he sits down.

"I'm sad," I say.

I cannot hear sadness in my voice and I know it's not revealed in my expression. I haven't had any more visions of cutting off my arm, but I have a strong sense of my life ending. Suddenly, it has become important to me that I finish the things I've started; complete tasks I've been postponing these past years. It's a strange and powerful desire that propels me toward the end. I can't shake the sense of my life ending, any more than I can stop the images from crowding my mind.

"What are you sad about?" he asks, leaning back in his chair with a rare pad of paper in his hands.

I'm dying and I don't care. I shrug. "I wanted to thank you for making time to help me. I know I've taken up a lot of your time. I wanted to be sure and thank you."

We're meeting on a Saturday. He crowds me into his busy schedule and I can't help but feel like a burden to him, as if I've failed somehow to meet my goal in a timely manner, and this has forced him to make room for me between managing inpatient care and covering county psychiatric units.

He sets down his pen to look at me, studying me for a moment. "I know it hasn't been easy to see me. You've had to adjust your schedule and there are time constraints. I know you're bursting to heal and I wish I could be more available to you, but you've hung in there."

I've brought my sadness with me today. It's an anvil tethered to me, pulling me down with such strength that I can almost feel the world slipping away.

"The thank-you," he says quietly, "is that goodbye?"

"No." I say softly, but it's a lie. I've been thinking that if something happened to me, if my life ends, as I feel it will, then I don't want him to think I didn't appreciate all his time and effort. I don't want him to feel a failure. "I wanted you to know that I appreciate the time you're making for me. I haven't thanked you. I know I'm supposed to be finishing and I'm trying."

"You're making tremendous progress. The work you've done so far would have taken another person four years in psychoanalysis. I know that some of the things we do make you very uncomfortable, but you push yourself to do it."

"I want to have my goal," I say faintly, feeling the sorrow well inside.

You're never going to have it. The haunting voice is not mocking or demanding. It's a child stating a simple inarguable fact.

"I have every reason to believe that you *will* have your goal. You're working hard and making good progress." His voice is distant, his words empty.

I sit next to a man, warm and content. My muscles loosen as I relax against him, my hand reaching for his penis. I smile at his playful manner, the easiness of two people sharing intimacy without imposed constraints. There are no rules to follow, no manmade laws designed to control our behavior, no Catholic guilt, and no embarrassment at our desire.

My fingers close around him with uncertainty. I hesitate and reposition, trying to find the right hold that will please him. He shifts restlessly and I can feel his frustration at my incompetence.

"I'm sad," I say again, and feel tears welling. No man is going to want me this way. No man will find me desirable if I don't know how to please.

"You're doing it wrong. Not that way! This way!" My father's voice, stern in reprimand, returns to haunt me. I lay unmoving on the cold ebony floor of my mind, sunken into darkness and despair.

Tears spill over the rims of my eyes. All I can think is how hard I've tried, and am still trying, and that I've accomplished nothing. I'm only going through the motions of pretending to be a person, pretending that I can have what other people have. Nothing I do will make a difference. I will always be this way. Alone.

My tears fall and my sadness is so heavy that I want it to bury me. I want to curl into the chair and close my eyes and slip into the darkness. Because even though I'm out of the pit, I'm still in the shadows.

"You've been telling me that you've been sad," he says quietly. "I'm sorry I haven't been paying attention."

It's the only time he's seen me cry, and I realize that my soundless misery must be both an accomplishment and a failure for him.

"Tell me about your sadness. Why the tears?"

I want him to understand without my explanation. I want him to see the images that feed my fear as he acknowledges the walls and pits that trap me. But he doesn't understand my sorrow, any more than I understand the easy comfort he displays. I'm frustrated enough to speak.

"I'm sad because ... no man is going to want me this way. I don't have experience like other women. Men want women with experience."

He's silent for a moment. "Do you learn to play the piano in a day? You want to know how to do something before you do it."

"Men want women with experience," I repeat.

"Who tells you these things?" His voice is stronger than usual. "You're talking about a billion men. You can give him your innocence, your willingness. He can teach you what you don't know, and that could be enjoyable for both of you."

All I can think is how slow and cumbersome the affair would be, how fraught with inability and incompetence. Between the lessons and teachings we would lose the very essence of what joined us together, and I would become a mirror image of the little girl on the bed.

"I want things to be different," I say softly. "I don't like how everything is, all separated."

"That's why you're here, to change things."

His comment makes me tired. I can almost feel the heaviness of the air press me into the cushions of the chair. All of my hard work for nothing, I think. I will be able to touch another and allow him to touch me, but in the end he will not want me. And yet I can't quit and I can't erase the images. I'm too far along the path to stop and have any kind of a life. I can't even have my old life any more.

It's the suspension between what was and what will be—being in both places and being in neither—that feeds my uncertainty and my sadness. Beneath the images and desires and hopes lies the danger that's never far: my growing need to hurt myself.

It all goes back to those rooms, back to the beginning when everything changed.

"I wish things were different," I say wistfully. My gaze is on the flooring, so I can hear his voice, but not see him.

"Different then or different now?"

Both. But it can't be both, because if I hadn't been molested I wouldn't need things to be different now. I would have a life like other women, full of the joy of giving and receiving, of needing and wanting, and of knowing that both are all right.

"I wish I hadn't been molested." I voice my profoundest wish, which has cemented me to this life of misguided beliefs. I know wishing it will only prolong my sadness and offer nothing in the way of healing, but I wish it nonetheless. "Why did he do that?"

Silence.

"I don't want to upset the little ones inside," he says quietly, "but your father was whacked. He made you his fantasy, and when you didn't respond the way he wanted, when you cried and resisted, you destroyed his fantasy." Pause. "I know you want to love your father, but you don't have to love what he did."

It's the strangest thing to want the love of a person who has harmed you. Maybe it's as simple and as complex as that he's my father, or maybe it's a more spiritual need to forgive and accept people for who and what they are: human. I have to remind myself that forgiving my father is not the same as excusing him.

"Have I upset anyone inside?" he asks gently.

I shake my head. We know what my father is and I know what I have done.

In a whisper, he asks, "Isn't it time to give back the shame?"

I don't answer.

CHAPTER 31

The playground was crowded. Lunch recess in the fourth grade seemed to last for an eternity. The nuns in the school patrolled with watchful eyes. Girls weren't allowed to run. It was unladylike. But I'd spent my entire childhood running wild and barefoot, climbing trees and getting dirty without restrictions, so the Catholic school rules seemed unbearable at times. The proper girls sat quietly on a bench and talked.

I liked to climb, but the monkey bars were always taken over by boys, and the nuns wouldn't let me hang upside down because my skirt would flop down and the entire playground could see my panties. So I was restricted to hopscotch or swinging.

I preferred swinging because I loved the feeling of flying it gave me. Sometimes, when the nuns weren't looking, I'd jump off when the swing was high and land in the thick sand beneath.

One day I was swinging with some classmates and I told them I'd seen my dad's penis. I remember the look on their faces as they stopped playing. I continued to swing, my fingers wrapped tightly around the cold chain. All my sisters had seen Dad's penis as well, and I wondered why the other girls hadn't seen their dads' penises. They challenged me, and I insisted I'd even touched it and I proudly told them what it looked like and how it felt.

They looked at each other, their expressions an amalgamation of disbelief and condemnation. They whispered to each other as I swung higher, watching the sky and pretending my body soared free. When I looked down, they were gone.

They stopped playing with me after that.

Three months later we moved unexpectedly from the farmhouse back to the city and another new school. I would never make that mistake again. Somewhere in my nine-year-old mind I had learned a lesson: tell no one.

"You can only count on family," Dad would tell us. "Friends are fickle. Family is for life."

Honor thy father and mother. Stop telling lies about your father. Only bad girls touch down there. Good girls don't do that. No sex before marriage.

My life had become a contradiction. I had learned to keep the secrets well.

March 28

I have a theory that if I wait long enough my pain will go away. The fact that it has never happened doesn't keep me from hoping or trying. So I wait for the images to change, for the pain to fade, and for my harmful urges to stop. But even I know when the waiting must cease, and that's when I think back to that day in July when I sat on the hard chairs in the psychiatric unit in the county hospital.

Waiting doesn't work for healing.

For days I battle the sadness and the growing sense that my life is ending. I don't have visions of killing myself, but I know my life is ending. I can feel it growing shorter with the passing of each day, but I'm not afraid.

And that frightens me.

The knives on the counter pull at me. I fantasize about cutting myself, feeling the pain and the joy of release. The pressure is like a giant bubble inside of me, pushing at me all the time: I want to hurt. While I imagine how wonderful that release would be, I question the directive.

Why should I hurt myself?

And is this the kind of life I want to live, controlled by destructive urges that offer only a brief respite?

"I've been having this urge again to … hurt myself … to punish."

The phone is pressed to my ear. In between sessions, we have a phone call so I can address anything that's surfaced after our last session. I've waited until after the session to bring this up, because the phone offers me a way of hiding. Still, I'm embarrassed by my thoughts, which don't seem to belong to me and are not a part of what I want.

"It's not an idea; it's a need. I know I've had this urge before, but this is different. I don't know how to make it go away, and it's strong, like pressure always pushing me."

I'm getting tired; the constant battles for control, to keep myself grounded and in the present, to keep myself safe without betraying them, are a gradual and persistent erosion like water wearing against stone. I'm fearful of the moment when the erosion will be complete.

"The urge to hurt yourself, is it yours or is it coming from someplace else?" Dr. Erickson asks.

He means her.

"I don't know; I just know I want to do it." I wait and listen to the silence.

"You've had this urge before," he says finally. "What did you do the last time that helped?"

The knife is in my hand. It's late at night and the house is quiet. I'm alone with my urge to cut off my arm, to drive the knife into my hand. Every cell and vessel in my body vibrates with this need to sink the sharp, steel blade into the soft flesh. My fingers tighten on the handle in desperation. I know what I can't do, but I must do it, if for no other reason than to silence the images. I stab the butcher-block table with a sob. I want to scream and rage and stab … and I don't know why.

I watch as the blade makes a single cut along the back of my hand.

I keep the memory to myself. "That's not an option. I have to do something else."

"What did you do?"

My failure rises like a scarlet letter. I push it away. "I don't want to do that. I want to do something else."

Pause.

"What did you do?" he asks again.

I hesitate, knowing he won't relent until he has his answer. Something has blipped on his radar and he's like a dog with a bone on this. I know what my words will make me.

"I cut myself."

Silence.

"Did you tell me that?"

"No." And then in my own defense, I add, "You didn't ask."

"How did that make you feel?"

"Better, less stressed, like the pressure was gone. It was nice."

"Then you learned an important lesson." His voice is like tightly spun silk. "It's going to be more difficult not to do it the next time."

"I remember you telling me that people who cut themselves fall into cycles. I don't want to fall into that cycle."

"No, you don't want to do that."

"But it's difficult to make the urge go away. It's like I'm being pushed to do something and it won't let up unless I do it." It's like being programmed, a deep coding in the circuits in my brain that I cannot stop.

"What are you thinking about when you feel the urge to hurt?"

She kneels in darkness and is not afraid. She rhythmically stabs the knife into her thigh and feels no pain. In a dark corner of the pit, another girl waits with a knife.

"Stabbing her leg is a metaphor for rape," he says.

I ignore the word he knows I hate. "It's just how things are in my mind," I tell him. It's the way I sort the images and organize the information, the places where I keep the disturbing thoughts that have manifested into innocent and dangerous children. It has nothing to do with rape.

"She's trying to tell you something," he says quietly. "You keep ignoring how she feels and it manifests into other things for you, like the need to hurt yourself, to punish. But whose punishment is it?"

A question I don't want to answer. I have a horrible feeling it is me she's punishing. And I know why.

"I don't know," I answer with a lie. "I just know I want to hurt myself and I don't like that feeling."

"One of the one-armed girls in the temple, Wholeness/Mutilation, is she still there?" he asks.

"Yes."

"What is wholeness?"

"Being one. Solid."

"What is mutilation?"

My thoughts stumble and stagger. "It's ... it's ... I don't know."

"Is it strength?"

"No."

"Is it powerlessness?"

I carefully consider the question. "Yes."

"Is it castration?"

Definitely. "Yes."

"Is it self-injury behavior?"

I hesitate, wondering where he's leading me. "Yes."

"What do you feel when you think of mutilation?"

"Helplessness," I say, because it seems that mutilation is everything in pieces, coming undone.

"Where in your body do you feel that?"

"My pelvis." Always my pelvis, that strange pressure that grows from the inside and pushes at me like a balloon expanding in my womb.

"Okay," he says quietly. "Are you in a place where you can work quietly?"

"Yes." I'm in the privacy of my bedroom, where I feel safe and solitary.

"I want you to go inside. Can you find the pit with the little girl in it?"

"Yes."

I follow his voice as he walks me through my internal world.

The pit is narrow and deep. I stand at the top, looking down. A rope of healing white light drops into the pit and I latch onto it as it lowers me into the pit. The little girl stands with the knife poised and ready to defend herself.

A warm glow surrounds me, a protective shield that will allow me to go near her without harm to either of us.

Still on the rope, I reach out and embrace the girl, hooking her into the nook of my arm. I carry her like the child she is as the rope descends into the pit.

I set her down by Sekhmet. The girl is stubbornly determined to be unmoved by my attempt to nurture and protect. She holds the knife tightly, but makes no attempt to harm me.

"Let the healing white light touch her," Dr. Erickson instructs. "You can put her into a protective bubble."

We repeat the exercise I'm so familiar with: putting the squeeze on the monster that has inhabited the girl.

I ask Sekhmet to take the monster away.

"Ask the little girl if there's anything she needs," Dr. Erickson tells me.

I frown. "She doesn't say anything. She's standing holding the knife."

"Can you hold her?"

"No."

"Can Sekhmet hold her?"

"Yes."

Sekhmet embraces the little girl, who does not resist. Her young face is unreadable, a combination of sorrow and regret.

"It's okay," I tell her. "I see."

I stand just in front of the two, a casual observer. For the first time I can understand the girl's rage, I can appreciate the desire to harm and destroy, and realize that my need to cut myself is her need for release and recognition. Her screams are silent. Her rage is unanswered.

"Tell me how you feel," his voice penetrates the haze of my internal world.

I mentally check myself. "Better."

"Still want to hurt yourself?"

"No," I say with confidence. The pressure is gone. It's like stepping into a different world where the darkness and heaviness does not exist.

"I feel ... happy."

"Good. We changed the chemistry in your brain. Now you want to expand on that good feeling. Is there something you do to feel good? A favorite food you eat that makes you feel good?"

I think about dancing naked in the bedroom.

"For me it's peanut butter and chocolate," he says.

"Noodles and cheese."

Because my mother always made noodles and cheese when the entire family was together. Noodles and cheese was a staple in our house: inexpensive to make and requiring little effort to put together. It was also the only food that seemed to come in abundance to our table, a large roasting pan full of steaming noodles and gooey cheese baked with crunchy crackers on top.

"So, you can have some of that tonight," he says, "and build on this good feeling for a while."

Just the thought of noodles and cheese makes me smile.

"I want shorter goals," I announce. "These big goals are too much."

"Okay, we can do shorter goals. It's a good idea to break up larger goals. What do your shorter goals look like?"

"I want to clear my body memories, get some relief from the trapped feeling. And I want to finish the hotel room." Because it's always there, like the sky above the earth or the ground at my feet.

"Okay," he says easily. "Those are good goals."

Yes, they are good goals.

CHAPTER 32

I washed my hair every morning. It was a habit I got into early in my teens when I realized that the mass of curls needed untangling and refreshing every day, otherwise I'd look like a deranged lunatic. This week I noticed how much of my hair was coming out in my hands as I rinsed the shampoo away. It had been happening for a while, and I thought it was normal. Or maybe I wasn't paying attention. For whatever reason, this day it struck me as worrisome.

There was a lot of hair in my hand. There was a lot every day. I examined myself in the mirror, seeing the thin cap of curls that had seemingly appeared overnight. I could see my scalp through the curls. I was going bald.

I made an urgent trip to the vitamin store. The nice woman behind the counter knew exactly what I needed.

"I almost went bald planning my daughter's wedding. I used this." She handed me a bottle. "It'll take a couple of months, but you can get your hair back."

I stared at her. What she was telling me was that stress was causing my hair loss. I numbly took the bottle, paid for it and left. When I got home, I obsessed about this. I stood in front of the mirror, examining myself as if seeing me for the first time. What else was I not seeing?

My fingers glided across my cheeks. I hated my complexion. Free of acne, it was uneven and couldn't seem to decide on a tone. Dad was Greek, and I had a light to medium skin tone that seemed to show every flaw. The wrinkles under my eyes were like battle scars, screaming out my age. For a single woman who'd never had children, I figured I should look a hell of a lot better.

This new discovery prompted me to schedule an appointment at the clinic.

"You have a nice complexion," they told me.

But I was insistent that I hated it. They recommended glycolic acid peels; simple, non-invasive and little down time.

But what did I care about down time. I had nothing else to do.

April 6

I'm grateful we're on the phone and I don't have to endure Dr. Erickson's penetrating gaze, but it's more difficult for me to stay focused. Though the sound of his voice transcends the phone and I'm able to connect easily with him, the isolation of my room where I do my work is like a boundary into another world. I seem to drift onto another plane and it's only his voice that anchors me.

Dr. Erickson sits in front of me. Our knees are close. He shifts slightly and ... our knees melt together.

He stands in front of me, ready to provide resistance to my pushing. As our hands touch, our flesh melts. His palms sink into mine; our fingers and hands are blended together like warm wax. I pull away, but I can't separate from him. He has connection and I can't break it.

"Are you in a good place now? How do you feel?" Dr. Erickson asks me.

"Tired." I don't like us melting together like that, a kind of permanent fusion where I can't get free. "We can work on that other, but ... I don't want to do any pushing exercises. I can see us melting together when we touch and I don't want that. But we can do something else."

Silence.

"What do you mean about melting together?" he asks calmly.

"I see you sitting close to me and our knees melt together. When you go to push out anger, our hands melt together."

"That's in your images?"

"Yes, that's what would happen. I don't want to do any of those exercises."

"If we touch each other you think we'll melt together?"

"Yes, that's what I see."

"But that's in your mind, that's not reality. Flesh can't melt together."

I try to pull away from him, but I'm a part of him and he's a part of me. Panic rises to fear and I struggle to free myself.

"Yes, we melt together." Why isn't he listening to me? My fingers poke at the carpet in my room. I don't like it when he doesn't understand me and I don't like having to explain myself repeatedly. "When you touch me our hands melt together."

"In your *thoughts* that's what happens." His voice is still calm, but insistent.

"Yes, that's what I see."

"But if we were to really touch, that wouldn't happen."

"No, that *would* happen. I don't want that."

Silence.

"How are you sleeping?"

"I didn't sleep very well last night, only an hour or so. I haven't been sleeping very well this week."

"How's your appetite?"

"Not very good. I'm not very hungry, but I'm eating."

"Are you eating enough protein?"

Protein? My mind rushes to catch up with his questions. "Yes. I eat fine."

"You're getting exercise?"

"Yes, I work out every day." Why is he droning on so?

Silence.

"Are you taking any vitamins? Any herbal supplements?"

"Yes." I frown, wondering why he's placed such a sudden interest in my health regimen.

"I'd like to see those supplements. Can you bring me the containers at our next session?"

"Yes, if you want."

"Are you still taking Seroquel?"

"No. I haven't taken Seroquel since November." I stopped because I didn't want to become dependent on it for sleeping, and it interfered with the work I was doing.

"I'd like you to take Seroquel for a few days."

"Why?" I can't keep the disappointment out of my tone. He has never pushed medication before and my thoughts spin at this sudden change to want to medicate me.

"So you can get some good sleep and calm things down. It will help you to think a little better."

What's wrong with my thinking? "I don't want to take Seroquel. I don't work as well with it and I'm trying to reach my goal." My heart is pounding with disappointment and fear. He's trying to prevent me from reaching my goal. He's trying to slow me down and I don't know why.

"I think you should take Seroquel for a few days and see if it makes a difference." His tone is gentle and suggestive.

"I'm working hard." I'm acutely aware that it's April and I'm supposed to be reaching my goal and finishing therapy, and I've never felt farther away from it; I feel fragmented and powerless. "Seroquel will slow me down."

"You're not in a good place to make decisions right now," he says quietly. "What you're thinking isn't helping you to move closer to your goal. We'll have more work that we have to undo later and start over."

His words strike me. What he's saying is that I'm making bad decisions and that I'm slowing the work. I remember how, months ago, I had subconsciously sabotaged my efforts to heal, pushing away memories and stalling the healing process. Is it possible that I'm sabotaging my efforts again now that I'm closer to my deadline for healing?

"I'll think about it."

"When you go a few days without eating and sleeping, it can make this kind of work more difficult and challenging." He pushes forward." Seroquel will let you get sleep so you can make better decisions."

I'm not convinced. "Seroquel makes it more difficult to work the images. I don't do good work on Seroquel."

"You're not doing good work now. You're not reality testing."

But I *am* reality testing; he just doesn't see it. I know he won't let me off the phone until I give him the answer he's looking for and I'm not ready to surrender, not completely. "I'll try it for one night."

"If you get confused in the next few days before we meet again, it would be all right if you wanted to call me and talk."

I don't know what we would talk about that we haven't already discussed, but his offer makes me nervous nevertheless. I pluck at the carpet fabric, uneasy at his suggestion. I've never called him out of session before and don't like the idea of being that needy.

"I don't like to bother you."

"I can appreciate that," he says easily.

"I don't like to call you outside of our scheduled time." It's a boundary issue for me. I won't be one of those patients who dial their therapist after every anxiety spell or when they're having a bad day. I keep things structured, and that's enabled me to work within the confines of the therapy sessions.

"I know you're an independent woman and you don't like to need me, but things can be confusing sometimes and this isn't something you can easily talk about with other people."

That's true, but ... "I like to make my own decisions."

"Okay," he says at length. "But you can make an informed decision. Will you trust that I have information that you might not have and that I can make a sound decision?"

But he doesn't understand why we would melt together if we touch, and this makes me think he wouldn't make a sound decision. Still, I could listen to what he has to say and do what I want anyway.

"Okay," I tell him.

"You'll call me if you get confused?"

"Yes."

But I know that I'm not the one who's confused.

CHAPTER 33

We didn't have television for the first few years of my life. Mom read Robert Service and Poe to us by lantern light around the kitchen table. We huddled near her, our elbows pressed to the rough surface of the table, and listened intently as her words painted vivid scenes in our minds. Sometimes we'd continue the stories after we went to bed, putting ourselves in the scenes of Poe or Service. We'd giggle and argue until Dad came in and told us to go to sleep.

Sometimes, Dad would stand by our bed and sing us to sleep, or tell us one of his favorite Poe stories. Dad told the best stories. He used different voices for dramatic effect and mimed a lot of the parts. We'd listen to the sound of his voice until we drifted to sleep.

Such were my early years, living in a cabin without electricity. While other girls were playing with Barbie and the highly coveted Easy-Bake Oven, I was making forts out of earth, playing with toads and chipmunks, and inventing every game imaginable to occupy my time.

With our imaginations as our only entertainment, the Wisconsin woods became a great landscape for playing cowboys. The tree limbs served as mock horses, and we four youngest children straddled the thick branches and kicked our bare heels high, racing across the plains to defend our cattle, which were nothing more than the tall ferns that lined the forest floor.

When we tired of cowboys, the trees were easily converted into pirate ships. We'd stand tall on the wide limbs and shield our eyes, always on the lookout for another ship to plunder. Sometimes the rules changed and sides were drawn. Inevitably, it ended with two siblings against the other two. Treasures were stolen and captives taken.

As with any childhood game, it all ended with the call to dinner.

April 16

How are you doing?" Dr. Erickson appears easy and relaxed, but watchful.

"Okay." The Seroquel helped me sleep heavily, and the calming effects linger into the morning, clearing away the clutter in my mind. Last night was the first night I didn't take the medication, but I still feel the effects of it.

He studies me in silence. "I did some research on psychosis. We don't know a lot about it. One of the criteria is loss of reality, but there's also supposed to be hallucinations."

Why is he telling me this?

"When you do your healing work, you go into a trance," he continues.

I go into another world, but I don't see it as a trance.

"You go into a trance frequently when we're in session."

"I do?"

"Yes. There's something called trance-logic, which is when you apply reality to the trance world and try to bring those elements into the present." Pause. "I don't think you completely get free of the trance, and you confuse the two realities, bringing the work you do in the spirit world into the present."

I digest his words, realizing he's concerned about my thought processes, but I don't want him to be concerned. It's not a good idea to have a psychiatrist concerned about how you think.

"I can point out to you when you're in a trance next time, if it doesn't interfere with the work you're doing."

I nod.

"You need to come out of the trance completely after doing your work and be in the present. Set your parameters before you start working and set your intention."

"I want to talk to you about something else."

"All right." He settles more comfortably into the chair.

I tell him I want the net with the body parts to go away.

"Are there enough parts in the net to make a whole person?" he asks me.

"I think so…but there are too many parts." I listen as he guides me.

I stand before the net and watch as it gently lowers to the ground and opens, revealing the dismembered parts. I quickly assemble the girl, leaving the male parts behind in the net. I ask Sekhmet to take the net and the discarded parts away.

"I'm supposed to do something else," I say.

The farmhouse is set against the green pasture.

"Are you ready to go into the house?" he asks.

I step through the door. The house has the hollow feel of empty rooms. I hear the echo of my shoes on the wooden floor. Up the stairs are the bedrooms, one flowing into the next. I walk into the room at the back of the house. There are three little girls waiting in the room. I take their hands, lead them safely out of the house and bring them to the temple.

"Is Sekhmet still guarding the door?" he asks.

"Yes."

"Ask her if she can help you. Are you by Wholeness/Mutilation and the assembled body from the net?"

We stand in a circle, the three girls from the house, Wholeness/Mutilation, and the strangely assembled body.

"All of you can melt into liquid in a basin in the center," he says, "so all of you are in one place, mixed together."

Like melted wax, we slowly liquefy into a pool of silver. The basin contains the liquid that was once our bodies.

"Now you're all in the basin and you can form a whole person from that liquid, bringing all the elements of these little girls, Wholeness/Mutilation and yourself into one being."

I stand naked in the temple, stepping out of the basin.

"You can look at yourself as this new person and know that you're complete. You have their resources, their strengths and lessons."

I'm unashamed in my nakedness, viewing my body in the reflection of the temple wall. Suddenly, I start to tear the flesh from my left arm. Skin and muscle peel away like soft paper. In seconds, I pare my arm down to the bone.

Through the door and in the pit, the girl stabs her thigh over and over.

"I've done something wrong," I say with distress, trying to get the images and the bombardment of emotions to stop. I haven't seen. I haven't seen.

"You keep pushing away her anger," he says quietly. "You won't acknowledge what's happened to her."

"I don't know why she's angry." I don't like the image of her stabbing herself, and I don't like the anger at tearing off my flesh, but I don't know how to stop any of it.

"She's looking for acknowledgement," he says. "Stabbing is a metaphor for rape."

I feel pressure, like some invisible force squeezing me tightly, trying to contain me, but I must break free as though I'd suddenly outgrown my body. The air thins as the room shrinks.

Nothing happened!

She stabs her thigh, driving the blade in and out with barely controlled fury. An anguished scream claws up from deep in her chest. I sit separate from her, resting my back on solid darkness. My wounded arm rests at my side.

"I don't like what she's doing," I say softly. I'm a helpless prisoner of my own images.

He picks up the wand he uses for EMDR. "Stay with her stabbing her leg."

After so many months my eyes follow the wand with practiced ease, and my thoughts fall into a familiar pattern. The back-and-forth motion, the inside, they're like a door opening.

I see myself lying on the bed in the hotel room, but I'm also near the bed because I've just walked into the room. Fingers push into me, but I sense them rather than feel or see them. I feel pressure between my legs, a sense of invasion—pain and humiliation.

"You're not on the ceiling?" he asks.

I shake my head, following the wand.

I'm curled on the edge, alone. There are no hands on me. I'm empty and cold and sad ... sad that he has done this. I'm alone and angry.

"I feel so sad and alone." My gaze drops to the floor as the wand stops. "I'm used to sleeping with my sisters," I say softly, remembering their comfort. "But I'm all alone in this hotel room and I don't have my sisters to go to."

Alone and rejected: used and discarded.

My thoughts shift on a moving plane. I have no images, only sensations. It's a strong but vague sense, like when you leave the house and can't shake the persistent sense that something's wrong—an iron left on, a door unlocked. You don't know exactly what it is, but you know for certain that something's wrong.

The sensation originates in my pelvis, and while my mind protectively keeps the images black, my body communicates the information: I am being invaded.

"What's wrong?" he asks, suddenly intense.

"I feel all this pressure inside of me." I put my hands on my abdomen. "I want to push it away."

"Is the pressure in your pelvis?"

"Yes."

"What's the pressure like?"

"Like there's something there and I want to remove it." But it doesn't feel solid to me, not an object, more a presence. "I want to push it out."

I don't know how to describe the sensation to a man, the sensation of being invaded. My fingers curl into fists. I want it out!

"You want to push out anger?" he asks.

I shake my head. My entire body is tense, my spine straight and stiff.

He stands, but makes no move toward me. "Come on, stand up. Let's push out anger."

I shake my head again, watching him warily.

His hands press next to mine—palm to palm—and melt into one another. Our flesh merges, bones and muscle woven into the same fibers …

"I know how impossible it is," he says easily, "but I want you to stand."

He takes a step towards me and I'm forced to stand to keep him from coming closer. I keep my distance, suddenly wary of him, the way prey is wary of a predator. He stands, content and easy, waiting for me. Tension rises like electricity crawling up from my toes, tingling, annoying, demanding.

I want it out! I stand a foot from him and he raises his hands, inviting me to match them. I want to push away the pressure. I want to breathe. I want to be released from the trapped feeling that's suffocating me. But I don't want him touching me. I don't want to remember.

Very slowly, I raise my hands. Cautiously, I press them to his palms …

His hands sink into mine, melding.

Immediately I pull my hands away, frantic to be separated, to have my body my own. I rub my thumb over all my fingers, verifying they remain divided, untouched.

"They didn't melt together," he says softly.

No, they didn't. I'm confused by this, and it takes me a moment to realize I'm separate from him. Slowly, I press my hand to his and push against his strength.

His big hands wrap easily around my legs, just above my knees. They're not cruel or demanding, but almost gentle in their insistence as he spreads my legs to move between them. His motions are slow and easy, the practiced maneuvers of a man all too comfortable with seduction.

I've been tricked.

"Push," he tells me, still pushing against my hands. "Push out the anger and sadness."

His weight presses me to the mattress. I don't even know how to struggle and deny him whatever it is I don't yet know he wants. It's between my legs, this object, pressing and demanding.

I want it out!

I push it away from me, using my energy and thought as a formidable barricade to keep it from coming closer. With a concentrated, final push, I'm free.

I stop pushing against his hands. My breath comes in short pants. My muscles tremble with exhaustion. Gradually, my blood slows and I realize the pressure in my pelvis and the need to push are gone. But it's a distant thought, a hollow victory. I know something now that I didn't know before.

He eases between my legs, all smiles and gentleness, an unassuming playfulness that puts me off guard.

"How do you feel?" Dr. Erickson asks.

"I don't feel the pressure," I tell him quietly.

"How's your arm?"

I sit against the darkness. The flesh on my arm is scarred and healing, as if it's been pieced together. The girl is still, no longer stabbing her leg. Anger stands at the doorway, up from the pit.

"That's good," he says, after I share my vision.

It's been a long session. I'm tired and drained, and my thoughts are turning over the new information and the change in the images.

I've missed something.

CHAPTER 34

The hotel room seemed to be the place where it all began for me, what I remembered the most from being molested. But it was really the farmhouse that set the scene. I knew that was where my nightmares had begun, horrible dreams of being chased by men with chainsaws and knives, being tied to long tree trunks and having my feet cut off with a saw.

I remembered a dream where my infant brother was being cut in two by a man who had broken into the house. Mom was lying on the couch reading her book, and I tried to shake her to get her attention so she could save my little brother. But as much as I shook her, she wouldn't take her attention away from the book, she wouldn't see that our little brother was being killed, she wouldn't do anything to stop it.

I had so many nightmares that I had taught myself how to wake up from them. If I were being chased, unable to scream or move, I would blink real fast and that would wake me. I'd wake with my heart racing in a dark bedroom with my other three sisters and pull Snowball, my stuffed white kitten, close to me and try to stay awake for the rest of the night, listening to the sounds the old house made and waiting for the light to arrive.

As I got older, and Dad stopped molesting me, the nightmares faded. But my fear never did.

April 23

The wounded arm is delicate. I can't touch it or the flesh will fall apart, so I sit in the space in my mind and I wait.

Anger won't come to me, though I stand patiently for her. There's a body in front of her that She stabs over and over. I don't know what happened to the other girl, to her. She's no longer where I left her. Maybe they integrated into one. They seem the same to me in appearance and actions.

Shame and Sorrow sit by the doorway with Sekhmet. I go to them when I seek this inner world, and I occupy time with play and chatter.

Where's the fear? I can't feel it. I can't see what happened on the bed in the hotel room and I don't search for the truth, and yet I want to know the truth. I cannot say "rape" and will my mind to remain steadfast on the path I've embarked upon, a path that's leading me to my new life.

The flesh on my arm soon begins to decay and fall off. This isn't my arm. I don't have dead things apart of me.

Again I approach Anger, who kneels in front of the body, stabbing it relentlessly. I want to understand her rage, but as I kneel in front of her she directs the knife to me, stabbing me over and over.

The room is not finished. I'm not finished.

"There's no peace inside," Dr. Erickson says casually.

I look down, trying to find comfort away from his seeking gaze. I have an image of a penis in my mind and it brings with it a twisted sense of confusion: arousal and fear, excitement and anger, curiosity and repulsion.

My flesh falls off my arm, decayed and dead.

What peace do I need to heal my arm?

"I think she's confusing things," I say. "She's confusing his fingers with a penis."

He's silent for a moment, and then says, "There are different versions of the truth. You have more than one truth. What version of the truth will help you heal?"

A version of the truth? Will finding the truth ultimately help me, or will it simply be another piece of the puzzle?

"What does it mean to have been raped?" he asks when I don't answer.

"I don't know." I struggle for words. "It's not who I am."

I think of myself as innocent and I hate it, and yet I can't think of myself as a rape victim. The word doesn't apply to me. I can't make it fit into the neatly organized structure of who I am. I am, by definition, untouched.

"That's your truth," he says. "What's her truth?"

That she was raped. I won't say it. I stare at him in defiance. I won't allow him to assign a label to me. I won't allow him to change my images. I may not know who I am, but I know who I'm not. I say nothing, staring at him with a tightly controlled expression.

"Will you accept that there's more than one truth," he says, "that she's had experiences that you haven't?"

"There can be only one truth."

"Oh?" he says, in the manner of baiting. "We deal with emotional truths: what feels real is real. You want to fill in all the blanks and know all the details before you make a decision, but that won't change what you feel, and we're working with emotions: anger and sorrow and fear. Your conscious mind is only delaying the healing process. Let your unconscious mind work for a change."

He's asking me to accept the label, to accept her. My fingers twist together. I don't want to be a part of her or her pain. I don't want to be a person who was raped.

"You can have your truth and she can have hers," he says easily.

A compromise? Or a truce?

"What's she doing inside, the little girl with the knife?" he asks. "Is she still stabbing you?"

She sits quietly, holding the knife, uncertain for the first time.

"No. She stopped. She seems ... confused."

"Good. Before knowledge comes confusion."

My thoughts wander from her to my sexual fantasy. I like practicing touch in my fantasy, but my frustration at the disruption and violence makes the practice anxious and stressful. So I've changed the fantasy.

"My fantasies are getting better," I announce suddenly, glad for a change of subject. "I had to change some things, but they're more relaxed."

"Have you been practicing with your toy?"

"No." I don't know whether I'm angry at his question or sad about my failure, but I know I don't like the question.

"How did you change your fantasy?"

I hesitate. It's not that I mind revealing my fantasy; I've become accustomed to relinquishing my privacy in this office. But I know my solution isn't a good one; it's just the old pattern of avoidance. "I ... he doesn't ... I like the touching and exploring, but ... I don't see him with a penis. I mean, it's there, but it's not there."

"It's not a part of the fantasy?"

"No." Then, guiltily, I add, "It's just because the fantasy wasn't going good the other way."

"When he had a penis?"

"Yes. So I don't see one."

"And your fantasy is still with a man?"

"Yes." It irritates me when he asks this.

"So he has a penis, but it's flaccid and hidden away, tucked in his jeans."

He's mocking me. I try to hide my embarrassment and irritation, and launch instead into an unnecessary explanation.

"It wasn't working the other way. When I tried to touch him, he got frustrated. I didn't like him standing there aroused, either, but I wanted to touch him. If I don't see it then I'm not afraid. I know he has one, I just don't see it."

The more I talk the more defensive I become, over-explaining and justifying, as if to convince myself. I can hear the desperation in my voice and don't like it, but I can't stop myself. For a moment I hear another explanation, one I've recited repeatedly over the years.

I like my life the way it is. I don't need to be married and have babies. I'm going to do something meaningful in my life and not waste years tied to a husband and family. There's nothing wrong with being celibate. People place too much importance on sex, as if it were everything in life. I don't need a relationship to define me. Women who need men are weak and desperate.

"What happens if he has a penis?" Dr. Erickson asks.

He kneels next to me. We're relaxed, kissing and touching. He moves between my legs and I can feel a sense of urgency in him, a sharp shift in his emotions, from tender and gentle to demanding and forceful. He no longer hears me. He no longer sees me. I don't exist.

"It changes him," I say quietly. "I don't like that men change."

"There's a physiological change during arousal," Dr. Erickson tells me. "Respirations increase, senses are heightened, there's a concentrated need and it can be intense."

"I don't mean change that way," I say. "He changes into a different person." Silence.

"You don't see the same person in front of you anymore?"

"No." I'm irritated and frustrated because Dr. Erickson isn't following my images. "He goes from being tender and caring to being mean. He's not nice anymore."

"So when a man is aroused he becomes mean?"

I can hear the trap being set. He's leading me somewhere, but my thoughts are too distracted with the images for me to be cautious. "Yes."

He nods slowly.

I take a deep breath. "I know that doesn't sound reasonable, but … that's what happens."

Maybe a man *would* be nice during sex, but it isn't what I see. I see and feel a complete change, as if an entirely different person takes his place. That sense of change makes me distrust him. He'll be nice until he doesn't get what he wants. I don't know what to do with that thought, since it interferes with my goal, so I change the subject.

"I remembered something," I tell Dr. Erickson. "I have this memory of being pulled toward my father. He's sitting on the edge of the bed, pulling me toward his lap. I can't get that image out of my head."

"Are you ready to work?"

I nod.

"What are you feeling in this memory?"

"Anxious, like I want to get away."

"Where do you feel that in your body?"

"My pelvis, but it's everywhere inside here." I motion to my middle. Every muscle and nerve is poised to flee. I feel the overwhelming need to back away, as if I were being forced toward an open flame. The danger and fear are palpable. "I want to get away."

"If I grip your arms and pull, will that be enough to release the memory?"

"Maybe." I hate bodywork. I don't like Dr. Erickson's hands on me and I don't like the release of the memory. This type of work makes it impossible to remain detached. Like sinking into a whirlpool, I'm caught in a flow of memories that are too powerful for me to resist.

"We can try EMDR," he says. "But experience has shown that you respond better to the physical exercise. The choice is yours."

I don't like EMDR any better than I like bodywork. The memory is trapping me and I want to be free, and, as always, I want the fastest resolution. I choose bodywork.

"Let's set our intentions," he says.

"Intentions?"

"What you want from this exercise."

He folds his hands together, resting his arms on his knees. I can see his eyes lose focus as he stares at the floor. He's deep in thought and I ... I'm uncertain, I don't know what my intentions are: to make the memory disappear? To prove that nothing happened? To eliminate the disturbing sensations the memory brings?

He stands and I follow slowly, still uncertain and having no intention of my own.

"How was he holding onto your arms?" Dr. Erickson asks.

I demonstrate, gripping his bicep. "He has both hands on my arms, holding me in place and pulling me toward him."

He nods and sets himself. "Think about the memory, think about what you're feeling."

His hands grip my arms ...

My father is naked, sitting on the edge of the bed. I stand obediently in front of him. His hands are wrapped securely around my tiny arms. The smell of freshly washed bodies permeates the air. I can't see it, but I know his penis is there ... waiting.

I pull back from Dr. Erickson, shaking my head. My right hand moves to his hand on my arm, intent on removing it, but the moment my fingers touch his, I pull back. I can't touch him and I'm not strong enough to pull free.

My hands find his forearms, giving my fingers something to grip.

Let go! Let go!

He tugs sharply ...

My legs straddle my father as he pulls me close, positioning me on his lap. His skin is warm from the bath and I can feel the heat radiating from him. My toes stretch to keep contact with the carpet as I lose balance and am forced onto his lap.

"It's all right," Dr. Erickson says quietly. "Let go."

I want to stay in the office and away from the memory that I'm being pulled toward. My fingers sink into Doctor Erickson's arm in an attempt to anchor myself, but I won't look at him. He's too close, just inches from me. I want to put my hands on his chest and push him away, but he's caught my arms.

"It's all right," he whispers.

My toes float above the floor. My arms are caught and I'm pulled toward him, toward … it.

My breath catches in my throat. I move my body as far away as I can, but I'm still held within the restriction of his grip. I pull my hips away from him, keeping myself safe.

I can only sense father's nakedness, his desire. I'm intensely aware that we're naked and alone, and I'm powerless. I slide down toward his belly …

Dr. Erickson is no longer holding me, and yet I haven't moved away from him. I stand there, stunned and thoughtful. Time has slipped past again. I can feel the dark space between us, those lost moments that leave me bewildered.

"What's the lesson?" he asks softly.

"Lesson?" My mind is numb.

"The golden thread in the center of all of this. The single thing you can take away."

The lesson: "Penises hurt people." The words sound strange and alien to my ears. I regret them the moment they leave my lips and echo in the small office. Once spoken, I cannot retract them. Now Dr. Erickson has heard my thoughts and knows my fear.

"Okay," he says quietly and moves to sit.

Penises hurt people? Where did that thought come from, and why on earth did I feel compelled to say it aloud? It doesn't even make sense. Or does it? On some obscure level, I know it's true. There's a part of me that fears a penis, an embedded terror that keeps me from an intimate relationship. This fact I cannot argue with, but I'm smart enough to know that I can explain it.

People fear the unknown. My inability to have a sexual relationship could be nothing more than a healthy and normal fear of uncharted territory. Or perhaps I've simply allowed my imagination to run unchecked after years of misinformation and contradictory facts.

Penises hurt people.

I suspend my thoughts as I hear the words again. I realize something very important: it feels like the truth. What does that mean for me? Where do I go from here?

"That's good information," he says, watching me. "How does your arm look?"

I sit quietly in the darkness. The flesh on my arm is pieced together and healing.

CHAPTER 35

In 1998, when Pleasing Sister and I purchased land to build our home, we had just begun to clear the land when Second Brother came to stay with us for a bit. He was getting divorced and needed a place to stay. His two sons were with their mother, and he missed them.

"Being a father is a lot of work," he said. "You have to do things with them and teach them things. I didn't know how to be a father. Dad never wanted anything to do with me. He basically ignored me."

"But you do lots of things with your boys," I told him. "Every time I call your house you're with them, out fishing or boating, or making them lunch. You're with them all the time."

Years earlier, I realized that Second Brother was a much better parent than his wife, who seemed content to leave the boys with their dad while she went shopping.

"Yeah, but I didn't learn any of that from Dad."

It took me a minute to recognize he was angry. I knew Dad had spent all his time with his daughters, but I'd never realized how that must have felt to his sons. It was Mom who went hunting night crawlers with them, and Grandpa who taught them how to scale and filet fish, and sharpen knives. Second Brother's friend's dad had taught him how to hunt, find his way out of the woods, make a fire with nothing, and live off the land.

I stared at him, as if seeing him for the first time. I'd always considered Second Brother lucky that Dad hadn't paid any attention to him. But at that time my brother hadn't known what Dad was doing with his daughters and why he wanted to be alone with us. All he knew was that his dad didn't want to be with him.

"Dad was supposed to teach me," he said, as if it were all too late.

And what lessons had Second Brother taken away from all this? He wanted to be a better father to his boys than our dad had been to him. He was trying to break the cycle.

April 29

She is down deep in the darkness, down further than I've traveled before. I know I must wake the girl who sleeps at the bottom. I can't finish this work with her unaware, and have her awaken later when I experience intimacy. That's been my fear: that stirring my sexuality will ignite emotions and memories I haven't processed, and transform the experience into one of terror that will close the door on any future attempts.

I might fantasize about intimacy and enjoy the rush of desire as my own hands stimulate pleasure in my body, but I *also* know that my fantasy is completely safe and utterly unreal. I know that a different pair of hands exploring my body would be both more exciting and more frightening. I won't have the control, and I wonder: will I be able to let go and feel, or will fear surface and take control?

She's at the bottom in my pelvis, where my sexuality exists. I know from masturbation that I haven't yet learned to let go, that there's still a sexual part of me I haven't connected with; there's a raw and unpredictable woman/child who freely expresses her desires without guilt or consequences. No thoughts. Just feelings.

I always imagined myself with the potential to be unconventional with regard to sex. I imagined exploring and experimenting without boundaries, expressing without shame: a wild woman designed for pleasure.

I want to know that woman.

I fall through layers of darkness into the center of my spirit world. I can barely see her. She's curled at the bottom like a child who is tired from play and lies down to rest. As I stand by her and will her to wake, she stirs. Do I hold her? Do I rescue her from the pit and bring her to the temple?

She moves to the soft, black walls as if they have called to her. She doesn't seem to see me or be aware of my presence. I watch as her face contorts with anger. In deliberate motions, she stretches her arms out as if she's reaching for something on the wall, and drags her fingers across the delicate fiber, ripping open the wall like a cat clawing at paper. She screams and kicks and claws, venting her rage on the pit.

The walls bleed and I retreat.

For days I watch her rage, tearing at the walls and digging into the softness like an insane person driven to escape. I keep myself distant from it and can only see her if I turn my thoughts inside.

Another thought distracts me. I'm still trying to answer the question of what having been raped makes me. I want to know the truth, because the truth will define me. And I still think the girl is confusing fingers with a penis. All the memories and images are jumbled, and my fear can't be what I think it is.

As I struggle to sort through the truth, an idea emerges from my turmoil: a test to determine what's real. I see the test in my mind, playing like a well-scripted movie.

I jump from a high place and fall through the air. I hit the ground. The impact doesn't stun me, even though I strike the ground with force. I take a breath, then get up and walk away as if nothing happened: not the fall; not my life.

This is the test: to know or not to know. If I jump and walk away from the fall, then all I remember is not real. It's just another movie set on the stage of my imagination. But what if I don't walk away? What if I hit the ground and stay, a pile of broken bones and torn flesh?

All my visions of falling … have they been nothing more than a twisted version of some unconscious desire?

Sitting in Dr. Erickson's office and sorting my thoughts, I think: I don't know what I am, victim or narrator.

"She wants something," I tell him, after explaining my journey to wake the girl.

"What does she want?"

"To give me something."

Her scratching and digging have uncovered what she wants, something that fits in her hands and is covered with black mud.

"What is it she carries?"

The mud falls off and a mason jar is revealed.

"What's in the jar?" he asks.

Three tiny lights. They glow and move, bouncing against the glass.

"Like fireflies," I tell him. "When I was a little girl, we used go outside at night and catch fireflies and put them in a jar. But these are different from fireflies; they're like … spirits or something."

"What do you want to do with these lights?"

The temple is empty except for Sekhmet, who has taken a position near the base of the highest altar. In the darkness, she waits, holding her knife still. Near her are the others and I realize there's a light for each girl.

"They're supposed to go to the girls."

"Can you do that?"

I unscrew the cover of the jar and remove it. The lights fly up out of the pit and find each girl.

"What is the little girl doing now?"

"She's standing next to me."

"She isn't scratching and kicking?"

"No."

"How do the walls look?"

The tears and gouges are sealed over. I can see the faint scars from her enraged frenzy, but they too are healing.

"Do you want to bring her out of that place?" he asks.

"Yes." I don't want her there any more, a forgotten resident of my sexuality.

"Let's clean the area first." His voice changes in pitch and tone, lowering to a velvety smooth tempo that runs through me like water. "Let the healing white light cover the sides and bathe them. As the white light covers the walls, you'll notice the scars heal until you can't see them any longer. The walls are new and untouched." Pause. "Are you ready to take the little girl out of there?"

I stand in the center of darkness. The healing white light slowly cleans the walls until they're black and flawless. The little girl stands next to me, waiting.

"Yes." My voice is heavy and slow to respond.

"Can you bring her to the temple with Sekhmet?"

Sekhmet likes to guard the girls. They're all in the temple now, except for the adult version of me, who still falls from high above, rushing to the ground with joyful anticipation. How I love to fall: the rush of air and no boundaries, just freedom.

"Do you want to integrate with her?"

I nod. She is my sexuality, my passion: the wild woman.

"You can dissolve into smoke with her," he says in his silky voice. "Or you can melt into liquid together. Or you can pull her into yourself."

She's small but determined, with an air of stubbornness and an attractive indifference to rules. Standing in front of me, I want to pull her into me, but I find myself in the temple on the pallet. She's at the foot of the pallet with Sekhmet.

We both slowly dissolve into tiny particles that look like smoke, and they float above the temple, mingling together in a mass. Gradually, the particles return to the pallet and I'm alone with Sekhmet ... and the small girl is a part of me.

"How do you feel?" he asks.

I can hear his voice, but it takes a long time for my brain to make my tongue work. "Fine."

Long minutes of silence stretch past us as I gradually come back to the office. The heavy darkness is no longer a part of me and I feel like a weight has lifted from me. I am light ... light enough to fall gently through the air.

Dr. Erickson is staring at me with a quizzical, almost amused expression, as if he has also made a return journey from the same places I have been.

"Things are changed," I say, even though I don't fully understand what I mean. My vague words are dragged up from deep inside, an unassigned emotion expressed as an incomplete thought.

He nods, but I sense it more than see it. He's only as much a part of the room as I will allow him to be.

"She's a part of you now," he says quietly, in tones of understanding and guidance. "Everything that she had, you now have: her memories and feelings, her desires and fears, her beliefs. Take what's of value and build on it, and accept the rest without judgment."

I'm not thinking of a little girl sleeping in the bottom of my pelvis. I'm thinking of the sexuality that has been dormant in me all these years, the longing and desire that I have never been able to manifest beyond a fantasy. This brings me a step closer to my goal, and I imagine, again, what it would be like to be in a man's arms, free and uninhibited.

The idea makes me feel primal and untamed, but at the same time uncertain and fearful. For the first time, I wonder: is it sex I fear, or intimacy?

Dr. Erickson is watching me carefully, studying me in his quiet manner.

"I'm thinking about what it would be like to be with a man," I say without looking at him.

My fantasies are still broken and incomplete. Like a movie with skips in the film, my sexual fantasy plays out without me connecting to the emotions, the arousal of touch, and the rush of orgasm. It is, in many ways, a task-driven fantasy that's more goal-oriented than emotionally motivated.

"Thinking about your fantasy?"

"No."

"Thinking about real life," he says, nodding. "You have to be out with people to meet this man."

"I know."

I've been at home this past year, having taken a year off from work to complete therapy. That hasn't given me many opportunities to meet people. His words remind me that therapy is the journey, not the destination. I'm going to have to test the boundaries of what I've learned these past months.

"Have you set your parameters of what you will or will not do?" he asks.

I look at him in confusion. Will or will not do?

"If you can set parameters now, it'll be easier to know where your boundaries are when you start dating." Pause. "Will you kiss him on the first date?"

"No," I say, scowling. I don't like my answer. "I don't know him. I can't know somebody in three hours."

"When will you sleep with him? Second date? Third date?"

"I don't know. Later."

"A week later, a month?"

"Later, when I'm comfortable and feel safe." His questioning makes me anxious. I hadn't thought about these parameters. I've spent my adult life trying to keep men away, and now I have to think about inviting them near ... and the risk of being hurt. "I have to feel safe first."

"How will you know he's safe?"

What a terrible question. It chills me on the inside. I don't like to think about the million things that can go wrong, the national statistics that have one in three women being raped, that sixty-five percent of all assaults are committed by someone known to the victim.

"There are some things that you can do to minimize the risks," he says, studying me from his place. "Pay attention to how he acts.

If you're ordering dinner and you say no to wine, but your date tells the waiter, 'The lady will have wine,' that's a sign. If he doesn't hear your 'no' at dinner, he won't hear your 'no' later. If he talks about his penis in the third person, then he's dissociated from it and he won't take responsibility for it."

I have no idea how I'm going to uncover that piece of information during a dinner conversation, but it gives me something new to worry about. I've been concentrating on my inability to have sex, and I've completely forgotten about the intricacies and layers in a relationship: getting the signals straight, establishing boundaries, and practicing mutual respect.

As Dr. Erickson continues his monologue on helpful dating hints, I suddenly realize my goal seems enormous and unattainable. What am I thinking? There are too many variables to effectively measure the risks and rewards, to ensure the joy and fulfillment I'm setting out to achieve.

My mind spins with thoughts of failure and danger, and I can feel a kind of storm gathering inside, a rising of emotions I haven't felt in months. I'm about to take the biggest risk of my life. I'm about to step out of my cage.

"Do you have any questions about sex that I haven't answered?" he asks, catching my attention again.

Only about a hundred and fifty. I can't bring myself to respond to his question; my thoughts are suddenly polarized as I realize: I guess I'm finished with therapy.

How did that happen?

He must think I'm ready since we're talking about functions and parameters and timetables, but I don't feel ready. He'll give me a few last-minute tips on the mechanics of sex and send me on my way. I've only just started massage therapy and I'm trying to get accustomed to touch without jumping out of my skin, or freezing in fear.

What if, when a man gets close to me and wants intimacy, I freeze again or dissociate? What if I can't be aroused by his touch?

"Do we need to talk about safe sex?" he asks, scrutinizing me. "You said you don't want to have a baby, so you should consider birth control, but that won't protect you from sexually transmitted diseases. Even if you both get tested, condoms are a good idea. There's a variety to choose from, but some of them you can't use a lubricant with because it tears the condom. You want to be careful about what type you purchase. You can practice putting them on your toy so you don't have any awkward or embarrassing moments during sex, although putting them on your lover can be a form of foreplay."

My gaze drifts in the room. Having never had sex, I hadn't considered condoms. They're not a part of my fantasy any more than they are a part of my reality. I follow his voice, trying to conjure images from his words.

"Condoms aren't one-hundred-percent effective for birth control," he continues. "Using a spermicide with the condom will be more protection, but it can have an odor. It might be a good idea to buy some just so you can get used to the smell."

I have no idea where to buy condoms, much less a spermicide, and from what he just described I don't want to buy any of them.

I try to slow the thoughts that are spinning around in my head, twisting my insides, but I can't. I'm on a fast-moving train with no way off. He's miles ahead of me, plowing forward into an uncharted territory, I suddenly realize how much I don't know, and how Dr. Erickson's experience is as natural to him as breathing.

Where will I be? Stumbling through a first try at the age of forty and trying to find my place in my lover's arms.

Wait, wait, I want shout. *You're going too fast.*

And then I think: I am the one going too slow.

CHAPTER 36

My fourth-grade classmates and I raced out of school when the bell rang. St. Robert's was a middle school, so only those of my siblings closest in age attended. My older siblings were in a Catholic high school. The big yellow bus would stop at the middle school first, and my siblings and I would pile in and rush to the back of the empty bus until the high school kids arrived and kicked us to the front.

Whatever friends we made were only school friends. Because we lived in the country, we had to get on the bus right after school and never had the chance to do extracurricular activities, or wander to other children's houses for an afternoon of playing. Our playmates, as always, were each other.

School had just started, but that summer Dad had bought us baby ducks. We'd rescued an abandoned nest of swallows and tried to handfeed them to keep them alive. We caught flies, mashed them up and pushed them down the waiting open beaks. One by one they died.

We buried them in the field with a proper ceremony, marking the site with a homemade cross we constructed out of broken branches. When we got back to the house, Mom comforted us with oatmeal cookies.

It was Dad who had the ultimate solution.

"Tomorrow we're going to get you some baby ducks," he said. "You can take care of them."

Dad wasn't working. He'd had a bleeding ulcer earlier that year and was convinced his life was too stressful to work. Mom had agreed. So, while she worked as a clerk for the county, Dad took us to a tiny pet store that sold baby ducks.

Each one of us eagerly scooped up a baby duck, claiming it as our own. I chose a black duckling and named him Soots. My three siblings chose yellow mallards. I liked the darkness of the baby duck and quickly pressed him to my cheek, promising to love him forever.

Mom was incredibly accommodating when we brought the ducklings into the house every night to rest in boxes by our beds. Eventually they grew too big for the boxes and we had to leave them out on the screened-in porch. I think by that stage Mom had given up trying to keep animals out of the house and had learned to compromise.

When the bus let us off in front of the old farmhouse, the ducks would be waiting for us. The bus driver thought this was funny, and liked to tell the story to the teachers at school while he waited for the bus to fill.

One day when we came home from school the ducks weren't there. We looked everywhere for them, calling their names. When Pleasing Sister came home she drove us up and down the deserted road. As the sun began to set, we returned home crying, upset that someone had stolen our ducks.

Just as dinner was being served, I looked out the window and saw all four ducks walking up the tracker trail from the creek.

"There they are!" I screamed.

We held them tightly in our arms and scolded them for scaring us. We wanted to lock them up to keep them from leaving, but Dad forbade it.

"Ducks like to fly and swim," he said. "They'll come back if they want to. You can't keep them locked up just because you want it."

We let them roam, but I didn't like it. I wanted to keep them caged so I'd know they were safe.

April 30

I entered therapy to be at choice and I feel I've accomplished that goal. I no longer think hands will hurt me, or that touch is bad, or being in a relationship means you're weak. I can now imagine allowing a man to touch me. I can even enjoy the fantasy, but I can't ignore that I haven't truly accomplished my goal of being able to share intimacy.

I realize there's only so far therapy can take me. My fear of men is equally as strong as my desire for pleasure. I still have fear of a penis, and my broken fantasies, which I now see are a product of my own lack of experience in the right area.

I think of the dozens of things I don't know about intimacy, and I begin to cry. With my tears comes the critical voice: *You're never going to have it.*

I'm afraid of failing, afraid of getting close to a man and having the same reaction I've had these past twenty years, afraid of not being able to be aroused by his touch, afraid of my inadequacy as a woman. All that fear and uncertainty leads to failure. And failure leads to sorrow.

Today I feel as if I will never be able to have my goal. I stay with the sorrow until I realize I'm in the bottom of a pit. Self-talk and reassurance fails. Something is wrong.

In desperation, I decide to call Dr. Erickson. It will be the first time I've ever called him outside of our scheduled appointments, and I wait as long as I can, hoping the sorrow and depression will fade. It does not.

"Something's wrong," I begin. "I wanted to talk to you."

"Okay."

"I've been sad today … crying. I was thinking about yesterday; our conversation about sex upset me. I don't know how to do some of those things, but I wasn't thinking about that, only about touch." I take a breath. "I didn't know I was supposed to put the condom on the man."

"Do you want an answer to that?"

"Yes," I say, without enthusiasm.

"You don't have to put the condom on the man. He can do that. It can be a form of foreplay, but it doesn't have to be. It's the responsibility of both of you to ensure protection, but you can ask him to take care of that."

Silence. I study his words.

"There are a lot of things I don't know and haven't thought of before," I say finally. "I'm not experienced, and I don't want to go into a relationship not knowing how to please him."

"You have the experience," he says. "You just don't have the education."

If his words are meant to make me feel better, they fall short.

"It's not the experience I want."

"But it's the experience you have," he says gently. "You want to know everything before it happens, but a lot of what happens during sex depends on the two people involved. It's not text book. Most people just follow the lead the first time. Instinct takes over. It's not complicated."

"But most people have sex for the first time in their teens. The boy isn't any more experienced than the girl." And I'm almost forty.

"There are books you can read that will give you a better understanding of what happens during sex. It should be a book without graphic pictures so you don't scare the little ones inside, but detailed enough for you to understand. I'll find a book that will help you if you want."

I'm not thrilled with the idea, but I can't absorb information I don't have. Somewhere inside, at some time, I'm going to have to accept that I have limited knowledge in this arena. I reluctantly agree to a book. Maybe there'll be something there that will ease my anxiety.

"It feels like I can't have my goal," I confess, knowing he's heard this from me many times before. "I feel inadequate."

"This inadequacy is taking on a life of its own," he says, almost to himself. "Where do you feel the inadequacy in your body?"

"In my pelvis."

"Are you in a quiet place right now where you can work?"

"Yes."

"I want you to think about inadequacy and the feeling in your pelvis. What images do you see?"

"I don't see an image. I hear a voice."

"What's the voice saying?"

"'You're doing it wrong.'" I can hear the deep, displeased tones. "'Not like that, like this.'"

"Are you alone?"

"No. Someone is with me." I feel a presence in front of me, kneeling. *I kneel in front of father. My hands are at my sides and I'm anxious and frustrated.*

"What are you feeling?" Dr. Erickson asks.

"Frustrated. I'm not doing it right." I can feel those words right down to my core, the desire and inability to please. "My father doesn't give me instructions. He only moves me where he wants me, so I don't know what he wants. He won't tell me how to do it right."

I feel an overwhelming need to please my father, and strong frustration at the no-win situation I've been placed in. If I just look at the memory for what it is and not judge it for what it's become, I can accept the feelings as my own.

"What's below the frustration?" Dr. Erickson asks.

"Anger." Anger at being placed in this situation that fosters emotions I can't understand: the twisted needs of a man who drags his child into a demented version of love. Isn't it enough that I love unconditionally? Isn't it enough for him to have the privilege of being a parent? What else does he want?

"What's below the anger?"

I send my mind down into the darkness, past anger.

"Shame." Shame at wanting to please my father in this manner, shame at failing to please him, shame at my curiosity and eagerness to please.

"What's below shame?"

"Nothing." It is dark and solid where I stand.

"Is that the bottom?"

"Yes."

"Is anything down there with you?"

"No."

"Then you can close up the pit. You can come up from it, sewing the bottom as you move to the top. Let the healing white light put you in a protective bubble before you begin."

I follow his voice, moving up the pit and closing it as I ascend through the opening.

"Better, still a little sad." I hesitate. "It's difficult to fantasize. I'm not having sex in my fantasies. I'm still afraid of that."

"Intercourse is only one form of intimacy. You can have a pleasurable experience without intercourse. You said you were interested in oral sex. He would likely enjoy that."

"But it wouldn't be sex, and he'd be disappointed. He'd be upset we didn't have sex."

"Not if you enjoy it as well," he says calmly. "Sometimes women worry needlessly about what the man will do, how he will react, if he is going to ejaculate—"

"Will that happen?" I ask abruptly. And then I think: of course that will happen, that's a man's release and the whole purpose of masturbation for him. But I don't have an image of ejaculation in my mind. My own reference is my father putting my hands on his penis. There was no orgasm that I remember, but I know now from my own masturbation that orgasm was imminent.

"Men are pretty goal oriented," Dr. Erickson explains casually. "That's probably going to be the desired outcome for him."

If I can feel satisfaction at orgasm, even self-manipulated, wouldn't he?

"What do you do next?" he asks.

"He wants to have sex, only I can't get to the sex part of the fantasy. I can't make that work. Everything is fine, but then he wants to have sex and I start to cry."

"Why do you cry?"

"Because he wants to and I can't."

"Why can't you?"

"Because … because I don't want to. I'm afraid of him. I don't want him near me. I don't like that he's changed." Suddenly becoming demanding and impatient with his erection. "I don't think men should change."

Silence.

"So we have some work to do on your phobia," he says calmly. "And you need to have a more realistic understanding of sex. Remember, you're living by committee. You need to take care of the concerns of everyone inside when you think about making changes. There are some little ones inside who still fear sex and men. You need to let them know that their concerns are being heard."

I don't like living by committee and asking permission for my life.

"I want shorter goals. The one goal is too big now."

"Okay, we can do shorter goals," he says. "We can have a week-goal or a month-goal. Think about what you want and a timeframe. Shorter goals sometimes seem more manageable."

"Yes, I want shorter goals. That will make me feel less stressed."

I don't like to fail. I can accomplish smaller goals. I'll educate myself on sex so I can feel less inadequate. I'll work on my fear and completing my fantasy. I'll think more about the gentleness of touch, the pleasure of sex and two people sharing.

I will have my goal.

I will change my life, with or without a committee.

CHAPTER 37

I was twenty-eight years old when I gave up dating. I remember that last date. He was slightly taller than me, a runner. A woman from work had introduced us, thinking we would make a good couple. I didn't get asked out very often and so I said yes.

I bought a pair of black lace panties and matching bra for the date. I prepared with precision and ceremony, waiting anxiously for the time for him to arrive. That afternoon I had fantasied about him coming in the house and us making love on the bed.

He took me to a restaurant on the river and I made awkward conversation. He said I was pretty, and he wanted to hold my hand as we walked along the riverfront. His palms were sweaty and I didn't like the touch, but I disciplined myself to hold still and pretended that I enjoyed it.

After the date, we stopped at my door and he pulled me close for a kiss. I'd never been comfortable kissing. I wasn't sure what to do, how long to linger. My inexperience probably screamed at him. I pulled away self-consciously.

"Can I come in?" he asked.

"You'd better not," I said, pushing him away with a hand planted firmly on his chest. My insides were tight and I just wanted to get away.

"Can I see you again?" He was holding my hands and staring kind of moon-eyed at me. I smiled. "We'll see."

Big surprise, he never called back.

May 6

I force the fantasy to finish the way I want, disciplining my mind against my fears. I examine the toy, trying to lessen the anxiety the sight of it gives me, and trying to manufacture the excitement I'm sure other women must feel.

Over it all, like a transparent film, is an image of the hotel room: that girl on the bed and my overpowering sense of suffocation. I'm not finished with the room.

I'm plagued by the idea of a test to determine if my memory is real. In the past weeks, the urge to fall is more persistent, and so is my desire to know who I am. The closer I come to the hotel room, the stronger my resistance is to the memory of my father lying on top of me, of the sense of invasion that still doesn't bring with it any details or images to support the impression.

My only hope is my stubborn refusal to believe that my phobia is anything more than a fabricated fear, contorted and transformed through the years. It's my inexperience that has manifested this fear, a natural panic of the unknown. It's nothing more than that.

I will not allow it to be anything more than natural resistance.

And yet I can't seem to resolve the memory or to accept what I don't know about what happened. And I can't ignore the sensations and emotions that are stronger than my need to forget.

Dr. Erickson sits silent in his chair. He stares at me, studying me as if he's seeing me for the first time. I'm staring at the narrow window next to him.

Go out the window!

I'm crouched on the open windowsill, looking down. The ground is a long way down but I'm unafraid. I jump like a child jumping into the arms of a waiting parent. My body rushes down and makes hard impact with the ground.

I pick myself up and walk away, walking into a new life.

"I don't feel good today," I tell Dr. Erickson.

It's difficult to breathe. The air in the room is heavy and I can feel my heart pounding rapidly, thumping with great force against the wall of my chest. My body is leaden and yet I'm restless, wanting to escape my skin.

All week I've had the desire to jump to the ground from a high place. The constant images of falling and rushing toward the ground persist in my waking consciousness. I'm not sleeping well at night as I fight off the urge to jump, and am haunted by images of the hotel room that stand stubbornly in my path.

As I wrestle with the hotel room and the confusion inside, I wonder again: what is real?

I know I was molested, but I won't let that define my life. She confuses fingers with a penis. Even as I say it, I know it's a lie. The suffocating feeling on the bed, the sense of invasion … all the images and sensations are moving together, ready to collide.

But there is a truth in the lie: my father never had sex with any of my sisters. He would not have had sex with me. I try to convince myself of the truth of this.

"Are you nervous about working the hotel room?" Dr. Erickson asks.

His voice seems far away. I can barely hear him. Blood rushes noisily in my ears.

Go out the window!

The ground is a long way down, but I'm unafraid. I jump like a child jumping into the arms of a waiting parent. My body rushes down and makes hard impact with the ground.

I can hear Dr. Erickson's voice, but I don't understand his words. I have a sense of him asking questions, waiting …

"I don't want to talk about this." My words are forced. It's difficult to make my tongue work. I shake my head. I want to stay away from the hotel room and the bed, and I want to stay away from the window. I grip the arms of the chair to anchor myself.

"I'm just here as a tool," he says easily. "It's your choice to keep things the way they are."

Go out the window!

I don't want to know the truth. I can't breathe. My heart hammers against my chest, but all I hear is the rush of blood in my ears. The room fades to shadows of gray.

"Are you in flashback?" Dr. Erickson asks suddenly, but his voice doesn't sound alarmed.

My insides feel as if they're going to explode. The fragile container of my body can't hold the energy inside. My fingers touch the sharp edges of the blinds. I'm standing at the window, looking down, but the office is only on the third floor and the ground is closer than what my vision recalls.

"It's not a good test."

"What test?" His eyes sharpen.

I feel his gaze on me, intense and searching. I don't know how I got here and I don't want to tell him that I want to jump out the window. But I so desperately do. It's the only way to know the truth.

Go out the window!

My fingers are on the sill, itching for freedom. My body rushes down and makes hard impact with the ground. I pick myself up and walk away, walking into a new life.

I'm so tired. The weight of the past months has settled on my shoulders like an anvil. I want to be boundless and weightless, to float through the air …

"A test to see if it's real." I have trouble pushing the words past my lips. I want to see if I'm real. My head is pounding with the rush of blood.

There's too much *in* me, too much for my body to hold. How simple it would be to let go and fall.

"I jump, and if I walk away then what I remember isn't real. If I don't walk away then it's real." Either way I would be free.

"That's a no-win test," he says flatly. "It's like the tests they gave people they thought were witches; if they drowned then they weren't witches, but either way they were dead."

Witches?

Go out the window!

If I walk away from the fall it would prove I've been imagining what my father did, what I think he did. If I fall and don't walk away, then I haven't been imagining the suffocation and the idea that's forming beneath these sensations of invasion.

I'm sitting in my chair and the window is across the room, and I wonder if I never left.

"If you want to jump, jump off the desk," Dr. Erickson suggests casually.

I shake my head.

"Is jumping out this window far enough?" he asks.

I shake my head again.

"Then you're talking a significant distance. If you don't die from the fall you could break your legs, or become paralyzed. Think about your life if you were paralyzed and couldn't feel below your waist."

His words are empty and meaningless to me.

Go out the window!

"What happens when you hit the ground?" he asks. His eyes never waver and there's a stillness in him that settles the room.

"I walk away."

Silence.

"Do you jump onto concrete or grass?"

"Grass. I walk away into a field. It's like walking into another life."

"In shamanism, when you journey you jump into different worlds. But what you're talking about is real. Shaman journeys are journeys of the soul."

It's like a new life, like starting over.

A shaman journey? My thoughts focus on his words. He's so calm and insistent, so certain of himself that I wonder if maybe I'm the one confused. I remember that when I do work inside, it's real on a spiritual plane: a place without physical restraints, where a body is unnecessary. I suddenly realize how dangerous my thoughts are, how irreversible they could be.

All four girls sit quietly by the door, which is still guarded by Sekhmet.

"I want my spirit death," I tell him.

"I think that's a good idea."

I don't want there to be any more people inside. I want the quiet peace of being free. I want that new life.

"Gather up who you need to gather and go to the temple," he tells me. "Ask Sekhmet if she'll help you."

We're in the temple. As we've done before, we melt into pools of silver liquid. Slowly, the separate pools merge into a single puddle of quicksilver. The liquid shimmers as it moves. I emerge from the pool, first my head, and then, like a phoenix rising, the rest of me, until the liquid is transformed into my body. I stand naked and alone on the polished floor, with Sekhmet as my witness.

Air presses against me, fills my lungs. I am ever so reluctant to leave the temple and the peace I've found, but I breathe and shiver, and slowly, by degrees, the temple fades. The office is smaller than I remember, the air cooler. And the window? It seems far way away; a distant thought that no longer has meaning.

My hands feel strange as I exercise my fingers, pressing them into the hard arms of the chair. It has become a familiar way of anchoring me, of connecting to the materials that surround me.

"Take your time to see the room," Dr. Erickson instructs me. "Notice the lighting and hear the sound of the traffic. Bring your body all the way back to the present."

No longer in the temple and not completely in the office, I vacillate between two realities.

"It's empty inside," I say softly. "There isn't anyone there."

The temple is deserted except for Sekhmet. The girls aren't where I left them.

"They're a part of you now," he says softly.

All the spaces in my mind are dark and empty, the corners vacant, the places where they reside abandoned.

"They've been there for so long," I say. "It's strange not to see them."

"How does that feel?"

I wait for the emptiness to feel lonely, but it doesn't. I have a strange sense of completion that doesn't equate to the crowded feeling I had at my first integration.

"Nice," I say quietly.

"And the image of jumping, the test, do you see that?"

"No."

"You don't want to do the test anymore?"

"No."

There's no image of jumping and falling, nothing to guide me for now. Suddenly I'm afraid of the dark space in my mind, the lack of direction, and I wonder: is this healing or is this punishment?

It seems important that I find a bridge between the here and now and my future, and that bridge is my fantasy, which is quickly becoming a foretelling. If I can't fantasize being intimate with a man, how am I ever going to be able to experience it in reality? Is all my work nothing more than pretty wrapping on a broken present?

I can make the voices and the images go away, but will that give me what I want: freedom to live in fulfillment and joy?

CHAPTER 38

In 1933, when Dad was abandoned with his four-year-old brother on the steps of the Milwaukee church, the Great Depression was in full swing. There was a small note attached to Dad's older brother's blanket, asking the nuns to take care of the two boys. The nuns christened Dad Eugene Cannon Law. We never knew who had abandoned them, or why, but the boys were obviously Greek.

I had read that during the Great Depression, more than 1.5 million women were abandoned by their husbands. I imagined my father's mother, a desperate woman who had been abandoned by her husband, with no family, foreign, unable to feed her children. Not knowing what else to do, she had put her children in the best place she could think of, a place where they would be fed and looked after.

Dad spent four years in the orphanage, and in an attempt to get people to adopt the children they featured my father in the Milwaukee paper. The old newspaper clipping we had showed him in short pants, standing in the orphanage, looking cute with his dark hair and wool clothes. In the photograph he is holding a small stuffy bunny, a gift from the nuns and the only possession he owned.

There was a short write-up about him, which prompted contact from Joseph and Edith Peltier, an older, childless couple from Nekoosa.

My dad rarely spoke fondly of his childhood with his adoptive parents, or spoke of it at all. He told us snippets of stories that made me cringe. His best memories, he confessed, were of the weeks he spent at his cousin's farm. Those were rare, happy days of running free and being able to play with others.

"My aunt would make Swedish pancakes every Sunday morning," he told us, "and we'd all gather around the table and eat as much as we wanted."

Dad's mother never let him talk at the table. He had to sit still and finish his meal, waiting to be dismissed. He never spoke of loneliness and rejection, but I could feel it in the stories he told sparingly. I think he wanted to forget his childhood. When Grandma and Grandpa died, they left all their money to their grandchildren, pointedly excluding Dad. Even in death they couldn't show him he mattered to them.

I often wondered what my childhood would have been like if Dad hadn't been abandoned, or if he'd had better parents, who were more tolerant and nurturing. I learned from this how our parents impacted our beliefs and shaped our lives.

Would my father have molested us if he had been loved?

Or was it in his DNA, or some past-life karma he carried around? Were we doomed from the start?

May 23

I practice my fantasy; explore my lover's willingness and my comfort. I discover that if he doesn't move, I enjoy it more. As I explore and experiment within the framework of my imagination, leading my fantasy man to my ultimate surrender, I experience another shift.

I have this strange fear that Dr. Erickson is trying to hurt me. It's an image, really, that breathes life into the fear.

Dr. Erickson puts his hands on my knees as if we were doing the counter-pressure exercise, only his fingers are wrapped around my knees. At first his grip is gentle and undemanding, but then it tightens into a crushing hold. As quickly, he changes, is now focused and determined to pry my legs open. He's trying to force my legs apart, and I struggle against his strength to keep them closed.

"Your fantasies are better?" Dr. Erickson asks.

"Yes. It works much better this way. I still can't get to the having sex part, but I like how things are going. It's nice." I pause. "I'm practicing with my affirmations and that makes me feel good."

"Are you still using the same affirmations, or have you changed them?"

"I've added some more. I like that I can express my emotions safely, and I like the feminine one. I had lunch with my girlfriend the other day and she said that I was different. I asked her different how?

And she said that I seemed more open to her, more reaching and easier to be around. I guess the affirmations are working."

"You're healing." There's a small smile on his mouth.

I dip my head, not quite a nod. It doesn't feel like I'm healing.

"Affirmations can be very effective in achieving positive results in a short period of time, but you have to use them at the right time," he says. "What are we going to do today?"

"I haven't been feeling well. I've had this disturbing image of my father lying on top of me. There's all this pressure here." I put my hand on my abdomen. "I want to push away."

"What are you pushing away?"

"Something …"

My father lies on top of me and I'm still beneath his weight. If I'm quiet and still, I know I'll be fine. Don't resist, I tell myself. Surrender.

"Something happens," I say.

"Do you want to find out what?"

The hotel room … everything is always centered there on the bed. It's become an entire world to me, and still I'm not finished with it.

"Yes, I want this picture to be finished." Like the other pictures that no longer matter, dull and faded photographs that have lost their emotional punch.

"Where do you feel this memory?"

"In my pelvis. There's pain." I can feel it, like a cramping.

"Is this the hotel room?"

"Yes, but it feels different. I'm not watching all the time like before. Now it's as if I'm there on that bed."

He nods. "You've integrated, remember? Can Sekhmet be with you in the hotel room? You can process this memory in as fast as five seconds, push all the way through to the end and let the memory go."

I can see the patterns on the ceiling from the bed. I stare up at it, searching for images in the stains.

"Sekhmet is with you," Dr. Erickson reminds me from his position far away. "She'll protect you."

My father's weight crushes me to the mattress. It's difficult to breathe. He lies on me as a dead weight, content with my submission. My chest struggles to rise against his weight. There's no air.

"Stay with it," Dr. Erickson encourages me.

I shake my head. My lungs are screaming for air. I can't move the weight. I can't breathe. I'm trapped!

I take my first breath, gulping in air. I turn away. My spine is stiff against the chair and every muscle is tight.

"When you stop, you have to go back to the beginning. It takes longer to process." He pauses to study me. "What are you pushing away?"

"I can't get out of the picture." I don't want to be there. I don't want this to be me, but there's no one else it can be. "I'm feeling those things. I don't like feeling them." It's too much. They'll crush me.

"You can feel all those feelings for a few seconds," he says gently. "Feel them and let them go."

I take a breath and try again to just feel and not worry about what's happening, to not judge what I know.

My father lies on me, heavy and unmoving. I am crushed, suffocated.

My lungs paralyze. My heart pounds rapidly as my body screams for oxygen.

I can't breathe. I can't breathe.

Blood rushes to my temples. I break away from the memory and gasp desperately for air.

"I don't know how to move him off of me," I say, my chest heaving. My fingers are curled tightly into my palms. How I want to hurt something. "I can't breathe!"

"You can't move him off of you," he tells me. "Just feel the feelings."

I pound my fists softly against the chair. *I don't want to feel!*

"Will it be better if we use EMDR with this?" Dr. Erickson asks.

I focus on the wand resting near him. "Maybe."

"We can control the speed." He grabs the wand for EMDR. "You already know what to expect—that you can't breathe. Just push through to the end."

I follow the wand …

I still can't breathe. The weight on me compresses my chest. I don't like what my father is doing.

"I don't feel well."

"Stay with it," he says gently as I follow the wand.

I don't like what he's doing.

"I don't feel well." Nausea rises in warning. Where am I? "I don't want to be here."

"The way out is through."

Suddenly, my father's penis nudges my vagina and I'm confused. What is that? Pain! Astonishment.

All of a sudden I'm in a field of beautiful flowers and the little girl is by my side. The rolling hills are topped with bobbing flowers. The sky is clear and blue. The air is clean and fresh. I want to run and play, my heart filled with happiness.

"What happened?" Dr. Erickson's eyes are fixed on me.

The motion of the wand has stopped. The field fades.

"I felt something … nudging my vagina. Then I felt pain and … utter astonishment. And then I was in a field of beautiful flowers." I liked the field. It reminded me of running through the daisies as a little girl.

"Are you alone?"

"No. The little girl is with me."

"Is Sekhmet with you?"

"She's behind us."

I'm staring at the floor, still partially in the memory that's too new and alien for me to feel comfortable. I like the field of flowers and I concentrate on the image, feeling a joy inside. And then my mind shifts to another picture.

A little girl is in the potting shed. In front of her is a large Mason jar filled with plant food. The pale blue-green liquid catches the sunlight streaming through the dirty windows.

"Does she drink the poison?" he asks.

"I don't know. I can only see the poison and I know she doesn't want to live, but she's worried about her family finding her. She doesn't know where she can go and die where they won't find her."

"Is Sekhmet with her?"

"I feel like someone is with her, but I don't know who. I'm not sure what happens to her."

"Is this a memory after the hotel room?"

"Yes, but close to it. I remember the house with the potting shed and I'm only eleven years old or so."

"Stay with this memory," he says, and begins EMDR.

"I only see the jar of poison." My voice is hypnotic as I follow the rhythm of the wand. "It's just a story the girl heard about the other people who lived in the house before her, how they killed themselves by drinking plant food."

The jar is large for her small hands. It sits on the table with the broken pots. She wants to disappear, and the jar of liquid beckons.

"She doesn't want to live."

His penis nudges my vagina. Confusion. Pain. Astonishment.

The timeline on the board all those months ago … the beginning and the ending …

'Did she die?' he asks me.

'Someone died.' Murder. "I think that's sad," I say softly.

"I think that's sad, too," he says, "that a child would be so hurt that she wants to crawl into herself and die."

Why would my father want to take such a beautiful girl and kill her like that?

The girl on the bed fades and appears like a flickering transparent image.

"I keep seeing the girl on the bed, but the image is wavering in and out, like I can't stay in the picture." Or maybe it's that I never left.

"Everything going in and out, wavering back and forth," he says. "The picture going in and out. The penis going in and out."

"No." My thoughts immediately slam down on his words. I don't see the penis and I don't like to think about it. It's not a part of this image

and it's not a part of me. But even as my mind denies the existence of the penis, I feel it and it makes me want to push away, to rid myself of it.

Fear and anxiety. Anger and frustration. The beginnings of panic.

"I want to push away," I announce. My voice shakes.

"You want counter-pressure?"

"Yes. I want to push."

I want to push and feel free. I can feel the pressure building in my pelvis like a powerful force fighting to be released of the confines of my physical body. Why is he doing this to me?

"There's a counter-pressure I do with my patients," Dr. Erickson says calmly. "I'put my hands on the sides of your knees and you push against them."

Dr. Erickson's hands on my knees? He's never touched my legs before. Not in reality.

"It would mean I'd have to be close to you," he warns.

What would it feel like to have his hands on my knees, to be struggling against him?

His fingers dig into the sides of my knees, bruising the soft flesh as he grapples to open my legs.

"I don't know," I say with uncertainty. The image is clear; I can already feel it.

"We can try EMDR," he suggests. "But in the past we've always had to go to bodywork in order for you to get what you need."

I don't want to leave with this nightmare inside of me, but I don't want to do the exercise he's suggesting either. I *can't* do it. My thoughts spin and dance, and my need to push intensifies. I'm trapped and immediately seek escape.

"I'll think about this," I say.

"You say that when you want to book out of here," he tells me.

I instantly deflate, my defenses shattered. We've been in therapy too long. He knows my strategies too well.

"You've always responded very well when we've incorporated counter-pressure into your body memories." His voice is gentle and edifying.

It's true. Counter-pressure has always provided me with the quickest processing to become free of a clinging memory. The exercise has always been like releasing a pent-up breath—all of a sudden I can breathe. But he's never asked to touch my legs before. He would be struggling to open my legs. I would be fighting against him. The thoughts repeat …

My stomach tightens. The metallic taste of fear at the back of my throat warns me to be cautious. What if I remember more? What if, when he touches me, I get lost in the memory? How will I get free?

His fingers dig into the sides of my knees, bruising the soft flesh as he grapples to open my legs.

I don't want to feel this. No. I can't.

"I want to think about this," I tell him again. My head is pounding and a high-pitched buzzing sounds in my ears.

"You want to leave feeling this way?" he asks. There's a strange tone to his voice, as if he's challenging me or he's disappointed.

"No."

Strong hands open my legs and a weight settles between them.

"Why do I have to do it today?" I ask, feeling cornered. "I'm tired and I want to think about this. Why can't it wait?"

"Because you're in a weakened condition and you do your best work when you're pushed," he says gently. "If you wait, in a day or two you may think this is just bullshit and not follow through."

I *will* think it's bullshit and not follow through. The pressure will be gone and the moment past.

My entire body vibrates like a tuning fork. The buzzing sound increases and I want to jump out of my skin. I don't want to stay, and I don't want to leave feeling like this. There's nowhere for me to retreat to. Even my mind provides no haven; my thoughts are whirling and disjointed.

Dr. Erickson waits patiently, watching me as I move nervously in the chair.

"Okay," I say finally, before I can change my mind.

"Okay what?" he asks.

I glare at him. "Okay, I want to do the pressure exercise."

He takes time to set up and explain. We move both our chairs to the center of the room. He's unusually close to me, and his knees are almost touching mine. His presence is oppressive and strangely electric. Nausea rises as I feel him smothering me with his proximity. He's talking, but I can only hear the buzzing in my ears. His hands are in fists just in front of my legs, and he demonstrates on his own legs how he will offer counter-pressure. He puts his fists on the sides of his knees and tries to open his legs.

I slide my hands between my legs, my vision narrowed to a pinpoint as my stomach drops. A strange pressure builds low in my pelvis.

"I'll get out of your bubble," he says, and moves away.

I can breathe and think, although my heart pounds, sending blood rushing to my ears.

"What are you thinking?" he asks quietly.

"About my father." My words are emotionless and seem to be coming from far away. "I didn't want him to do that."

"Is that why you've covered yourself?"

I realize that my hands are between my legs and I make an effort to remove them. The pressure inside is palpable and making me sick, as if something living were trying to get out of me.

"I want you to take a couple of deep breaths," he instructs me.

It's an effort, but I comply. The buzzing begins to fade. I look at him as if I'm seeing him for the first time.

"Ready to try again?" he asks after a moment. He's relentless, but oddly patient, knowing he can wait me out.

I nod and he carefully moves back into position. This time he keeps a space between us.

"I'm going to put my fists on the outside of your knees and I'm going to apply pressure. I want you to try to keep your legs open as I do this." He's studying me intensely, his hands poised.

I nod and he settles into position, putting his fists on the outside of my knees. Immediately, he uses his strength to try to close my legs.

I focus only on my knees and his hands, blocking everything else out of the room. I offer counter-pressure to his, but it feels wrong. The pressure in my pelvis grows, dropping lower.

Dr. Erickson stops and moves back. I feel his eyes on me, but I'm still focused on my knees, breathing heavily.

"That's not right," I say softly, frowning.

"What's not right?" His voice is gentle and quiet.

"It's wrong." I put my hand on my abdomen, refusing to look at him. Why hadn't I felt relief? My thoughts turn inside, and I know why. "I want to keep my legs closed, not open."

"Okay." He moves into position, but this time he puts his fists on the inside of my knees.

I feel it then—the need to kick and punch and scream.

He applies pressure, trying to open my legs, and I immediately tighten my muscles to try and keep my legs closed. I feel the pressure releasing, but I want to cry, scream in outrage. It takes all my control not to push Dr. Erickson away and kick at him. Instead I focus on trying to keep my legs closed as he continues with the pressure to force them open.

A soft gasp escapes me. I feel sweat running down my back.

He's struggling as well, against my strength. I can feel it.

And then we're free. He moves back, studying me, but I don't see him. The strange pressure inside me is gone and I feel better, despite my sadness. Time stretches as silence fills the room, and I wait, but I don't know for what. It seems as if something should happen.

"How do you feel?" he asks finally.

"Better. The pressure is gone." I can't quite make my voice strong. I feel shattered and fragile.

"Want to do it again and solidify the work?"

I nod, but I don't really want to do it again. I want to sit in the chair and disappear. I want to be numb and invisible and imaginary.

CHAPTER 39

Pleasing Sister and I began to clear the house. We filled a dumpster with objects we no longer needed, which were many. We had the uncomfortable task of splitting things up: furniture, dishes, linens. My family had always given us gifts as a couple, something I had resented for years. Dividing up our possessions became a therapeutic task in itself.

I had bought most of the furniture and other things in the house, but when I'd purchased them it had been for both of us, although Pleasing Sister had made the decisions with me. I remembered shopping at Eddie Bauer for our big comfy chairs, and selecting the wood for the handmade kitchen island.

After twenty years of living together, nothing was just mine or just hers. Somewhere along the way everything had become ours. This lack of separation both angered and saddened me. I had no idea what a life on my own would look like.

I let her choose first. She took very little and this surprised me. I had enough money to buy new things and she didn't, but I said nothing. She could be ridiculously stubborn, and with a sharp temper. When she was eight years old she threw an eraser at a nun in school. I'd once seen her throw a batch of raw piecrust across the room because it wouldn't roll out.

I wasn't sure what to do with this new, silent sister, but I saw that it was part of her need to establish her independence, and I let her be.

Angry Sister had come to help Pleasing Sister, and promised to be there to help when she moved out. That was the thing about Angry Sister; she took sides quickly. You were either for her or against her, and she was the one that chose which side you were on.

I knew all this would work itself out. I was seen as selfish, but Angry Sister had passive aggression down to an art and would never speak her true mind. She was content instead to make grand gestures on Pleasing Sister's behalf.

As for me, I stayed hidden and let the world move around me. For once, I didn't pretend.

May 30

For days a single image distinguishes itself: Dr. Erickson's legs resting next to mine.

I study the image that remains imprinted in my thoughts, trying to determine if it's real and from where it came. Anxious and frustrated, I can't alter the image to create a sense of welcome space between Dr. Erickson and myself, and so I'm left with the feeling of being physically crushed, my privacy invaded.

Worse than that, I begin to realize something I'd never thought of before: Dr. Erickson is bigger than I am. He has the legs of a man, stronger and more muscular than mine. Like a tiny seed, the thought germinates, stretching its roots into the fabric of my mind and tickling the edges of a more disturbing idea: he's too close.

It's the first thing I say when I enter the office.

"You're too close," I tell him.

The air conditioning isn't on because of the holiday, and the office is stifling.

"I have a picture in my mind of you sitting in front of me. I can see your legs next to mine."

Black pants and polished shoes. Dr. Erickson sits in front of me, so close that our knees are almost touching.

He stares at me, saying nothing.

"I know we did EMDR, but you sit out there when we do that." I point to the neutral territory in the middle of the room. "I remember that. I can see the bookcase, that's how I know where I was. In this picture you're over here."

He doesn't move into my territory without reason. He has been careful to allow me the option to move away from the wall. I can't imagine that I allowed him to cross my well-defined boundaries.

"We did a body memory-release exercise," he says casually. "I was close to you."

I search my mind for the reference, but I can't come up with the image of what he's saying. I only see his masculine legs next to mine and know he's too close to me.

I shake my head. "I can see your legs ... you're over here next to me. You're too close." Suddenly I want to push that invisible barrier away from me, push at the heaviness that's settled on my hips, and find the room to move and breathe. "I'm staring at your legs, and I'm thinking how much bigger you are than me. I never thought of that before, that you're bigger than I am."

"I'm a big guy."

"It seems strange that we've been together this long and I never noticed that."

"You've integrated," he reminds me, "and there are other parts that might have noticed this a long time ago."

"You're too close to me," I say, feeling that pressure, the need to push away. "I don't like you that close."

"Okay, too close." He's in psychoanalyst mode. I can see his gears turning. "Too close to what? Too close to finishing?"

Where did that come from? I barely have a life as it is; I'm certainly not going to make therapy my pastime. And yet I know that he's not that far off. I've been thinking about ending it and what my life will be like without the security of our weekly visits. As long as I'm in therapy, there's no real pressure to find my own life, to apply the lessons I've learned and see how I fare.

That's how it is with therapy. It can become a crutch to lean on, a convenient excuse for not owning your own life, as if by entering therapy we assign ourselves a label that we're nothing more than a work in progress and therefore not responsible for any real growth. After all, who expects grand gestures from someone in therapy?

"I don't want to be dependent on therapy," I say calmly, thinking how strong a chord his words have struck. "There's always going to be something to work on, something to talk about." Who wouldn't want to sit down with a person whose livelihood was based on impersonal analysis and non-judging opinions? "I have to focus on getting my goal. That's what I want."

He nods in agreement. "I'm hearing a 'holy shit' in here."

"No," I said faintly, "No, I just want you to be wrong."

"I can understand how you would want that."

"I don't think it's about that." I quickly shift his attention away from a subject that's becoming too intimate. "You're too close to me. I want to push you away." I demonstrate my meaning by pushing against the air at my hips. "You're too close."

"Is this the hotel room?"

I'm lying on the bed, smothered in freshly bathed skin. My hips are trapped by a dense weight. I'm paralyzed, helpless.

"That's what it feels like."

He reaches for the wand, signaling EMDR, and smiles slightly. "You want to come out so you're not against the wall?"

I move to the center of the room.

He pushes his chair back and twists his body away so his legs are not facing me. He looks like a schoolboy who has turned around in class to tell his best buddy something important.

"Think about pushing away," he says.

I'm in the hotel room on the bed. There's a struggle to get my legs apart so my father can lie between them. I want to wiggle free and push him away, but I surrender because it's the easiest thing to do. I can feel the truth of my next thought: lie still and he'll go away when he's tired.

Dr. Erickson stops EMDR. "What's happening?"

I can see and feel that little girl with an intensity I hadn't experienced before. I'm supposed to be on the ceiling. Why aren't I on the ceiling?

My voice sounds far away when I speak. "He's lying on me."

The heavy weight on me is warm and unmoving.

"I thought that's all he wanted. I feel myself surrender. I thought if I lay still nothing would happen." Pause. "He tricked me."

"Yes, he tricked you."

He begins EMDR again. I follow the wand ...

My father crawls between my legs. I sense danger, and yet there's resignation, as if I know my struggles are not going to matter. Somewhere inside is the thought to lie still and, above that, a stronger, much more peculiar thought. What am I doing in here? How did I get here? How did I get to this place?

I frown. "I have a strange thought. I'm wondering how I got here, who this person is."

He stops the wand's motion. "In psychiatry we call that depersonalization. It happens when people are under extreme stress."

He continues EMDR. I try very hard to make it not me, to go back to the ceiling where I belong, but I can't budge the memory.

I lie on the bed, trapped beneath the weight of this man I no longer think of as my father. Trapped and crushed.

I'm stuck," I tell Dr. Erickson with distress. "I can't move. I can't. Nothing more happens. I'm just there and ... I want to push away."

He leans forward and asks softly, "What do you need?"

"I want to push away." I push with my hands again, as if I were pushing an invisible force away from my body.

The soft, warm weight presses me into the mattress ...

"You want to free that little girl? You want counter-pressure?"

"I ..."I don't want any more hands on me. I don't want him close and pressing, taking and smothering. I don't want to be here anymore. I want to finish.

I nod before I can convince myself otherwise. "But not on my legs. Not that kind of pressure. This is different." I don't want to push from there; I want to push away.

"You keep pushing with your hands at your pelvis. Is that where you need to push from?"

"Yes. You're too close. I want to push you away. I want to be free."

He thinks for a moment. "If I can offer pressure on your hips, will it be enough for you to push free?"

I want to be free, but I don't want touching. The only way to get free is to push. "Yes, but how would we do that?"

Later, Dr. Erickson will refer to this session as "magic."

We decide to take two blankets and use them as pressure against my hips. No physical contact from him, and I get to push free. We work out all the details and, since this is beyond the scope of our normal therapy, he writes up an agreement that we both sign.

"Ready?"

No.

The blankets are colorful, and I like that. They remind me of the quilts my mother used to make when I was a little girl. They represent comfort and safety. I lay down on the floor on one blanket and he covers my hips with the other one.

Suddenly he stops and looks at me. "This isn't psychiatry, you know."

"But it's going to work, right?"

"You respond very well to bodywork. I think it's going to give you what you need to release this memory."

He stands on the blanket to create the pressure against my hips. "Start struggling."

I twist and push against the blanket, lifting and tilting my hips. It's more difficult than I thought. His entire weight is on the blanket and I have to stop to catch my breath.

"Keep struggling," he tells me. "The blankets are getting loose."

I renew my efforts. Slowly, I feel myself slipping from the blanket and am able to sit up, unrestrained. I wait a moment, wondering what happened, waiting for the revelation that will snap all the pieces into place. But none comes. I'm free and it doesn't seem enough.

"Two out of three?" he asks.

I nod and position myself under the blanket again and stare at the ceiling.

I'm lying on the bed with my father on top of me. He's a dead weight on me, immoveable and oppressive. I can smell the clean, musky scent of his skin. He's so heavy. He doesn't even try to move.

"You're not struggling," Dr. Erickson says.

I put my hands against the back of his legs and the contact makes me feel safe. I struggle against the tight hold of the blanket, pushing at the back of his legs as I make progress from beneath the restraining fabric.

I wriggle out from beneath my father, finding a narrow exit. I am safe. I am free.

I sit up again. I don't feel well. I stare at the floor, sorting my thoughts that come sluggishly. I try to put it all together: that room, the girl: me. Where is the pressure? Do I still want to push?

Dr. Erickson is watching me intensely as he sits on the floor.

"That was more intense than I thought it would be," I say slowly.

"I couldn't step back from her. I was that little girl. Before, I'd always watched her."

He nods. "I mentioned to you at the beginning that could happen. Remember?"

Did he? I don't remember him saying that. "I don't like that I couldn't watch it."

"It's more personal now. Now, if those attorneys were to ask you a bunch of questions about what happened to you, you would be more emotional than before. Before, it wasn't about you, and you were able to answer their questions without having feelings attached to them. Now it would be different."

Yes, the memories are personal, a strong part of myself that I can no longer divide into a safe impersonal fragment. I'm bonded to the images the way a parent is bonded to their child, and I've lost the ability to regain the blissful separation.

I'm the girl. I've always been her.

CHAPTER 40

As our house emptied of things we had once thought so important, my mind emptied as well. I waited for days after the final therapy session, waited for the feeling of wholeness and freedom to fade. It did not.

I couldn't feel pressure in my pelvis and abdomen. I didn't feel the accustomed suffocation. The quiet inside was peaceful and unfamiliar. The chatter had silenced with the disappearance of the little-girl images, but I didn't feel alone. I felt relief.

In this respite, I went home to my parents' place for a short visit. They knew that I was looking for a job, and that Pleasing Sister and I had been clearing the house, getting ready to sell it. My parents had always been supportive of their children's decisions, and this was no different. If they were disappointed, they didn't show it.

"My mother never let me move," Mom had said years ago. "She wanted me close. I won't do that to my children." And she never did. "Travel and do things while you can. Be free."

My parents wanted to move to Australia when I was six years old, but Grandma, Dad's mother, had put up a fuss and they decided against it. It was one of many such plans that never saw fruition.

I told Mom that I was going to give her and Dad some money from the home sale as a thank-you for all the help they'd given us in building it. "I'll give you the money, Mom," I said.

Dad had never been good with money: as much of a genius as he was, he couldn't balance a checking account to save his soul. Mom had only been managing her own money for the past two years. It had been a huge step of independence that she had taken reluctantly. Like any good wife who had married in 1953, she believed the husband should manage the household funds.

I had lunch with my parents. Dad had told me he wanted to make me noodles and cheese, his specialty. He took great pride in making the dish. I could smell the aroma of cheese when I walked into their apartment.

"Hello, sweetheart," Mom said, embracing me at the door. "The noodles and cheese need another half an hour."

Dad came out of his den, empty cup in hand, smiling. In my entire life, I rarely saw him without a cup of coffee or cigarette in his hand. He always liked seeing Pleasing Sister and me. We were the ones who had spent the most time with him.

I hugged him with some hesitation, waiting for the anger to rise. It didn't. His embrace was strong and I felt the ribs in his chest press against me. He took me by the hand and led me to the oven, opening the door.

"Smells good," I said.

"I have a secret recipe," he said.

Dad always liked to be different, to have something that other would covet, but more than that he wanted approval. He was over seventy years old but he was still that little boy, seeking appreciation and love from those around him.

We ate lunch and talked about how my job hunting was going.

"A second interview," Dad had said. "That's good. You'll do really well. People will want you. Don't take the first job that's offered. Be picky."

I nodded. I couldn't help but watch him. Something had changed and I was trying to decide what. He looked the way I always remembered him, but he seemed different. Therapy had taught me to monitor my thoughts, to pay attention to the feelings in my body. But my thoughts were silent and my body calm. The usual tightness in my pelvis was gone.

As I looked at him, I could only think of that little boy who'd been abandoned and spent four years in an orphanage. And then my father's words came back to me from years before, when he told me how he felt when his father was buried: *When they lowered him into the ground, I thought, I'm finally free.*

June 10

I'm concerned about something," I tell Dr. Erickson. "Did I touch you last session?"

He studies me a moment.

"I can feel you on the tips of my fingers," I tell him.

"You touched me on the back of my legs when you were trying to get out of the blanket."

I stare at my fingers. I don't like the feeling in them. "I don't know why I would have touched you."

"You pushed against me to get free. No harm, no foul," he says easily.

I'm not supposed to touch him. "I didn't need to push against you to get free," I say. It's true. I can feel a strong need to touch him, something I've never felt before.

"Maybe you needed some leverage without knowing it," he suggests.

"No." I shake my head.

"I'm giving you some explanations and you're rejecting them," he says, "so there must be something else here."

"I wanted to touch you."

The blankets are tight against my hips. I'm trapped and powerless. Don't hurt me. Dr. Erickson's legs are within reach and I curl my fingers around the backs of his calves.

"If I touch you, you'll know I'm there, and I won't be hurt. If you don't know I'm there, you can hurt me." I look at him. "Sometimes when you touch me, I can't feel you. It's like you're wearing gloves."

"Sometimes I shield when we do a counter-pressure exercise."

"It's important that you know I'm there. I don't want to be an object. It feels like I can be hurt, that you'll forget who I am."

"Is this how you felt when your father was touching you?"

"Yes." I suddenly realize the connection. "I just shut off and it didn't matter anymore who I was or what I felt."

"So touch becomes something to save you," he says simply.

I smile at the thought. "I like that kind of connection." I hadn't realized how lonely a life I was living until I unveiled.

"Where are we with things?" he asks. "You have a goal. Do you have choice?"

I run a scenario in my head. When a man pulls me near, I feel very strongly that I will not push away. I can lean into him and still say no without feeling inadequate. I can allow some touch that I'm comfortable with, and wait to be comfortable with others. My value is not in what I can do for him, and my love is not what he can do for me. I can say no and still be loved.

"Yes, I have choice."

"Something else?" he prompts.

"I'm still ... afraid."

"Your phobia of penises."

"Yes. It's not full of terror like before, but I still have fear and uncertainty."

"Some of that will be there until you have that exposure. You're practicing with your toy?"

"Not really. I look at it." It still seems too big to me, too unrealistic.

"You still have the fear of not being able to accommodate a man?"

"Yes, because ... I still don't like it, not close to me."

"If you can accommodate a man you can have your goal."

"Yes, I suppose."

"Is that what you're afraid of, having your goal?"

"No. I'm afraid of *not* having my goal. I want to like him, but it's all this ... this ... He changes. I don't like that he changes."

"What do you mean he changes?"

"Changes, changes." I hate it when he doesn't understand what I'm talking about. "It's like this." I raise my hands and open my fingers to curl them into the air as if I were clawing at an invisible force.

He stares at me.

"I don't know how to explain it to you. He changes."

"Who changes?"

"Men."

"Who? Which man?"

He's made me stop and think. I see a face, and it's not the face of my fantasy man. It's the face of my father.

I look at Dr. Erickson. "My father. I remember sitting in front of him with my hands on him and he changed. It was like his hair came all on end and his face contorted. He was like a monster; crazed. It was too much. He was too dangerous."

"It's too much. He's too big," he says. "Where is the danger?"

Not in the penis sitting in my hands. "In letting go."

"Is that orgasm?"

"Yes. That release is sweeping, it's too much for a little girl."

"Yes, it's too much for a little girl, but you're not a little girl. You can say no, or you can watch, or it can go as far as you're comfortable with it going. You didn't have those choices when you were a child."

"I have the choice now."

"Yes, you have the choice now." His eyes are steady on me.

Once I understand where the fear comes from, it's easier for me to change the beliefs that hold me back. I can rationalize with my logical brain that my fear is from past experience as a child who was ill prepared to handle the intense emotions of orgasm, but it doesn't alleviate my phobia. Not completely.

"Still uncertain?" he asks.

"Yes. I can understand what you're saying and I can work on this, but I still feel the fear at the sight of an erect penis."

"What do you want to feel when you see an erect penis?"

I search my mind. "Excitement. Passion."

"Okay." He moves out of my line of vision. "I'm going to get out of your way. I want you to look at the wall. On the one side of the wall is a picture of an erect penis. On the other wall, I want you to put a picture of something that makes you feel excitement and passion."

I went to the Smithsonian once and saw the actual painting of Whistler's *The White Girl*. The painting was over eight feet tall and it dominated the entranceway. From a hundred yards away, I was drawn to her mysterious beauty. I stood in front of the painting and marveled at the details. There was energy coming off the painting. I could see the brush strokes and smell the paint. How I wanted to touch it, and feel that energy and all the passion Whistler put into the portrait.

"Do you have a picture?" he asks.

I nod.

"In your peripheral vision is the image of the penis. Can you see that?"

"Yes."

"In front of you is the picture you've chosen that gives you excitement and passion. Is there anything else the picture gives you?"

I put my fingers into the air as if I were touching the texture of the paint on the canvas.

"Touch?"

I nod. I love the beauty of the painting, the subtle nuances of color and shape, and the fact that its sole purpose is to be appreciated.

"I want you to take the image of the penis and bring it over to the picture in front of you. Just superimpose it over the picture."

I move the images, but my thoughts stay with the feelings of *The Lady in White*.

"When you think of an erect penis, can you think of the beauty and excitement and passion you feel when you look at the chosen picture?"

I can.

Whistler painted *The Lady in White* as an act of defiance to the art community. Critics had labeled him an impressionist. He hated that they had dared to presume they knew how he felt inside, labeling his art in their arrogance. Angry, he chose out of spite to paint in a different style. He had the model stand with no expression on her face, her arms hanging limply at her side. He didn't want the critics to interpret her, or any of his work. The painting had the complete opposite effect of his intention. For years, critics analyzed *The Lady in White*, surmising who she was and what had happened to her.

I feel a strange connection to that painting.

"Come back to the office," Dr. Erickson says.

I focus on him, only a few feet from me.

He looks expectant. "Want to test?"

I nod, still foggy.

"Can you run your fantasy?"

It takes me a moment to sort my thoughts.

My lover is naked in front of me, aroused and unhurried. I stretch across the distance between us and kiss him lightly on the mouth. My hands rest on his powerful thighs. As he draws me into an embrace, my hands find his ribs. The muscles along his ribs are taut, his flesh warm.

We fall back onto the floor. The blanket is soft beneath our naked bodies. I feel his firm erection press against my thigh. For a moment, I stiffen. (The painting has power and beauty, and I want to touch it to feel what it has to offer.)

My hand seeks him out. My fingers close around him, and I begin to stroke rhythmically.

I look at the wall as my fantasy fades.

"Must be better," he says lightly. "You're smiling."

I am smiling. I turn to look at him. "I like that."

He smiles. "Something new for you to practice."

I feel a blush on my cheeks and turn away.

Epilogue

I ended therapy one year to the day after I first sat in that hard, plastic chair in the psychiatric ward. The last time I saw Dr. Erickson, I thanked him awkwardly, smiled and left his office. That was it. No certificate of achievement, no commemorative ribbon. Not even a handshake. Just goodbye.

After a year and so many hours of baring my soul and deepest kept secrets, the lack of ceremony seemed wrong somehow. A letdown. I wondered if everyone felt this way. Maybe the reason why people lingered in therapy for years was because they didn't know how to end it. And wasn't that the same reason many unhappy people stayed in unfulfilling relationships? Are we that bad at letting go?

Or do we just hate change that much?

For me, it was a little of both. I could have stayed in therapy where I was safe, talked about the things I wanted to do, and pretended I had healed without needing to kiss a man. But that would have been the old me.

I'm a different person from the emotionally damaged woman who committed herself, literally and figuratively. I started therapy on my knees, immobile with fear for the future. Slowly, tentatively, I began to crawl toward the sense of hope that Dr. Erickson gave me, and then to walk more confidently, determined to heal.

Healing was never about sex.

I will tell that the first time a man kissed me, I didn't push away. For one brief moment, the old thoughts surfaced, then faded as his lips pressed mine. Suddenly, I wanted it to last. I lingered and felt and tasted. As he moved his hand to the small of my back, I didn't stiffen with fear, but leaned into the pressure, letting him pull me close. As our bodies pressed together, I felt the tug of excitement and anticipation.

In that moment I realized that therapy really had changed me, that I'd put the old thought patterns behind me and could be fully in the present without the past interfering.

I measure my success, not by the men I've been with, but by the freedom I've claimed and the relationships I've built. I now speak to hundreds of people about the benefits of therapy. I share my experiences in the hope that others can avoid living decades with their pain and fear, pretending that everything is okay.

Some people are willing to settle for mediocrity, and become comfortable with their pain and sadness. Pain and sadness become their life. But it doesn't have to be that way.

Healing, for me, is restoration; a return to the perfect, loving, trusting person we were when we entered this world. That was the person I was always trying to get back to. I didn't want to reinvent myself, but *return* to myself. This was my goal all along, and what my family ultimately was seeking from me. My relationship with my siblings and parents has never been more meaningful and fulfilling.

I remember the first time I realized I had forgiven my father. I was sitting at the table, having lunch with my parents. My father seemed old and frail and sad. "Empty," I used to say about him. But I didn't see an empty man. I saw the little boy who had been abandoned, and I wondered again what his life would have been like if his parents had been better parents, if he hadn't been adopted by the strict couple who had really wanted a girl.

What would my life have been like?

And then I realized that I didn't want to know. For the first time in a long time, I liked my life. I liked the person I had become, and every event I have experienced has shaped that person.

For the first time, I'm free.

Love and peace

Laureen

CPSIA information can be obtained
at www.ICGtesting.com
Printed in the USA
FSOW04n2255100517
34142FS